"This book has many voices but one goal: to [c]
contemporary psychoanalysis. The authors develo[p]
rich and diverse perspectives. Sensitive cases illust[rate]
it more accessible for clinicians. This is a pat[h breaking and essential]
volume for anyone searching for coherence in the maze of contending
approaches to psychotherapy that dominate the landscape."
– **Charles B. Strozier**, PhD, Author, *Heinz Kohut:
The Making of a Psychoanalyst*

"In this lucid and well-articulated volume, we are introduced to the intersection of Kohutian Self Psychology and Intersubjectivity Theory. Readers will find in this book accessible theoretical explanations, which are illustrated by excellent clinical examples. This is a must read for clinicians interested in this innovative approach to clinical work."
– **Joyce Slochower**, PhD, ABPP, Professor Emerita, Hunter
College & CUNY; Faculty NYU Steven Mitchell Center;
Author, *Holding and Psychoanalysis: A Relational
Perspective & Psychoanalytic Collisions*

"This book offers students, as well as experienced clinicians, a clear and skillfully illustrated guidebook that combines the most transformative aspects of Heinz Kohut's and Robert Stolorow's contributions. The chapters in the book abound with clinical examples for using this approach to treat individuals, children, and couples and in working with depression, addiction, suicidality, and sexuality."
– **Doris Brothers**, PhD, Private practice, New York City, Author,
*Falling Backwards: An Exploration of Trust and Self Experience
and Towards a Psychology of Uncertainty*

Intersubjective Self Psychology

Intersubjective Self Psychology: A Primer offers a comprehensive overview of the theory of Intersubjective Self Psychology and its clinical applications. Readers will gain an in depth understanding of one of the most clinically relevant analytic theories of the past half-century, fully updated and informed by recent discoveries and developments in the field of Intersubjectivity Theory. Most importantly, the volume provides detailed chapters on the treatment principles of Intersubjective Self Psychology and their application to a variety of clinical situations and diagnostic categories such as addiction, mourning, child therapy, couples treatment, sexuality, suicide and severe pathology. This useful clinical tool will support and inform everyday psychotherapeutic work.

Retaining Kohut's emphasis on the self and selfobject experience, the book conceptualizes the therapeutic situation as a bi-directional field of needed and dreaded selfobject experiences of both patient and analyst. Through a rigorous application of the ISP model, each chapter sheds light on the complex dynamic field within which self-experience and selfobject experience of patient and analyst/therapist unfold and are sustained. The ISP perspective allows the therapist to focus on the patient's strengths, referred to as the Leading Edge, without neglecting work with the repetitive transferences, or Trailing Edge. This dual focus makes ISP a powerful agent for transformation and growth.

Intersubjective Self Psychology provides a unified and comprehensive model of psychological life with specific, practical applications that are clinically informative and therapeutically powerful. The book represents a highly useful resource for psychoanalysts and psychoanalytic psychotherapists around the world.

George Hagman, LCSW, is a clinical social worker and psychoanalyst in private practice in New York City and Stamford, Connecticut. He is a member and faculty member of the Training and Research Institute in Intersubjective Self Psychology and the Westchester Center for the Study of Psychoanalysis and Psychotherapy. He is the author of books on the Psychoanalysis, Self Psychology, art, and bereavement.

Harry Paul, PhD, is a clinical psychologist in private practice in New York City and Chappaqua, New York. He is a founding member, past president, faculty, supervisor and training analyst at the Training and Research Institute in Intersubjective Self Psychology. He is the co-author of *The Self Psychology of Addiction and Its Treatment: Narcissus in Wonderland* and he has co-authored papers on addiction and self psychology. He currently sits on the international Council of IAPSP.

Peter B. Zimmermann, PhD, is a licensed psychoanalyst in private practice in New York City. He is a founding member and member of the board of trustees, faculty, supervisor, and training analyst at the Training and Research Institute in Intersubjective Self Psychology in New York. He is the current president, senior faculty member, supervisor and training analyst at the Training Institute of The National Psychological Association for Psychoanalysis in New York.

Intersubjective Self Psychology

A Primer

Edited by George Hagman,
Harry Paul and
Peter B. Zimmermann

Routledge
Taylor & Francis Group
LONDON AND NEW YORK

First published 2019
by Routledge
2 Park Square, Milton Park, Abingdon, Oxon OX14 4RN

and by Routledge
52 Vanderbilt Avenue, New York, NY 10017

Routledge is an imprint of the Taylor & Francis Group, an informa business

© 2019 selection and editorial matter, George Hagman, Harry Paul and Peter B. Zimmermann; individual chapters, the contributors

The right of George Hagman, Harry Paul and Peter B. Zimmermann to be identified as the authors of the editorial material and of the authors for their individual chapters, has been asserted in accordance with Sections 77 and 78 of the Copyright, Designs and Patents Act 1988.

All rights reserved. No part of this book may be reprinted or reproduced or utilised in any form or by any electronic, mechanical, or other means, now known or hereafter invented, including photocopying and recording, or in any information storage or retrieval system, without permission in writing from the publishers.

Trademark notice: Product or corporate names may be trademarks or registered trademarks, and are used only for identification and explanation without intent to infringe.

British Library Cataloguing-in-Publication Data
A catalogue record for this book is available from the British Library

Library of Congress Cataloging-in-Publication Data
A catalog record has been requested for this book

ISBN: 978-1-138-35453-1 (hbk)
ISBN: 978-1-138-35454-8 (pbk)
ISBN: 978-0-429-42475-5 (ebk)

Typeset in Times New Roman
by Swales & Willis, Exeter, Devon, UK

Contents

List of contributors ix
Preface xi
GEORGE HAGMAN, HARRY PAUL, AND PETER B. ZIMMERMANN
Acknowledgements xv

SECTION I
The theory and practice of Intersubjective Self Psychology 1

1 An introduction to Intersubjective Self Psychology 3
   PETER B. ZIMMERMANN, HARRY PAUL, AVIVA ROHDE, KAREN ROSER,
   GORDON POWELL, LOUISA LIVINGSTON, AND GEORGE HAGMAN

2 Empathy in Intersubjective Self Psychology 14
   KAREN ROSER AND AVIVA ROHDE

3 Transference in Intersubjective Self Psychology 25
   AVIVA ROHDE AND KAREN ROSER

4 The therapeutic action of Intersubjective Self Psychology, Part 1 37
   PETER B. ZIMMERMANN

5 The therapeutic action of Intersubjective Self Psychology, Part 2: the case of Ricky 57
   AVIVA ROHDE

6 Working with the trailing edge: resolving the fear of repetition 69
GEORGE HAGMAN AND SUSANNE M. WEIL

7 Working with the leading edge: when the selfobject tie is intact 80
HARRY PAUL, PETER B. ZIMMERMANN, AND GEORGE HAGMAN

SECTION 2
Clinical applications **97**

8 Melancholia revisited: depression and its treatment from the perspective of Intersubjective Self Psychology 99
PETER B. ZIMMERMANN

9 Addiction: an intersubjective self psychological perspective 113
HARRY PAUL

10 Child treatment: working with the leading and trailing edge 131
KAREN ROSER

11 Working with couples in Intersubjective Self Psychology 141
NANCY HICKS AND LOUISA LIVINGSTON

12 Sexuality and Intersubjective Self Psychology: what matters 162
GORDON POWELL

13 A suicidal patient: gasping for air 178
LAURA D'ANGELO

References 189
Index 193

Contributors

Laura D'Angelo, MDiv, LP, is a psychoanalyst in New York City. She is a member of the Training and Research in Intersubjective Self Psychology, the National Psychological Association for Psychoanalysis and the Harlem Family Institute, where she teaches, supervises and serves as a training analyst. In her prior career, Laura worked as a journalist with credits in national magazines, newspapers and academic journals.

George Hagman, LCSW, is a clinical social worker and psychoanalyst in private practice in New York City and Stamford, Connecticut. He is a member and faculty member of the Training and Research for Intersubjective Self Psychology and the Westchester Center for the Study of Psychoanalysis and Psychotherapy. He is the author of papers and books on Psychoanalysis, Self Psychology, art, and bereavement.

Nancy Hicks, PsyD, is in private practice in Metuchen, NJ and New York, NY. A graduate of the Training and Research Institute for Self Psychology, she currently serves on the faculty at the Center for Psychotherapy and Psychoanalysis of New Jersey, and at the New Jersey Couples Therapy Training Program.

Louisa Livingston, PhD, is a psychologist in private practice in New York City. She has lived in many parts of the USA before coming to New York City. She loves listening to '60s music, playing tennis and relaxing. She published 7 articles from 1998 to 2009 focusing on the therapeutic process derived from her clinical work with individual patients, groups. Two of which were co-authored with her husband, Marty Livingston.

Harry Paul, PhD, is a clinical psychologist in private practice in New York City and Chappaqua, New York. He is a Founding Member, Member Board of Directors, Faculty, Training Analyst and Supervisor of the Training and Research Institute in Intersubjective Self Psychology (TRISP). He is co-author of the book *The Self Psychology of Addiction and Its Treatment* and authored numerous other papers on self psychology and the therapeutic process.

Gordon Powell, LCSW, is a psychoanalyst in private practice in Manhattan. He teaches and supervises at The Institute for Contemporary Psychotherapy (ICP) and The Psychoanalytic Psychotherapy Study Center (PPSC), both in Manhattan. He is on the executive committee for Psychotherapy Center for Gender and Sexuality (PCGS), a division of ICP.

Aviva Rohde, PhD, is a senior faculty member at the Training and Research in Intersubjective Self Psychology Foundation. A psychologist and psychoanalyst, she is in private practice in New York City where she treats adults, adolescents and couples.

Karen Roser, PsyD, has a doctorate in school psychology from New York University. She is a graduate, faculty member and supervisor at TRISP. She is in private practice in Manhattan, where she sees children, parents, adults, and couples.

Susanne M. Weil, LCSW, is a psychoanalyst practicing in Stamford, CT. She was trained at the Training and Research Institute for Self Psychology in New York City. In addition to teaching and supervising, she is active in community work that includes membership on the bio-ethics committee of a local hospital and consults on leadership to community-based organizations.

Peter B. Zimmermann has a PhD in philosophy from the University of Bern, Switzerland. He is a Founding Member, Member Board of Directors, Faculty, Training Analyst and Supervisor of the Training and Research in Intersubjective Self Psychology Foundation (TRISP). He is the current President of the Training Institute of the National Psychological Association for Psychoanalysis (NPAP), from where he has his Certificate in Psychoanalysis (1982) and is a Senior Member, Faculty, Training Analyst and Supervisor. He maintains a private practice in psychotherapy, psychoanalysis, and supervision in New York City.

Preface

Intersubjective Self Psychology: A Primer is an introduction to the theory and clinical practice of one of the most versatile and useful models of modern psychoanalysis. Intersubjective Self Psychology, or ISP, fully integrates the core ideas of Self Psychology with Intersubjectivity Theory into a seamless, comprehensive framework which provides the clinician with tools to understand and treat patients and engage in a dynamic and creative interaction with the social surround. Most important, the perspective of ISP elucidates fundamental dynamics of the psychoanalytic relationship.

The authors of this volume, all analytic clinicians, have collaboratively developed the ISP model and have used it with great therapeutic benefit in clinical practice for the past 30 years, refining many of the core concepts, through trial and error of clinical practice and through extended dialogue among ourselves. We have taught this model as members of the TRISP faculty, and several other psychoanalytic training institutes, and have trained scores of psychodynamic therapists and psychoanalytic candidates to become highly effective clinicians. It is with the intention of sharing our knowledge and clinical experience that we offer this primer.

In the 1970s and 1980s, Heinz Kohut brought about a major revision in psychoanalysis. This involved several publications which laid out the basic tenets of what he called Self Psychology, but he also sparked a movement, a new community devoted to the refinement, application, and promotion of his new ideas for psychoanalysis. The core concepts of self psychology are the concept of the self and the selfobject transferences. Kohut discovered that people, in order to develop their self or self experience, need the caregiving surround to provide certain experiences: selfobject experiences of mirroring validation, idealization and twinship. As a result, Kohut came to recognize that patients look to the analyst not only as the figure onto whom they project their internal conflicts, as Freud and in his wake traditional psychoanalysis maintained, but also as the figure that they need to perform previously unmet developmental functions, selfobject functions, to resume self development where it was derailed. This understanding of emotional development resulted in a fundamental shift in how psychoanalytic therapy is practised.

Later, during the 1990s, Robert Stolorow and George Atwood argued that the traditional psychoanalytic model of the isolated, private mind was inaccurate and misleading. They offered an alternative, Intersubjectivity Theory, which understood human psychological life as inextricably embedded in the felt interaction between people and thus, they argued, any and all psychological phenomena, from emotional health to the most severe forms of emotional disorder can only be understood from within the intersubjective context within which they occur. They conceptualized the psychoanalytic situation as an "intersubjective field", constituted by the differently organized experiential worlds of patient and analyst, (Stolorow, Atwood & Brandchaft, 1987) which, engaged at the deepest levels of human interaction, provide the opportunity for growth and transformation.

As Stolorow and Atwood joined the Self Psychology movement, an attempt was made to develop a unified model, a model founded on both the principles of intersubjective theory and self psychology. However, over time Intersubjectivity Theory abandoned core clinical ideas of Self Psychology, in particular the selfobject transferences, and instead evolved into Intersubjective Systems Theory, while Self Psychology continued to focus on the vicissitudes of self experience, gradually adapting many of Kohut's ideas to the new perspectives of Relational Psychoanalysis.

That being said, the authors of this volume have continued the important effort of integrating the key clinical concepts of Self Psychology with the fundamental theoretical insights of Intersubjectivity Theory and have developed the framework of ISP. We have demonstrated how the flawless compatibility of the two models enhance the understanding and clinical utility of each and we have further developed the ideas to provide a new platform for a highly effective clinical practice. And, ISP makes a significant clinical addition to both theories by proposing that psychological growth and development not only occurs when there is an analysis of the break in the selfobject tie, as Kohut originally conceptualized, but that generative psychological health is advanced through the ongoing and sustained selfobject relationship itself and in the interpretation and understanding of the leading edge. That is, the ongoing selfobject tie itself is curative and the attuned engagement of clinicians utilizing the ISP model, discussing and exploring the generative leading edge with the patient also facilitates growth and solidifies psychic structure. Speaking with the patient about the leading edge and its' function, at moments in the treatment when the patient will neither be shamed by a discussion of the relationship, nor experience the therapist as taking credit for the patients' progress, focuses the therapy on the process between the participants, and the importance of the healthy connection between them.

This ISP primer will be very useful to new clinicians interested in an approach which is sophisticated, practical and relatively easy to grasp. Key concepts are: the intersubjective field, the selfobject and repetitive transferences and trailing and leading edge. However, the elegance of the ISP model belies its flexibility in understanding and treating virtually an infinite variety of clinical situations. More senior, experienced clinicians will find in this volume a clear introduction to an important analytic model, a perspective which can enhance and empower any psychoanalytic practice.

In other words, although ISP is a refined model of psychotherapeutic practice as well as of human relationships, it is also practical, useful, and filled with clinical concepts and ideas which the reader will readily be able to apply to his/her therapy practice.

The following is a brief overview of how we have organized and structured *Intersubjective Self Psychology: A Primer*. As a whole we have designed the book as an introductory text intended to provide the reader with a basic understanding of the theory and practice of ISP. It is not a scholarly work, it is a clinical guide. If the reader wishes a more extensive and in depth discussion of the theoretical foundations of ISP, we refer you to the texts which are identified in the references. In this book we give just enough of a literature review to put our ideas in context and credit our major predecessors and sources. Each chapter is organized to review relevant areas of ISP theory, followed by in-depth clinical examples. Except for the introductory chapter, this method is followed throughout the book. We want this to be a useful tool, which the reader can readily apply to his or her daily psychotherapy practice. The book begins with an introduction to the theory of ISP, written collaboratively by the contributing authors. We give a bit of history, followed by a discussion of the theories of Self Psychology and Intersubjectivity, the integration of which constitutes ISP. Chapter 2 (written by Karen Roser and Aviva Rohde) explores the role of empathy in ISP, its use as a mode of understanding and a source of growth and healing. Chapter 3 (also by Karen and Aviva) discusses the complex nature of transference, which ISP posits as having multiple dimensions and functions. Chapter 4 (written by Peter B. Zimmermann) is an extended discussion of the theory of therapeutic action in ISP and Chapter 5 (written by Aviva Rohde) is an extensive case example which demonstrates how the ideas from Chapter 4 are applied in clinical practice. Chapter 6 (written by George Hagman and Susanne Weil) deals with clinical work with what ISP calls the "trailing edge", meaning the repetitive fears and defenses which can block therapeutic progress. This is followed by Chapter 7 (written by Harry Paul, Peter B. Zimmermann and George Hagman) which discusses the work with the "leading edge", the aspects of transference which are growth promoting and which constitute the drivers of therapeutic change. These introductory chapters are followed by chapters which apply ISP to various clinical challenges: melancholia and depression (Peter B. Zimmermann), addiction (Harry Paul), work with children (Karen Roser), couples (Nancy Hicks and Louisa Livingston), the topic of human sexuality (Gordon Powell), and the treatment of a suicidal patient (Laura D'Angelo).

In the course of writing these various chapters we chose to hone in on some of the essential and clinically useful ideas of ISP. This is an important part of the design of the book: to introduce the reader to a handful of key concepts in ISP, and then to elaborate on these concepts as they pertain to certain topics, such as empathy, selfobject transference, therapeutic action, depression, addiction, etc. As you will see, we return to these essential concepts time and again – intersubjective field, generative and repetitive transference, leading and trailing edge – each time viewing them from the perspective of the authors and the ways in which these concepts elucidate important concepts and show how they apply to various areas of clinical practice. In fact we believe the true value of the book is in the numerous, detailed clinical examples that illuminate the central ideas of ISP. We hope that, by taking this approach, the reader will grow more and more knowledgeable about ISP concepts, how they can be usefully applied to psychotherapeutic work, how ISP can increase clinical efficacy. Finally, we hope this book encourages the readers to use the ISP perspectives to think in a new way about their own role in the clinical process and appreciate the rich complexity and opportunity of the intersubjective field.

Finally, the editors and authors have assured that the identity of the patient and all other persons has been disguised in all of the case reports in this volume. Several are composite reports which combine the details of work with different people, yet these are also disguised. And in several instances the patient has reviewed and approved the case report, yet even in these cases the report has been written in such a way as to preserve anonymity.

The authors of this book are a group of senior psychoanalysts in clinical practice in the New York Metropolitan area, who are all affiliated with TRISP – the Training and Research in Intersubjective Self Psychology Foundation, either as graduates or teachers. Over the past 30 years they have collaborated and debated, supervised and consulted about the core concepts of ISP and the clinical application of the model. As instructors in the ongoing workshop series at TRISP, they all have been active in the elaboration, refinement and promotion of the ISP model. This volume marks the first time that these analysts have attempted to bring together in one volume, the basic concepts of ISP and communicate them in a concise, clear, and practical primer.

George Hagman, Harry Paul, and Peter B. Zimmermann

Acknowledgements

The authors want to thank the psychoanalytic innovators whose work have made *Intersubjective Self Psychology: A Primer* possible. They are Heinz Kohut, the inventor and founder of the field of Self Psychology. Robert Stolorow with his collaborators George Atwood, Bernard Brandchaft, and Donna Orange who, against much opposition, developed and promoted the intersubjective perspective in a field then dominated by the paradigm of the isolated mind. And Marian Tolpin, whose vision of patients as basically hopeful and healthy, more than dreadful and ill, led to the recognition of what she called the Forward Edge of development and treatment. The profound influence of their ideas are felt throughout this book. They compose the generative intellectual intersubjective field with which the authors are engaged.

The editors wish to thank their patients and supervisees, for sharing their worlds and engaging in the intersubjective journeys with us. Ongoing discussion with supervisees provided an intellectual forum and emotional support for the development of our ideas. Without this shared commitment, this manuscript would not have been possible. Lastly, we recognize the importance of our own emotionally sustaining relationships, the generative, leading edge of our personal intersubjective lives. Our life partners and relationships with family and friends, are critical to our ability to engage our patients. We are deeply grateful to our partners, Moira H., Amy P. and Suzanne Z., and our children, families, and friends whose love and support helps us to fully participate in the work.

Last but not least, Peter and Harry and all the contributors want to thank George Hagman who, with his enthusiasm, intellectual rigor and editorial drive, has brought this project to life.

Section I

The theory and practice of Intersubjective Self Psychology

Chapter 1

An introduction to Intersubjective Self Psychology

Peter B. Zimmermann, Harry Paul, Aviva Rohde, Karen Roser, Gordon Powell, Louisa Livingston, and George Hagman

In this chapter we present the fundamental concepts of *Intersubjective Self Psychology* (ISP) which combines the core concepts of Heinz Kohut's Self Psychology (Kohut, 1971, 1977, 1984) with the essential ideas of Robert Stolorow and George Atwood's Intersubjectivity Theory (Stolorow & Atwood, 1992; Stolorow, 1997). From these established theories we create a new, cohesive psychological, and therapeutic model that transcends both theories and that we call *Intersubjective Self Psychology* or *ISP*. We believe that ISP provides an orientation to psychotherapeutic practice that recognizes and promotes forward development in therapy (the leading edge) as well as addresses and works through the repetitive patterns (the trailing edge), all with a deep appreciation for the interdependent nature of the human experience.

Self psychology

What are the essential ideas of Self Psychology which undergird ISP?

At the heart of Self Psychology is the concept of selfhood. "The Self" is a theoretical abstraction that stands for the complex set of experiences and fantasies each of us has about our self, and who we know and feel our self to be. These experiences and fantasies become organized according to significant patterns of beliefs, feelings, memories, and values. These cognitive and affective notions of oneself constitute the experiential and motivational center of our sense of being and of being-with-others. Ideally, these varied experiences that constitute the self are organized into a cohesive whole, but are not fixed or rigid; rather they are emergent and fluid. The experiences of vitality, coherence, continuity, and personal initiative characterize the essential qualities of our experiential center, the sense of self. The sense of self is highly contingent upon and embedded within a matrix of relationships.

The foundational listening and exploring stance of the Self Psychological analyst is empathic immersion in the patient's experience. Empathy was famously defined by Heinz Kohut as "vicarious introspection" (Kohut, 2010). In other words, empathy is the often difficult and slow process of feeling and thinking oneself into another person's subjective experience, as fully as possible; hence understanding the person from within that person's frame of reference.

Kohut later expanded that understanding and came to see empathy as both a mode of exploration of the experience of another human being and a way of relating to another human being. As a means of exploration, the analyst seeks to understand the patient's experience from within the patient's experiential world as it unfolds in the shared psychological field of the analytic relationship. As a form of relating, the analyst's empathy communicates the value placed on the patient's lived experience as well as a fundamental acceptance of it as something that can be understood, even if not always condoned. The analyst's commitment to empathy as a mode of exploration, and as a means of relating to the patient, lays the groundwork for the whole of the analysis.

Kohut discovered that not only are the development of self and the sustained experience of healthy selfhood contingent on the felt responsiveness of caregivers in childhood and significant others throughout life, self development relies on experiencing the other as part of the self. The self also relies on the emotional availability of others to perform necessary developmental functions and tasks. Kohut identified three specific lines of development along which self development can successfully unfold. He labeled them mirroring, idealizing, and twinship experiences (Kohut, 1971, 1977, 1984).

In the mirror line of development, we look to others to feel truly known and accurately seen. In the archaic mirror experience, we feel admired, the object of the other's adoring gaze. In the more mature mirror experience, we feel recognized and valued for who we know ourselves to be. A successful mirror experience contributes to a cohesive, reliable, and realistic self-esteem, and a solid sense of self-worth.

In the idealizing line of development, we look for a merger with someone whom we experience as calming, strong, and wise; one who offers him or herself for our protection and guidance. A successful merger with an idealized other provides opportunities for soothing, which results in a reliable capacity for affect regulation.

Finally, in the twinship line of development, we look to find in the other an experience of alikeness, a feeling of sameness that is shared, which results in the consolidation of self experience. We seek to recognize ourselves in the other and yearn for the other to recognize themself in us. Twinship lays the groundwork for a sense of shared humanity, a feeling of being human among humans.

In all three lines of development – which correspond to relational experiences that facilitate the development of a cohesive sense of self – the other is experienced as part of the self and as providing essential functions in maintaining the self. For these reasons, Kohut called these relationships selfobject relationships (Kohut, 1971, 1977, 1984). Selfobject experiences are fundamental human needs akin to the needs for air and water. Like plants turning toward sunlight, humans strive to find relationships that provide the selfobject experiences that generate and sustain self development and that enable previously stalled development to resume. As such, they are ubiquitous and, given a responsive other, they will emerge spontaneously.

Because Kohut believed that the availability of emotionally responsive others – those who provide opportunities for selfobject experiences through the life span – is a basic human need, he located the source of most human suffering in the absence of reliable, emotionally attuned others and/or in the presence of emotionally misattuned others, which results in the failure to find sustained, attuned selfobject experiences with others. The absence of empathically attuned others results in the failure in the development of an adequately vital, coherent, and continuous sense of self. This lack of necessary responsiveness, in concert with the child's inherent vulnerabilities, sets the stage for psychological, emotional, and/or behavioral disorders. Selfobject failure in the formative years that is either protracted or traumatic results in rigidified structures of self and other, emotional scar tissue that manifests itself in specific character formations and personality disorders. Conversely, psychological and emotional healing is possible when the opportunity for a reliable selfobject experience is restored with an emotionally responsive and empathic other. This conceptualization of psychological development is the basis of all forms of self psychological treatment (Kohut, 1984).

Kohut recognized the unfolding of the selfobject tie with the analyst and called this the selfobject transference. Selfobject transferences are relational pathways established and facilitated in the analysis in the service of self development. The three lines of development that Kohut identified as pathways for self development take the form of specific transferences in the analytic setting. In the mirror transference, patients seek a sustained experience of affirmation and validation that generates a positively toned self-esteem and sense of agency. In the idealizing transference, patients seek an experience of merger with the felt strength and emotional reliability of the analyst, in the hope of being calmed and soothed. In the twinship transference, patients seek an experience of essential alikeness with the analyst and appreciation of the analyst's felt alikeness with them. This leads to a feeling of shared humanity and an affirmation of who the patient knows him or herself to be. As patients' selfobject needs emerge and are properly responded to by the analyst, restoration, consolidation, and structuralization of the self experience occurs and the sense of self unfolds and solidifies.

Kohut understood that felt experiences of self and others – or selfobject fantasies[1] – constitute the bedrock of psychological life. These selfobject fantasies are established at the beginning of life and constitute the template for a sense of self as well as for all relationships. Over time, in interaction with caregivers and others, these fantasies are modified, and gradually transformed into increasingly mature, adaptive, and self-esteem-enhancing conceptions of self and other. Consistent with the selfobject themes described above, Kohut believed that the most important of these fantasies for the development of the self are the fantasies of the grandiose self, the idealized parent imago, and the twin in the twinship transference.

In its most archaic form, the grandiose self describes a self-experience in which perfection is attributed to the self and all imperfections are attributed to the other. Likewise, the most archaic form of the idealized parent imago is an image of the other as perfect and the self is only perfect when merged with the other. The most archaic form of twinship is a fantasy of a perfectly identical other.

All three of these selfobject fantasies undergo a similar developmental process. In interaction with empathic and attuned caregivers, these selfobject fantasies evolve and are transformed in age-appropriate stages to adapt to the increasingly complex reality at hand. These transformed fantasies then become the basis for mature self-esteem (mirroring), a reliably established capacity for self-soothing (idealization), and a solid sense of feeling human among other humans (twinship). In the absence of attuned caregivers, or in the face of traumatic ruptures in the tie with them, however, the child will retain early, archaic versions of these fantasies. In such cases, these fantasies will interfere with the development of a healthy and robust sense of self. To the extent that a person remains organized around archaic fantasies of self and other, he or she will struggle with feelings of fragility and vulnerability and will be prone to feelings of fragmentation and/or depletion. Defensive behaviors will be employed to maintain the incompletely developed sense of self and to ward off fragmentation due to anticipated failures of attunement or traumatic disappointment by needed others.

Kohut also discovered that patients often fear the sense of vulnerability and potential retraumatization that may accompany the emergence of selfobject needs in treatment. Patients might be fearful that emotional intimacy and the reactivation of selfobject needs in relation to the analyst will lead to pain and a repetition of childhood experiences. Patients who have experienced significant selfobject failures or damaging misattunement by caregivers may protect themselves against retraumatization through psychological and behavioral strategies that deny, devalue, deflect, or otherwise neutralize the emotional connection with the analyst. Patients employ these defensive strategies to protect a vulnerable self from what might be a hurtful relationship with the analyst.

If the analyst offers the patient experience-near and useful interpretations of his or her fears and the related self-protective efforts within a sustained, supportive, and empathic relationship, the patient may begin to feel safe enough to risk the reactivation of selfobject yearnings and needs with the analyst. In this way, the interpretations of defense are in the service of reinstating and developing the selfobject transference.

Intersubjectivity

What are the essential ideas of Intersubjectivity?

At the core of the theory of Intersubjectivity is the idea of the fundamental context dependency of all psychological life (Stolorow et al., 1987; Stolorow & Atwood, 1992). Stolorow and his colleagues argue that psychological phenomena in general cannot be understood apart from the *intersubjective context* by which they mean the *psychological field* that is generated by the intersection of the psychological world of one person with the psychological world of another as well as with the world at large. The clinical implications of Intersubjectivity Theory are that psychological health and psychological disorder originate in and are sustained by the intersubjective contexts in which they occur.

In other words, a person's self-experience is at all times determined by and dependent upon the specific intersubjective contexts in which it takes shape and by which it is sustained (or not). The experiences of connectedness, attunement, responsiveness to affect states and self states, and selfobject needs are fundamental to the development and consolidation of self-experience. These experiences are by definition intersubjective.[2]

A person's sense of self is constituted or disrupted in the context of attuned or misattuned responsiveness from significant others (selfobjects), as experienced by that person. As an example, for one patient the therapist's silence is experienced as a gift from the heavens, providing the space and freedom to free associate and unfold her world, and therefore consolidating her self experience, while for another patient that same silence is experienced as a traumatic repetition of the withholding angry father and therefore disassembling her self experience.

This context is referred to as the *intersubjective field* (Atwood & Stolorow, 1984) and is constituted in childhood by the intersection of the vulnerable and evolving subjectivity of the child with the (hopefully) more mature and developed subjectivity of the caregiver. Any two or more people engaged with each other constitute a specific intersubjective field within which each person's self-experience takes shape, contingent on the subjective frame of reference, the personal world, into which the experience is organized.

The concept of subjectivity includes the entirety of feelings, beliefs, fantasies, memories, and thoughts about oneself and others. This includes unconscious dimensions, which may have never required conscious awareness (Stolorow & Atwood, 1992) yet may nonetheless constitute basic reflective templates which Atwood and Stolorow (1984) call "central organizing principles"; a person's most fundamental beliefs. On the other hand, some unconscious aspects of subjectivity may have been banished from consciousness, and sequestered for safety's sake, because the affect and self states involved are experienced as threats to psychological health, the cohesion of self-experience, and/or the needed tie with an essential other. This dimension of subjectivity is traditionally called the *dynamic unconscious*. Intersubjectivity Theory contends that the dynamic unconscious consists of the defensive sequestration of any feeling or fantasy which poses a risk to the self, not simply because of the content of the affect or fantasy per se, but because of the threat it is felt to pose.

As we will demonstrate throughout this book, the notion of the intersubjective field, and its conscious and unconscious determinants found in the subjective worlds of interacting people, is fundamental to our understanding of the psychotherapeutic situation. Psychotherapy is an intersubjective field in which the psychological lives of patient and therapist meet and influence each other. And at the heart of the process is the way in which the unconscious dimensions of the patient's subjectivity are expressed and transformed in the course of the unfolding therapeutic interaction. Given this, we now turn back to Self Psychology, because it is the vicissitudes of self-experience and selfobject needs which emerge in the intersubjective psychotherapeutic field, manifest in the expression of the patient's fears and dreads, as well as his or her longings and hopes, creating the opportunity for therapeutic change.

Intersubjective Self Psychology

What is Intersubjective Self Psychology?

Integrating Kohut's theory of the self with Stolorow's Intersubjectivity Theory compels us to eschew notions of isolated subjective experience in favor of the rich complexity of reciprocally influential, continuously interacting and mutually constituted subjective worlds. Together, both theories not only enhance our knowledge of the relational context of all psychological life but also provide a powerful therapeutic tool. The idea of self development as being co-determined by the intersubjective matrix within which it occurs is perfectly met by the conceptualization of the analytic situation as an intersubjective field, constituted by the intersection of the experiential worlds of patient and analyst. The result is that in the analytic situation we are not dealing with a patient's experience in isolation; rather we are at all times dealing with the patient's experience as it is co-determined by the felt interaction with a particular analyst and as it evolves in response to it; similarly we are at all times dealing with the analyst's experience as it is co-determined by the felt interaction with the particular patient. The analytic situation is thus conceptualized as an intersubjective field of reciprocal mutual influence, constituted by the intersection of the experiential worlds of *both* patient and analyst.

By integrating Self Psychology with Intersubjectivity Theory, we are committed to uphold that all of what Kohut recognized to hold true for the development of the self, above all the selfobject transferences, with what Stolorow recognized to hold true for the therapeutic situation, above all the reciprocal nature of the intersubjective field, which means what holds true for the patient also holds true for the analyst. In other words, the analytic situation is constituted by the felt interaction of both the patient's and the analyst's sum total of their emotional worlds; the intersubjective field is bi-directional and co-determined by the specific intersection of the respective emotional worlds of patient and analyst, this includes the emergence and expression of selfobject needs for the analyst, as well as the patient.

Because both theories share the belief in empathy as the analyst's method of observation, we are committed to exploring the experience of the patient in the intersubjective field from the patient's perspective, from within the patient's experiential world. But based on the theory of Intersubjectivity we understand that empathy cannot be seen as disinterested or objective. The experience of the patient is co-determined continuously by the felt interaction between the patient's subjectivity and the analyst's, and vice-versa: the experience of the analyst is co-determined by the felt interaction with the subjectivity of the patient. Hence, from an ISP viewpoint, the analyst's empathy is more than just feeling oneself into the experience of the patient. Rather, it is a complex and rich immersion in the intertwined subjective experiences of analyst and patient, and the meanings these experiences assume for each of the parties involved, in turn, shaping how each responds to the other. It is this complex field of reciprocal mutual influence that constitutes the intersubjective matrix and becomes the object of analytic exploration.

Kohut's discoveries of the selfobject transferences are enduring and recognizable themes in all human relationships and thus we contend that in all treatments the intersubjective field is fundamentally constituted by the intersection of the selfobject transferences of patient and analyst. The sum total of all development-enhancing modes of relatedness – of these the selfobject transferences are foremost – are gathered under the heading of the *leading edge* (Tolpin, 2002).

On the other hand, self disorders are characterized by anxieties related to the potential emergence of selfobject transferences and accompanying vulnerabilities associated with the fear of repetition of trauma and other selfobject failures. These fears, anxieties, and dreads give rise to the repetitive transference patterns of patient and analyst, the intersection of which will equally shape the intersubjective field. The sum total of all repetitive modes of relatedness comprise the repetitive transferences and derive from traumatic experiences and selfobject ruptures are gathered under the heading of the *trailing edge* (Tolpin, 2002).

The concepts of leading edge and trailing edge describe an important duality, central to the intersubjective field: hope vs. dread. The leading edge expresses one's hopes and other progressive elements. The trailing edge harbors one's dreads and those fears that serve to preserve the status quo. Taken together, the concepts of the leading and trailing edges capture the ways in which hope and dread serve to organize and motivate contrary aspects of the transference. ISP is the perfect medium for this duality to be expressed, on the one hand focused on the development of a shared psychological field within which the selfobject transferences, the leading edge of the patient's emotional world is permitted to unfold and flourish, and on the other hand, wherein the repetitive transferences, or trailing edge, is elaborated and worked through. The question as to why either the leading edge or trailing edge becomes the focus of work, depends on what themes are salient at any given point in time.

Both patient and analyst experience the duality of hope and dread (Mitchell, 1993; Bacal & Thomson, 1996). Hence, each brings to the analytic situation their leading and trailing edges. The following is an example: The empathy and attunement of the analyst, while reflecting her leading edge, may stir up longings and needs in the patient, his nascent leading edge. This paradoxically may intensify the patient's trailing edge protections against rejection and abandonment, resulting in avoidance and "resistance." The patient's transference manifestations then activate the analyst's fear of rejection and failure, leading to her emotional withdrawal or dissociation: the analyst's trailing edge. The patient senses this and feels confirmed in his expectation of abandonment, thus warranting a redoubling of defenses and self-protective measures. The analyst becomes aware of how the patient's attitude evokes an old experience of rejection by her depressed mother. She also senses the patient's need to protect himself from his abusive parent. In this way, there is a congruence of trailing edges. The analyst's understanding helps her feel more empathic with the patient's need for self-defense and signals that the analyst's leading edge has moved to the forefront. The analyst puts into words what she thinks the patient may be feeling and the reasonableness of his seeking to protect himself. The patient begins to feel understood and safe, and his leading edge is activated as he feels more connected, as his fears are acknowledged, and he does not feel ashamed. Tentatively, the leading edge of both analyst and patient slip into congruence and tendrils of hope are extended, strengthening the sense of attunement.

The objective of ISP is the unfolding and development of the leading edge of the patient in the intersubjective field of the analytic situation, for it is at the leading edge of the transference that the patient's hope for selfobject experience is strongest and the associated motivations for renewed development most imminent. The unfolding of the creative capacities of the patient's leading edge is further facilitated by the engagement with the analyst's leading edge. So, for example, if when the patient seeks and finds a selfobject transference experience of mirrored expansiveness, at the same time the analyst experiences the patient's well-being and feels mirrored him or herself, a co-determined selfobject transference within the intersubjective field facilitates the patient's healthy sense of self. The same holds true for the idealizing transference and the twinship transference. Each of them may be the central leading-edge theme for both patient and analyst. The synchronicity of the patient's leading edge and the analyst's leading edge constitutes the dynamic basis for growth and creative change.

That being said, ISP recognizes that hope and dread are linked in a dialectical relationship. Hope is already contained in dread and dread is contained within hope. In the language of leading and trailing edges, the leading edge invariably revives the trailing edge themes, just as imbedded in the trailing edge is the kernel of the leading edge. In other words, in the experience of many patients, hope has too often resulted in failure and injury. Inevitably, the analyst's offering of an opportunity for a longed-for selfobject tie will activate old fears. At the same time, the activation of the trailing edge intensifies the desire for repair and restoration associated with the meeting of selfobject needs. This dialectic, which is also active for the analyst, opens up infinite configurations that might emerge in the analytic relationship. The analyst seeks to feel her way into and through this complex, ever-changing, and volatile psychological and emotional dialectic. It is the tension inherent in this dialectic between leading and trailing edges (the hopes tied to and restricted by the dreads that keep us safe) that creates distress and is thus the primary motivator for the patient. Yet it is this same tension that provides the opportunity for the analyst to support the leading-edge hopes and thus tip the balance of the transference toward change.

The patient's dreads are particularly strong and unyielding when the core organizing fantasies remain undeveloped and therefore maladaptive. Untransformed grandiosity mobilizes dependency needs, which may be accompanied by threatening memories and emotional trauma. As a result, the mobilization of self-protective, defensive strategies accompanies the dread of repetition. Because the trailing edge emerges in these symptomatic and resistive dynamics, the analyst inevitably becomes personally embroiled, not least because of the analyst's own trailing edge. Working with and through the complex trailing edge toward therapeutic change becomes possible because of the unique characteristics of the analytic relationship. The analytic dialogue, which is tilted toward the subjective world of the patient through the tool of empathy, is facilitated by the analyst's ability to decenter from his or her own trailing edges. The analyst's ability to interpret the patient's dread while maintaining responsiveness to the patient's subjective life allows the patient to feel safe enough from the threat of repetition of trauma and/or selfobject failure and thereby encouraged to relax protective measures and defenses. In this environment, selfobject longings are revived and hope rather than dread becomes justified. The result is the evocation of selfobject needs in an intersubjective context wherein they might be met. As the leading edge of patient is met by the leading edge of the analyst, a transformative engagement between patient and analyst is activated. In this intersubjective field, the patient finds a sustained facilitating context for the unfolding of new psychic structures and growth.

ISP treatment should not be confused with a simply supportive process. Interpretation and working through of the trailing edge is a requirement for therapeutic success – even as it occurs in the context of a newfound sense of safety that relaxes the grip of the fearful past, allowing for the emergence and enactment of new, now-unencumbered hope. In other words, the therapeutic action of ISP consists of two interrelated processes: development of new psychological structures when the tie is intact and transformation of existing structure via interpretation when the tie is disrupted.

Although interpretations of the leading edge are not needed when patient and analyst are connected by the analyst's attuned engagement with the patient's leading edge, we contend that such leading edge interpretations at crucial times may significantly strengthen the intersubjective bond and promote forward development. In other words, the interpretation of the leading edge and of the generative intersubjective field can also strengthen the patient's self, at a time in the therapy when the patient is beyond the shame of identifying the specific nature of the therapeutic relationship. In doing so, the core of the patient's self-experience is enhanced and fortified. Furthermore, the patient is empowered by knowing what he or she needs. Getting help is easier when we can ask for what we need.

Whenever the selfobject tie is ruptured and the patient's dread is in the foreground, interpretation of the trailing edge becomes essential. The process of empathic, compassionate interpretation of repetitive transferential experiences serves to illuminate and bring to consciousness central protective organizing principles and self and object fantasies that constitute the person's character structure, and declares them to be eminently understandable from within the intersubjective context with the analyst. Such understanding re-establishes the selfobject tie, allowing the leading edge to move once again to the foreground. This process of interpretation brings about the transformation of existing structures, as described by Kohut in 1984.

When repetitive transferences of patient and analyst are worked through, the trailing edge dynamics recede and the yearned-for selfobject transferences of patient and analyst are able to unfold. This will constitute the fortuitous intersubjective field within which the patient and the analyst receive the emotional nutrients that permit self-experience to evolve and solidify. The analyst is experienced as providing the needed selfobject experience that results in the acquisition and development of the patient's new or emergent self structures. The same holds true in the opposite direction: The analyst feels affirmed in his or her sense of competence and efficacy, which meets his or her longed-for selfobject experience and results in the acquisition and consolidation of the analyst's emergent self structures.

The unfolding of the leading edge in the intersubjective field is the foremost objective of ISP. We thereby have turned the therapeutic action of traditional psychoanalysis on its head and are proclaiming that the work with the trailing edge, while necessary, is not the sufficient condition for a curative action. The sufficient condition is the work with the leading edge. For it is the strengthening of the leading edge, and with it the hope and motivation for renewed self-actualization and healthy development, that is the driving force behind the therapeutic process.

Notes

1 The term fantasy is used here in keeping with psychoanalytic theorizing. Since selfobject bonds refer to the patient's subjective frame of reference, the term fantasy is used to denote the patient's experience of the tie with the analyst. The use of the term fantasy in no way implies a lack of reality; it only denotes that the reality is determined by the patient's subjective experience.
2 The terms "intersubjective" and "relational," in current psychoanalytic parlance, have overlapping but not identical meanings. "Relational" emphasizes interactions between people, whereas "intersubjective" refers to the subjective experience of the relationship, whether or not an interaction takes place. This subjective dimension is not included in the term "relational." For example, sitting with a patient in a catatonic state will constitute a specific intersubjective field but it would not be a relational experience. In this way relational experiences are always intersubjective but not all intersubjective experiences are relational. Intersubjective is the more encompassing term.

Chapter 2

Empathy in Intersubjective Self Psychology

Karen Roser and Aviva Rohde

Empathy is central to the theory and practice of both Self Psychology as well as ISP. It is the subject of Kohut's first Self Psychological paper (1959), and his last presentation before his death in 1981. For Kohut, the work of the Self Psychologist is rooted in the empathic understanding of the patient's experience and the formation of an empathic bond.

Empathy was defined by Kohut as "vicarious introspection," the slow and deliberate process of feeling oneself into the experience of another (1959, p. 207). It is the way to begin to make sense of another's internal world. As Kohut said, "it is a mode of observation attuned to the inner life of man" (1981, p. 542). Empathic understanding is a mental activity of the therapist in which she attempts to understand the patient's emotional and experiential world from within the patient's subjectivity. Self Psychologists are attuned to a patient's hopes and strengths. These form the basis of the selfobject transferences, and the patient's leading edge. The Self Psychologist is also attuned to the patient's vulnerabilities, or the patient's trailing edge dreads. These vulnerabilities might be easy to empathize with as, for instance, when the patient describes various ways in which he has felt injured by those in his life such as parents, bosses, spouses. At other times these vulnerabilities manifest in ways which might be more difficult to empathize with, such as when the patient gets angry at or feels hurt by something the therapist says or does. The Self Psychologist's focus on empathy helps the therapist find ways to understand her patient's reactions from within her patient's personal, experiential world, no matter how foreign it may seem to her.

Not only is empathy at the center of the psychoanalytic endeavor, it is also at the center of human relationships in general. For instance, when a child is complaining of a stomach ache before school, the parents use their ongoing experience of the child to feel their way into the child's internal world in order to understand whether the child is physically ill or might instead be feeling anxious about going to school. If they can maintain their empathy, they can respond to their child's needs in the moment.

And the child will feel understood and strengthened. In therapy, the therapist puts her empathy to benevolent[1] use, which enables her to understand, support and interpret her patient's experience.

For instance, as a simple example, suppose an unusually tall person walks into the office. The empathically attuned therapist asks herself, "What is it like for this person to be so tall?" She might think about what it would mean to her (introspection), but would be aware that she does not yet know what it means to the patient (vicarious introspection). In asking the question, she is beginning to create a space in which it is not external reality that is the subject of her inquiry, but her patient's subjective experience of it. Upon exploration she might learn that her assumption, for instance, that being tall contributes to positive self-regard, does not hold true, and the patient's dominant feeling is shame at "sticking out like a sore thumb." To arrive at this understanding is an act of empathy or empathic exploration, in which we understand the patient's experience from within his own experience. If the therapist also felt ashamed of sticking out like a sore thumb, there would be a meeting of their worlds which would make the empathy easy to access. However, if the therapist had always wanted to be tall, the experience of her patient might be difficult to grasp. Acting from within her trailing edge of shame at being short, the therapist risks missing her patient, and a moment of empathic failure would occur. Alternatively, staying attuned to the patient's inner world, different from that of the therapist, allows the therapist to decenter and express deep understanding of the patient's lived experience.

Thus, by definition, empathy is a process of exploration leading toward deep understanding. Empathy is not an affect. This distinction, often misunderstood, has led to many misperceptions about empathy. For instance, empathy is often mistakenly assumed to be synonymous with compassion, attunement, kindness or intuition. Let's take each of these ideas in turn.

Compassion is a feeling of sympathy for the predicament of another. In order to feel compassion, one must first empathize with the other's experience. Out of that process one might feel concern for the other. The feeling of compassion derives from the process of empathic exploration, but comes only after empathic discovery. Empathy, the mode of exploration, is the method by which we might come to feel compassion.

Attunement refers to the experience of feeling emotionally on the same page with someone else. Being attuned to someone's experience is an emotional connection, a feeling. Empathy can lead to attunement but also can lead beyond: to an understanding of a feeling based on your knowledge of factors in the patient's life – it is an analytic process rather than an affective experience.

Kindness refers to a feeling of consideration for another and is associated with action. Empathy, on the other hand, is an internal process.

Empathy can lead to kindness but it does not presume kindness or benevolence. It only presumes understanding of the other.

Intuition is a spontaneous feeling about another's experience and, in this way, is close to empathy. However, intuition bypasses cognition: rather than the slow, deliberate process of empathic exploration, intuition comes as a flash, a moment of awareness. We might have an intuition about someone's internal experience, but it is the process of exploration, hallmark of empathy, which has the potential to confirm intuition.

In addition to a mode of exploration, Kohut also recognized that listening empathically is a mode of relating and creates a bond between people. "The mere presence of empathy has also a beneficial, in a broad sense, a therapeutic effect- both in the clinical setting and in human life in general" (1981, p. 544). Through the act of empathizing, the therapist conveys an acceptance and sense of importance placed on the patient's lived experience. The experience of being understood in a deep way provides the foundation for the bond between two people. Each moment of inaccurate empathy has the potential to derail the bond, but each moment of subsequent correction deepens it still further.

The concept of empathy as a curative bond is inherent to what Bacal (1985) describes as "optimal responsiveness." The therapist's ability to deeply empathize with the patient's experience makes possible a response that addresses the patient's needs optimally. The patient feels understood and the healing bond deepens. Optimal responsiveness is made possible by the therapist's empathy.

> **Clinical moment**
>
> A husband and wife were taking turns telling me (KR) about the extremely stressful time each of them was having. At one point, the husband said, as an example of how the stress is affecting him, that he had "acted out" that morning by being sarcastic about his wife's individual therapist. He had apologized almost immediately, but felt bad about it. Later, during the wife's share, she said she remained hurt by her husband's remark. There followed a moment of silence, each in their experience of strong feelings, neither coming through for the other.
>
> I had a moment of feeling my way into the husband's experience, and asked him if there was a feeling which had led to the sarcastic comment. The husband thought a moment and said yes, he now realizes he was worried that, if his wife doesn't get the help she needs, it will have an impact on him. He expressed a great deal of shame about this. As he spoke I saw the wife's face soften. She said she understood his feelings and that she would feel – in fact actually does feel – the same way. The husband in turn softened. He reached out his hand and held hers.

> My line of inquiry arose out of a moment of empathy, my appreciation that there must be something unexpressed that would lead to the sarcastic comment. It is noteworthy that my empathic inquiry into the husband's experience led to the wife's empathy for her husband, and to a deepening in the bond between them.

Empathy and Intersubjectivity

We now turn to an Intersubjective view of empathy. In 1987, Stolorow, Brandchaft and Atwood introduced the concept of "sustained empathic inquiry" (p. 10), based on Kohut's work on empathy. For them, the therapist's sustained empathic immersion in the patient's experiential world leads to the formation of an intersubjective context wherein the therapist seeks to understand the patient from within the patient's world and the patient comes to believe that he can be understood. Thus, as with Kohut, empathy becomes the mode in which understanding and action occur within the dyad. From an Intersubjective frame of reference, however, the concept of empathy evolves further. The notion that there are two subjectivities in the room – patient's and therapist's – adds new layers to the concept of empathy. With two subjectivities actively engaged, we understand that the therapist's empathy is – by definition – reflective of her own subjectivity, and as such, impacts and co-determines the patient's experience and vice versa. With this in mind we understand that there is no such thing as neutral or objective empathy. The patient's subjectivity can only be understood through the lens of the intersubjective context within which it occurs. Sustained empathic immersion happens within the field generated by the intersection of the subjectivities of patient and therapist.

For an Intersubjectivist, empathy is directed not just to the patient's internal world, as it evolves in relation to the therapist, but also to an understanding of how that empathy is formed and shaped inescapably by one's own subjectivity. The therapist's presence and actions affect the patient's experience and vice versa: the therapist's subjectivity is influenced by the patient. For example, when the therapist's expressions of understanding are met with openness and appreciation by the patient, the therapist will feel more effective and able, which will in turn enhance her ability to empathize and act on her empathy. The patient, in the presence of a therapist who feels effective, will likely feel more trusting, more capable, stronger.

Empathy and Intersubjective Self Psychology

Finally, we turn to ISP and the contributions gained to the concept of empathy when we combine Self Psychology and Intersubjectivity. The

Intersubjective Self Psychologist is empathically attuned to shifts in the patient's self state, seeking to understand these shifts from within the patient's world of shifting selfobject needs and transferences. This is the Self Psychology part of the equation. Intersubjectivity adds the dimension of empathy which is directed towards the field from within which both patient and analyst experience each other. Not only are the patient's selfobject needs considered and understood, but also considered and understood are the ways in which the relationship between patient and therapist bears on the therapist's selfobject experience. Empathy is directed toward the ways the patient's hopeful feelings and feelings of dread affect the therapist, and vice versa. An awareness of how the patient's generative and repetitive themes intersect with those of the therapist is at the heart of the treatment for an Intersubjective Self Psychologist.

In addition, Self Psychology adds to Intersubjectivity the understanding that the empathic bond is curative in and of itself. For Stolorow et al., empathy remains an exploratory activity. In 1992, they describe the goals of the therapeutic alliance as "the progressive unfolding, illumination and transformation of the patient's subjective universe" (p. 94). This is achieved by the analyst's "unwavering commitment to understanding from within the patient's own subjective framework" (ibid., p. 93). This describes the primarily cognitive function of empathy. It is based solely upon the act of understanding the patient within his subjective world and does not consider that the experience of being listened to empathically is curative. For an Intersubjectivist, thus, it is the act of understanding which is most powerful. For an Intersubjective Self Psychologist, the healing power is also in the empathic bond, in the therapist's continual focus on her patient's experience. In the analytic setting, the empathic bond is an ever evolving feedback loop between the patient's and therapist's emotional worlds, where each confirmation of understanding deepens the bond in both directions.

Working empathically from within an Intersubjective Self Psychological stance is a complicated endeavor. It becomes especially difficult when we sense that the patient is resistant, suffering the throes of a repetitive transference, or expressing something from the unconscious about which the patient is as yet unaware. In these moments, our patient's deepest experience may be disavowed from their felt need. In such cases we must be empathic to the patient's expressed need, while also exploring the disavowed roots of that experience. For instance, while our patient may want us to affirm that indeed the boss is at fault, we might sense that the patient's defensiveness is at work, thereby contributing to the boss's response. In the ongoing work – the sustained empathic inquiry – we see that the mutual influence of patient and therapist affects how we think about each other at any given moment. Being empathic to a defensive or resistant theme in the patient, the therapist may know something and address herself to something that the patient does not know yet. Only by watching what happens as we relate, as therapist tries out a new perspective and patient responds, and vice versa, do we become sensitive to the deeper meanings of our patient's experience.

Out of this tender feedback loop, we start to arrive at a place of understanding and clarity. The bi-directional nature of the selfobject experiences for both patient and therapist defines the nature of the empathy and the potential for growth-promoting therapeutic experience. From within her empathic understanding of the patient's leading and trailing edges, the therapist makes interpretations, interpreting first one, then the other, based on her understanding of what would lead to the most growth in any given moment. Ultimately, whether the interpretations are experienced as empathic or off the mark is within the provenance of the patient; it is the patient who determines ultimately the correctness of the therapist's empathy.

Case of Tess[2]

The following moments from the opening phase of the case of Tess demonstrate the value and transformative power of empathy within the theory of ISP. The case was chosen to illustrate empathy because the patient's initial presentation challenged the therapist's capacity for empathic understanding and responding. In fact, rather than feeling for the patient's experience, the therapist felt drawn away from the patient's experience toward instead imagining the reactions of important others in the patient's life. Working from an Intersubjective Self Psychological perspective, the therapist was able to shift away from her trailing edge response to the patient toward a leading edge experience, which opened the pathway for empathy. Finding the way into the patient's experiential world allowed the treatment to break free from a potential stalemate and move forward.

When I opened the door to meet Tess, a 38-year-old single mother of a teenager and a young child, I was struck by her youthful appearance and her earnestness, none of which predicted the vitriolic anger I was to hear about. She was despairing over ever resolving a paralyzing argument with her sister Anne, 15 years her senior, with whom she lived and who had raised her after the death of their single mother. Tess was in a chronic state of rage at Anne, and was demoralized from the ways the unrelenting rage had taken her over. The everyday challenges of raising her children while managing tensions in her work life were only made worse by the churning anger. Living under the same roof as her sister, Tess felt unable to disengage from the anger roiling inside of her. This is what brought her to therapy.

The trouble began when Tess, in a distressed state after an argument with her adolescent child, approached Anne for guidance, as she'd done many times before. Anne, to Tess's great dismay, responded dismissively,

"That child was always out of control." Anne's words enraged Tess, and so began a bitter, unrelenting argument. Tess was furious that her sister would not apologize for uttering these words which felt so hurtful. Anne's claim that she could not apologize for an injury she did not understand inflamed the situation further. Tess's rage grew to encompass a litany of past hurts: overheard comments about her difficult child, feeling disregarded, feeling taken advantage of. Eventually the rift expanded to a refusal to engage with her sister. Tess refused interaction with Anne until, and unless, Anne agreed to pursue therapy with a therapist whose qualifications and standards matched my own. It is worth noting that, at the time, I was so derailed by Tess's intense rage that I missed the clue she'd just offered to me about her selfobject yearning.

Tess spent the initial sessions turning around and around her rage at her sister, repeating the minutiae of the arguments, word for word. Each pass through the recollection re-ignited her dismay about Anne's failings. She had committed each sister's words to memory, words that helplessly replayed in her mind and in session. Tess was sure that I would see the issue plainly and clearly; that Anne's "refusal to see what was obvious" would be as clear to me as it was to her, that Tess's expletive-laden responses were harmless expressions of righteous anger. She was certain that her own words were correctly expressive of the problem and that I would see things as she did. Unfortunately, I did not. To my ear, Tess's anger was disproportionate rage. She responded to her sister with caustic sarcasm, belittling rejections, angry curses. I had the sense that Anne had tried, but felt helpless to understand and eventually felt cautious about interacting at all. All the way through, Tess shut her down with a wall of anger.

I was at a loss. Rather than feeling for Tess, I felt for Anne, readily imagining her dismay and helplessness in the face of Tess's relentless anger. Empathy? Feeling myself into the psychological world of my patient? It escaped me.

To complicate matters, I was committed to an intersubjective awareness that "truth" as such is subjective. But all the while that Tess was fighting to have her sister acknowledge a "truth" she herself was committed to, I held fast to my own competing "truth," that Tess's expressed hostility was unrecognized by her, and being denied in front of me. I was puzzled and frustrated. I felt certain that what I heard as Tess's verbal tirades represented her trailing edge, desperately in need of interpretation. But the hostility she expressed was so successfully disavowed there was no way in. Had I tried to address the anger directly I believe she would have been both incredulous and hurt. It might have driven her away. Once, in a moment that emerged from my own distressed trailing edge, a well-worn defense against feeling grievously misunderstood, I said, "You sound quite angry," and Tess responded, "I know, I'm OK with that." This was a non-starter. At the same time, I feared that the longer I went without addressing the ways her hurtful words were at the heart of this problem the more I was failing Tess and reneging on my responsibility as a therapist who both promises an authentic response and addresses trailing edge manifestations. Mostly I felt that her reality and mine were so far apart that *there was no empathic basis* from which to explore different perspectives.

I was lost, but she kept coming back. While I didn't understand this I had an intuitive sense that Tess placed extraordinary faith in my understanding. I knew that I had to figure this out. The one connection I held onto as a kind of toe-hold in an otherwise uphill climb toward empathy was the image of Tess tortured from the inside by the relentless, churning rage. Whatever I thought of the content of her argument, I could readily imagine the experience of anguish from feeling held captive by unrelenting, helpless rage. With that image in mind I had a chance of decentering from my own dismayed reaction to her hostility; I had a chance to understand something more. This was the beginning of my being able to access a leading edge openness to her experience, the beginning of my being able to think and work intersubjectively. I actively called upon my own memories of feeling trapped, helpless anger in order to feel my way into Tess's experience; though I did not yet understand, I felt compassion for her, and even the seeds of affinity with her.

Once I was able to locate a reaction in me that was less critical, I felt freer to raise some questions. I said that I thought we needed to understand something deeper about her anger. That I had the sense that her anger was the product of something more, something from earlier, something deeply felt, not before understood or expressed, but crystallized in the fight that triggered the grievous rupture. Here I was working on the premise that rage is the expression of narcissistic injury, a theoretical concept that is at the heart of Self Psychology. But my motivation to shift the conversation came as well from my intersubjective understanding: In the absence of understanding the roots of Tess's rage I felt distant from her, separate, and judgmental. By pursuing an understanding of those roots, I was also addressing *my own need* to find a pathway toward empathy. Moving toward what I could experience in myself as a leading edge allowed the intersubjective perspective to guide our process.

Tess was willing to pursue this exploration. She said the fight caught her off-guard because, in Tess's words: "I was always so close to Anne. She was always a heroine to me. That's why I went to her when I was upset and why I was so offended by her response." Tess had just painted a picture of traumatic de-idealization. Tess's self experience had developed along the idealizing line with her sister as the needed idealizable selfobject. In the face of the devastating loss of the mother, Tess's need to trust in the guidance, strength, wisdom, and maternal qualities of her older sister was great. When Anne treated Tess's distress about the fight with her teenager casually, and complicated things by referencing long-held disdain for the child, Tess felt not only lost and disappointed in the moment but profoundly betrayed by the very person she needed to shore herself up.

Continued exploration revealed that this traumatic rupture in the idealizing line was the proverbial last straw in a lifetime of both small and significant cracks in selfobject responsiveness. Tess shared her experiences of confusion and dismay when, for example, Anne brought dislikable boyfriends into their home or when Anne made household financial decisions that favored Anne over Tess. Tess had never before articulated her experience of having promised herself to always be compliant with Anne's choices and directives. She was dutiful to a fault, which required denying how distressed and betrayed she actually felt. She formed an identity around her commitment to work hard to preserve family harmony, which allowed her to preserve Anne as idealizable. This has helped us understand that her current-day frustration, that she suffers while Anne disengages, has long roots in her feeling that she sacrificed herself and her legitimate developmental needs in order to preserve Anne's self experience. She was earnestly doing what was expected of her and no one was there to understand her.

In thinking about her own experience of being a mother, Tess began to wonder first about Anne's experience of "mothering" Tess, and then about their mother's experience of being a mother. She felt that Anne betrayed what should have been an ironclad commitment to remain Tess's loyal parenting guide; this was a significant rupture in the idealizing tie to Anne. But even more, this realization ushered in a devastating awareness of the trauma of their mother's death. Tess's experience of the de-idealization of the maternal figure she'd come to trust opened up the devastating wound of the loss of the mother – the original traumatic rupture in the maternal idealization.

Tess's ability to speak of her deepest pain allowed her leading edge – the yearning to find the maternal guide she'd so grievously missed out on – to emerge. My recognition of the traumatic de-idealization at her core revealed the profound narcissistic injury at the root of her rage. This understanding allowed me to decenter from a judgmental reaction to her expressed rage and instead empathize with the pain that drives it. Here was the emergence of my leading edge in concert with hers. In the context of this growing empathic bond, Tess began to say that while the estrangement from her sister remained, she no longer suffered the churning anger that had been so deeply punishing. She achieved a relative calm for which she expressed gratitude.

This newfound calm allowed for the development of a natural feedback loop between empathy and the evolving selfobject transference, all experienced within the intersubjective field. Tess turned from talking about her distress with her sister to saying she wanted help with something else. "You're a mother. You can give me some good parenting advice." I was keenly aware that Tess was offering me an opportunity to both substitute for the mentoring she'd hoped to get from Anne, and at a deeper level be the mother she didn't have. This moment grew out of our newly forming empathic bond – both of us meeting at the leading edges of our experience.

Tess wanted help with encouraging her young child to stay in bed through the night. Evenings were challenging enough without adding to them the interrupted sleep that happens when a child climbs into the parent's bed in the middle of the night. I resonated immediately with her experience and described for her what seemed intuitively right for me when my child didn't stay in her bed through the night, instead climbing into mine and similarly disturbing my sleep. We developed a plan whereby she could come in at night, pull a sleeping bag out from under my bed, and crawl into it on the floor next to me, but in her own space. I'd reach down over the side of the bed to hold her hand, she'd reach up to grab my hand, til she fell back to sleep. What was most noteworthy to me about what I shared with Tess was that the image of the held hands over the side of the bed was the detail Tess found most meaningful.

From this I was able to understand a dynamic that was always there, but lay hidden behind the defensive rage. I thought of the image I have of Tess as I greet her at the beginning of each session. I am struck each time by her innocent appearance, her youthful demeanor, her earnestness. I realized that she is looking at me as her good mother – desperately needed – metaphorically reaching up her hand to mine, settling finally into calm. I understand that I am more purely idealizable than the mothering sister who fell from grace and also desperately needed given the loss of the mother whose death reverberates as an on-going trauma. In the face of the traumatic de-idealization of mother and sister, the yearning to experience me as an idealizable maternal figure was intense.

This understanding solidified three essential building blocks: I could truly *empathize* with Tess's experience of traumatic de-idealization, I could be responsive to her yearning to establish a progressive *idealization* along the maternal line, and we were both engaged along our own *leading edges* of development. This foundation allowed for the beginnings of the next essential phase in the treatment: addressing the trailing edge.

Tess described to me another punishing argument she had with her sister, an argument that ended when Anne stormed away, grabbing her car keys. In what felt to me like an unguarded moment Tess told me that she'd called after her sister, "Go drive off a cliff!" She started to describe whatever happened next, but then stopped herself and said "I just now realized that I say terrible things when I'm angry. I really have to stop doing that." This was a stunning moment – so fresh and raw and plain. It was all the more meaningful for being a true discovery for Tess. I believe that Tess could share this moment – both the revelation of what she said to Anne and her assessment of its destructiveness – because she could more fully trust in our empathic bond. She could trust in my understanding of the profound frustration, hurt and helplessness she feels with Anne and so share with me a fuller picture of her rage. And out of that trust she was able to recognize the hostility expressed in her words and challenge herself to do better.

My sense is that the corrective that has happened as a result of developing the empathic bond has created movement on many fronts. The idealizing selfobject transference has blossomed and as a result Tess has moved from the frozen, raging, confused place she was in when we met to feeling that she has developed a measure of calm and the fortitude to begin addressing the relational stress she experiences in the most important and needed relationships of her life.

Conclusion

Kohut impressed upon us that even when we are convinced of our own rightness in the face of our patient's apparent wrongness, the patient's fundamental, experiential truth – garnered through the process of deeply empathizing with the patient – is the most meaningful experience to be known (1984, pp. 93–94). In the case presented, it was a commitment to a deep empathic exploration that allowed the therapist to decenter from her fixed and ultimately misguided understanding, in order to open up awareness of the patient's deeper truth.

In summary, empathy is the process by which we come to understand another's experience from within their subjective world. It is subjective: the way we experience and empathize with another is based upon our own unique subjectivity, and how our subjectivity is impacted by the intersubjective field created by patient and therapist. An Intersubjective Self Psychological approach to empathy encompasses the role of empathy as a tool for understanding patients from within their own experience and as a healing bond. The focus of our empathy is on both the subjectivity of patient and of therapist, as well as on how they influence each other.

Notes

1 While empathy is most often thought of as being used for good, benevolence is not assumed. Empathy, or the deep understanding of another's inner world, can just as readily be used for malevolent purposes as when that understanding is used inflict harm. Kohut famously uses the example of Hitler's whistle bombs to illustrate this idea (1981, p. 529).
2 This case was conducted by one of the authors. It is written in first person, but reflects the view of both authors.

Chapter 3

Transference in Intersubjective Self Psychology

Aviva Rohde and Karen Roser

The analysis of transference, loosely defined as the patient's thematic experience of the therapist, lies at the heart of the psychoanalytic endeavor. Freud's (1895, 1912) early discovery of the potency of transference remains a cornerstone of psychoanalytic theory, and in the years since Freud's groundbreaking discovery advances in psychoanalytic theory that have major implications for our understanding of transference have taken hold. Heinz Kohut (1971, 1977, 1984) developed the theory of Self Psychology by raising the profile of self experience. Stolorow and colleagues (Stolorow et al., 1987, 1994; Stolorow & Atwood, 1992) developed the theory of Intersubjectivity by recognizing the inherent interconnectedness of interpersonal experience. Both theories have significant implications for the theory of transference. More recently, Intersubjective Self Psychology (ISP) was developed, drawing from the most clinically potent aspects of each component theory and thereby enhancing our understanding of transference. This chapter will explicate the fundamental principles of an Intersubjective Self Psychological theory of transference.

Transference has been widely understood in psychoanalytic circles as the transfer of past experiences, beliefs, affects and relational patterns onto the present, typically onto the person of the therapist. Freud (1895) referred to this ubiquitous phenomenon as a "false connection," and considered it an "obstacle" to be struck down. In treatment, this obstacle might emerge in various forms. The patient might regress, and in so doing relate to the therapist in a symptomatic expression of an early childhood phase. Or perhaps the patient displaces feelings properly directly toward early objects and now misdirects them toward the therapist. Alternatively, the patient projects internal painful, destructive, or shameful affects onto the innocent therapist. Or the patient becomes trapped in repetition-compulsion, helplessly repeating with the therapist the centrally troubling dynamics of childhood (see Stolorow et al., 1987 for details).

All of these transference manifestations fall under the category of transference as distortion, a dynamic relational configuration in which the real and true present is distorted by a past which looms too large to be shed. It is the job of the therapist in this realm to correct these distortions and guide the patient toward a real and true assessment of the present, via a real and true assessment of the therapist. Of course, all these dynamics presume that the therapist knows what is real, that the therapist knows better than the patient what is true. More than that, such transference interpretations presume that there is a singular truth to be arrived at; subjective experience carrying much less validity than objective, analytic wisdom. It is just this notion of transference as distortion that undergoes significant revision when seen through the lenses of Self Psychology and Intersubjectivity.

What happens to our understanding of transference when we look through the lens of Self Psychology? The Self Psychologist's focus on empathy – a deep and searching process of feeling and thinking oneself into another's subjective experience – teaches us that the other's subjective experience has logic and value and primacy, whether or not it is consonant with our own subjectivity. For each of us, subjective experience has psychological truth. The notion of transference as distortion, in assuming that only the therapist has access to truth, invalidates the patient's subjective truth, and risks alienating self from other. From a Self Psychological perspective, we aim to discover the patient's subjective world, the patient's personal truth. And that is what opens up the pathway to the selfobject transference and to new opportunities for transformation.

In order to understand the concept of the selfobject transference, it is first necessary to explain how Self Psychologists understand the selfobject experience and its importance in healthy self development, to which we now turn. Listening empathically to our patient's felt experience we discover, as Kohut did, that healthy and robust self experience relies upon the felt responsiveness of others. This use of the other for the sustenance and development of the self, which includes feeling the other as part of the self, is called the selfobject experience. The notion of selfobject experience is rooted in the idea that healthy self-development requires the use of the other to provide and fulfill psychological functions. Capacities such as self-esteem regulation and self-soothing develop when the individual is free to use the other, to experience the other as part of the self, to borrow the other's evolved development for the benefit of the self. The use of the other for the sustenance of the self is the selfobject experience.

Selfobject needs are primary developmental needs. They are as essential for psychological survival and development as air and water are for physical survival and development. Like plants which bend inexorably toward the sun, we – by definition of our humanity – seek available and responsive selfobject experience in our surround. In healthy development, the child uses the parent to supply healthy stores of narcissism in the form of recognition, calming and soothing, shared experience. We all use important others – teachers, friends, lovers – to provide these nourishing narcissistic supplies along the way. And when these developmental needs are met, unimpeded, the self begins to grow and takes on independent capacities for self-esteem and the like.

Given the importance of selfobject needs, the failure to find selfobject responsiveness in needed others is disruptive to self development. Such ruptures are at the root of psychological distress and may lead to symptomatic expressions of narcissism – excessive grandiosity, or its opposite, depleted self-esteem; emptiness and alienation may also result. When ruptures become repeated in the form of traumatic derailment of developmental needs or phase-inappropriate derailment of developmental needs, healthy development stalls, and narcissistic pathology becomes entrenched. Alternatively, when selfobject responsiveness is available and well-attuned to the developmental needs of the child (or adult), psychological healing moves to the foreground, and development proceeds along healthy lines. This is the foundation that guides Self Psychological treatment.

It is the job of the therapist to facilitate the development of a healthy selfobject tie, strive for its maintenance, and interpret the disruptions that are inevitable. The therapist must be alert for underlying, perhaps even hidden expressions of selfobject yearnings (see Tolpin, 2002), respond to those bids for selfobject responsiveness, and in so doing, allow for the re-establishment of a healthy selfobject pathway for development. The activation of the selfobject transference with the therapist – a renewed opportunity for the patient to use another for the sustenance of the self – puts derailed development back on track, creates new possibilities for stalled development to turn to growth and for rigidified narcissistic pathology to be transformed into mature and flexible expressions of self.

With these thoughts in mind, it is easy to see that facilitating the establishment and maintenance of a needed selfobject transference – rather than interpreting away a distorted and misdirected transference – is central to a successful Self Psychological treatment. The establishment and maintenance of the selfobject tie may be accomplished via the interpretation of selfobject needs, interpretation of ruptures in selfobject experience, repair of such ruptures, and/or provision of selfobject responsiveness. The result of the activation or reactivation of the selfobject tie is transformation from archaic to mature forms of self-experience. This transformation continues even outside the therapist's office: since we do not outgrow our need for healthy self experience – those needs are lifelong – we look to develop and maintain ties to an available, responsive selfobject milieu in the forms of self-sustaining relationships and an on-going community that can be emotionally relied upon.

Kohut delineated three major selfobject themes, or developmental lines along which self experience undergoes transformation. These selfobject themes are mirroring, idealization, and twinship. The mirror selfobject experience refers to the need for affirmation, recognition, acknowledgment, celebration, appraisal. It refers to the yearning to find the proverbial "gleam in the mother's eye" when involved in something joyful or expansive. The yearning to be known and accepted for who one is involves a hope for a mirror experience. The psychological development facilitated via a mirroring experience is the building and maintenance of a positively-toned self-esteem. An example of a mirroring experience might be a patient who, having been raised by a depressed and distracted parent, yearns for the focused attention of the carefully listening therapist. The result would be the activation of developmentally progressive mirror needs in the service of self-esteem.

Idealization refers to the yearning to merge with the strength, wisdom, confidence, inspiration, and safety of an admired other. The ability to fold oneself within the protective arms of the larger other allows for a sense of safety and calm, a capacity to begin to self-soothe. An example of idealization: a patient whose parent was too anxious to protect the patient from undue distress might especially look to the therapist to be confident, wise, and stable. The successful idealization experience would facilitate the patient's ability to self-soothe.

In twinship, one looks to find in the other an experience of sameness and to confirm that sameness with the feeling that cherished alikeness is reciprocally shared (Togashi, 2009). This feeling of kinship, often felt in friendship or community creates the feeling of shared humanity, the feeling of being human among humans. For example, a patient who grew up feeling isolated and alone might especially thrive in the discovery that the therapist shares in a range of emotional or personal experiences. This twinship facilitates a sense of shared humanity.

Of course, there are inevitable failures in empathy and selfobject responsiveness which cause ruptures in the needed selfobject tie. Perhaps the therapist fails to comment on the patient's newly developed pride in an acquired skill and the patient feels unrecognized. Or maybe the therapist feels stumped in providing some good advice and the patient's idealization is dashed. Or the therapist feels distant from the patient and the twinship is disrupted. In all these scenarios interpretation of the selfobject yearning and the failure to find in the therapist the desired response provides the pathway to restore the very selfobject experience that was ruptured. This rupture-repair cycle is at the heart of the analytic work in self psychology; in fact, it is often the rupture in an otherwise smooth analytic relationship that clarifies that a selfobject transference had been either yearned for or was formerly in place.

A therapeutic focus on the selfobject experience constitutes what we refer to as the leading edge of treatment – a focus on the patient's hope. This hope might be explicitly expressed or it might be hidden under layers of symptomatic expression. Either way, drawing out that hope is the mechanism for building selfobject experience. But patients also bring their dreads to treatment. Dreads which are well-earned, deeply entrenched, and which keep the patient stuck in dynamics that prevent forward movement. We recognize these dreads in the form of defenses and the repetitive transference, and we refer to them collectively as the trailing edge. Often enough a rupture in a selfobject tie will trigger a trailing edge response. Alternatively, a deeply rigidified defensive structure might prevent a selfobject tie from evolving at all. These are thorny engagements but inevitable too; they are also opportunities for crucial work. In such cases a compassionate and determined empathic inquiry into the patient's experience and the stall in development becomes necessary. Interpretation of the repetitive theme – which itself performs a selfobject function – is the very pathway by which the selfobject tie is either restored or newly formed.

Given that the selfobject concept is elusive and easily misunderstood, it is important to clarify a few ideas. First, a selfobject is not a person, cherished and needed as that person might be. Rather, a selfobject is the therapist-serving-as-psychological-nourishment in the inner world of the patient, or the parent-serving-as-psychological-nourishment to the child. In the absence of the object functioning to shore up, there is no selfobject. Second, there is no such thing as a "good" or a "bad" selfobject. Selfobjects are by definition psychologically enhancing. If the presumed selfobject stops functioning in the service of the self, or worse, becomes destructive in the psyche of the self, it ceases to be a selfobject at all. Next, it is not possible to decide from within the subjectivity of the therapist that a patient needs this or that selfobject experience, as in, such-and-such a patient is short on mirroring, or needs someone to idealize. Instead what is important is that the therapist – via empathic immersion in the patient's subjective experience – discover the patient's yearnings to be responded to along specific selfobject lines. The therapist works to be responsive to the selfobject needs that are presented. Finally, selfobject themes are not determined by the activity of the therapist – rather by how the patient experiences the therapist's activity, whether consciously or unconsciously. The therapist may feel that he or she is responding along the lines of the mirror theme, but if the patient experiences the therapist's words as idealizable or reflective of a twinship experience, then those latter themes prevail. Related to this, the therapist does not do anything special to create selfobject experience other than to be alert to its emergence and/or interferences in its emergence. Being alert to the emerging selfobject need guides the therapist in choosing a pathway of responding. Being alert to interferences in the emergence of the selfobject theme affords the therapist the opportunity to prevent the patient's resistive response and/or triggers the therapist to pursue an understanding of the rupture in the treatment now requiring repair.

Within our understanding that the selfobject transference is central to a meaningfully conducted treatment, we must ask how then do we understand the success of treatment orientations that do not consider the selfobject experience to be central? Surely different successful treatments are well-matched between particular patient dynamics and particular therapeutic orientations. But it is also true that an intact selfobject experience may be operating silently, without explicit notice, in treatments which draw their inspiration from theories far from Self Psychology. A well-timed interpretation in a classical treatment may be felt to be especially meaningful because of the idealization the patient has for the therapist. The acceptance and understanding provided by the DBT therapist to his or her patient may be felt as compassionate mirroring. The enlivened dialogue between interpersonal/relational therapist and patient may facilitate a transformative twinship experience. The repair of a transferential rupture in any treatment may allow the needed selfobject experience to get back on track. And so on. In this way, we speak of the selfobject dimension of the treatment operating silently and successfully in the background of a variety of treatments.

What happens to our understanding of transference when seen through the lens of Intersubjectivity? Intersubjectivity as proposed by Stolorow and colleagues (Stolorow et al., 1987, 1994; Stolorow & Atwood, 1992) provides a model of psychological life which refers to the inherent context-dependency of emotional experience. Psychological experience begins in and is elaborated by the relational contexts in which it occurs. Individual experience is shaped in the interaction of self with other; psychological experience occurs in the interaction of psychological worlds. This means that emotional phenomena cannot be understood apart from the intersubjective contexts within which they occur. Experiences such as connection, disconnection, attunement, misattunement, responsiveness, and lack of responsiveness, for example, are all intersubjectively dependent.

The overlapping subjectivities of self and other constitute the intersubjective field, which might be composed of two peers, or child with parent, or patient with therapist. In any of these dyads there is a continually evolving feedback loop that generates a specific and evolving context, a shared experience in which each participant experiences self with other. A person's sense of self may be facilitated in the context of an attuned other; in such cases development proceeds from less to more mature. Or the sense of self might be disrupted in the context of misattuned responsiveness from the other, leading to stalled development or traumatic interruptions in development. We can then readily see the importance of the intersubjective field constituted by the vulnerable child with the (hopefully) more mature parent, or the vulnerable patient with the (hopefully) more mature therapist. As the child's or patient's subjective experiences emerge they will interact with the subjective experiences of parent or therapist to create a specific constellation to be understood and responded to. Each member of the dyad organizes the contribution of the other along lines determined by their own subjective frame of reference which in turn becomes a contribution to the other's subjective experience, organized within the other's personal world.

It follows naturally from this that transference, an inherently relational experience, takes shape within the co-occurring psychological worlds of patient and therapist. Both patient and therapist bring to their engagement their own subjectivity, which includes each of their selfobject yearnings, hopes and dreads. The field established between them is crafted from the specific self experiences of each member as well as the mutually overlapping interactions that are generated between them. The patient's transference must be understood with an awareness of the contribution of the therapist's subjectivity; similarly the therapist's self experience is influenced by the interaction with the patient. It is the therapist's responsibility to understand and use their own subjectivity toward the project of facilitating their patient's psychological growth. This may involve drawing on aspects of self that are most enhancing in the treatment or conversely quieting those aspects of self that interfere with the development of the selfobject milieu. Understanding the relative contributions of patient and therapist to the intersubjective field the therapist has the tools to either use or decenter from their own subjective experience in order to be fully responsive to that of their patient's.

In summary, the Intersubjective Self Psychological perspective on transference combines the central principles of Stolorow's theory of Intersubjectivity with the central clinical concepts of Kohut's Self Psychology. Intersubjectivity extends the selfobject concept with the claim that all psychological life, including self-experience and selfobject experience, takes shapes under the umbrella of context-dependent subjectivity. In parallel fashion, Self Psychology extends the Intersubjective view on transference by retaining the primacy of selfobject experience in understanding human relatedness. Bringing these two concepts of transference together enhances the complex and meaningful matrix of subjectivity and self experience in the clinical setting. The following case example illustrates clinical work with transference from an ISP perspective.

Case of David[1]

During the first year of treatment David, my 40-year-old patient, became increasingly obsessive in his recounting of his daily routine and how he was trying to organize his time. He began many sessions expressing new insights about his lack of ability at some particular skill, explaining his thoughts about, for instance, his inability to schedule, be on time, prioritize. In the process, he overwhelmed himself – and me too – with his self-criticisms and complicated explanations of how he understood his flaws. I would offer suggestions as to how he could handle things, speaking from within what seemed to me to be an idealizing transference. I saw his yearning for a figure who held certainty, and the hope was that with an idealized maternal figure behind him his anxiety and feelings of weakness would decrease, allowing him to trust his own judgment. In the sessions however, it did not work that way. He would welcome my suggestions, often fine-tuning them, but he also struggled to understand them within his world of seeking the best possible solution to overcoming his defects. Maybe he should hire an organizer? Or could I tell him what he was doing wrong so he could fix it? This pattern persisted.

As this was happening, we were also dealing with another arena of concern for David, his relationship with his wife of ten years. He spent many sessions picking her apart, pointing out her flaws and going over the ways in which he had tried to "fix" her. Predictably, this did not go over well with her, and she argued back. David was bewildered by the fighting and saw her as irrational and emotionally explosive. Because he felt he was only trying to help her, he could not see the ways in which he was contributing to the tension between them.

As time passed and there was none of the movement I expected, I found the sessions repetitive and depressing; I felt suffocated by what I experienced as his nitpicking, his relentless negativity. It activated a sense of helplessness and futility in me as I searched for things to say that would finally make him feel better and render the connection transformative. There was no room for process; when I tried to tell him what I thought, he felt that I hadn't understood and redoubled his efforts. Our line of inquiry, which felt more like working on a carpentry problem than analytic exploration, got him and us nowhere. I felt held captive, rendered helpless by his obsessive-compulsive rumination. He sought to get something just right and I felt like I was never saying quite the right thing. I reacted by becoming increasingly sleepy and finally one session he caught me with my attention wandering and my eyes half closed. This was a profound disjunction: he increasingly looked for me to fix him, but the process made me feel that it was impossible for me to help him. David had a sense of himself as boring, now added to the already compromised sense of himself as flawed. I needed to understand this disjunction in the intersubjective field in order to reconnect and move forward together.

I began an internal exploration of what had been happening. In my helplessness, my dread of being ineffectual and weak rose to the foreground, leaving me in a heightened state of vulnerability and causing me to check out. I lost my connection with the theory which grounds and organizes me, and with it, my connection to David. Though I struggled hard to provide the idealized experiences it seemed he yearned for, the activation of my trailing edge dread left me unable to provide him with an experience he could organize around. I came to realize that both of us ended up feeling that we were failing. I recognized a potential twinship in our experience of both needing to and failing to be perfect. There was a nascent possibility that we could find ourselves stronger through our similarities, but at this point, these similarities were far from shoring up our self experiences. Rather, our trailing edges were in conjunction. Understanding this allowed me to work my way back into my leading edge: my sense of myself as a caring, empathically attuned, strong enough therapist, who could find a way to connect with her struggling patient.

With a new sense of purpose and commitment to the process on my part, we began to explore David's experience of feeling weak and vulnerable, in need of "fixing." A memory emerged of the father he idealized. When he was 15, David came to his father with a dream of following in his footsteps as a renowned lawyer. Father's response, that David couldn't handle the stress of deadlines, was a devastating, narcissistic injury. His bid to merge with the idealized object failed as he was deemed unworthy. In order to maintain the tie, David blamed himself, and joined with his father's image of David as flawed. His father remained on his pedestal and David was on a never-ending search to fix himself. His organizing fantasy was that if he could fix himself, he would finally be worthy of his idealized father. But the idealization was defensive, not progressive. David's propping up of his relationship with his father, as damaging as it was, was also necessary as we came to understand how absent mirroring experiences were. Neither of his parents spared much attention or thought for him, absorbed as they were in each other and his father's work, so a mirror experience was not available to him. Thus, it became clear to me that rather than a leading edge hope, the merger with father was his trailing edge dread, which would not result in transformation. Rather, it was a defensive idealization that would never yield a strong and stable self experience; it would only yield endless repetition, a repetition which had then become activated in relation to me. Something else was needed.

With this understanding in place I felt stronger, more empathic, and more connected to the theory, which is an organizing and stabilizing idealized presence for me. Drawing on my own childhood experience of trying for an ideal self who would be worthy of a defensively idealized parent, I was able to begin expressing an understanding of his yearning to fix himself. As we proceeded, I found the fine line between being the one who knew the answers like his rejecting father and the weak, helpless self of my dread. I could be in it with him. From within, I could begin to address with him the need to be perfect and the pain of accepting the impossibility of fulfilling this goal. He seemed to feel understood in a new way, receiving my words without needing to question them and pick them apart. As the possibility that I could genuinely understand him became more of a reality, David began to understand that when I said he needed to mourn the loss of a potential ideal self I was not condemning him as a hopelessly defective individual. I was speaking as one on the same journey, with similar flaws. It was our shared humanity which began to feel palpable in the room. A sense of us both being just fine as is began to emerge as I was able to share my vision of both of us in our vulnerability and our strength. Rather than being the all-knowing but rejecting father, I could be one who, like David, understood how hard it was to manage all my dreams and still be the person I want to be. Rather than looking for me to provide him with ways he could fix himself, David began asking if whatever he was feeling was "normal." Could he be like others, like me? He began to see my flaws not as a failure in a potentially perfect vision, but affirming that I was not any more perfect than he was, but able to hold onto myself without needing to be perfect. Instead of the relentless negativity, there emerged the possibility that he could be a "human among humans," and that I was someone with whom he could connect around our shared struggles to make a rich life that felt "good enough." In other words, a leading edge hope emerged in mutual acceptance and twinship.

This space was sometimes hard to come by. At times my efforts to respond within a sense of twinship with him risked triggering in me the same state of vulnerability as he had so often felt; at these times we might both become overwhelmed with negativity. However, I gradually settled into feeling myself into David's experience in a new way. Rather than asking myself to find answers, I worked to express a connection with him around his striving to feel competent, alive and engaged, even when there are no absolute or perfect answers.

As I started to see the relationship between David and me through the lens of twinship, I began to feel greater empathy for him as he struggled to help his wife in the same way I struggled to help him. I expressed my understanding of his genuine concern for her and how hurt he felt by her rejection of him. And I stopped trying to "fix" his perception of her. Gradually he began to focus more on his feelings about his wife – the frustration, hurt, and fear – rather than his perception of her flaws. This enabled me to empathize and understand how he felt. As I validated and "normalized" his experience, I suggested that perhaps he could approach his wife with these feelings rather than with an expectation of what she could be doing differently. David took my words in, and gave it a try. He came back into session saying his wife had responded by expressing her vulnerability and concerns about herself. As she opened up, he reported feeling empathy for her – and pleasure in finally being able to connect. The twinship with me enabled him to find twinship with her.

The yearning for an ideal – in himself and in others – remains strong in David. He still struggles with self-criticism and occasionally succumbs to obsessive nitpicking, both about himself and about his wife. However, the intersubjective field between the two of us has changed and that has opened new possibilities. I am interested and engaged in finding a way to reach him in twinship, and to resist the urge to join him in self-criticism. I search for ways to normalize his experience, to find a way of expressing a sense of the inherent struggle in accepting limitations, and to take pleasure in our connection. In almost every session we come to a place of steadiness, something he can feel hopeful about. In some moments it is a view of himself as strong; in others he accepts my view of him as making progress.

Here is a moment that illustrates the transformation. The session opened characteristically enough with David talking about the details of his efforts to research the purchase of a car. He chronicled the complex and minutely detailed process he goes through to arrive at decisions, second-guessing, backtracking. I was mostly silent, sympathizing, looking for an opening in order to see if I could bring us to a mutual understanding from a little more distance, perspective. I was actively holding onto my leading edge as one who could be with him in the process, rather than searching for a perfect solution. Thus, I did not try to solve the problem but tried to bring awareness of his choices into the dialogue. But then he truly amazed me by taking a step back himself, saying he planned to be done by next week. I expressed wonderment at his prediction of a speedy resolution to something which in the past took him weeks, if not months. He expressed surprised at my surprise, and then seemed pleased. I felt him responding expansively, as he told me how actively he is trying to limit his obsessive researching and changing of his mind. Inside, I was feeling the hopeful connection with a twin who was growing stronger which, in turn, strengthened my sense of self and allowed me to venture further. After I commented on his awareness of his process, I was then emboldened to ask a question about his understanding of how his need for the ideal affected others, particularly his wife. David was able to reflect on her view of him, saying he knew she felt that he needed to strive for perfection. Rather than expressing a feeling of being misunderstood by her, he began to think of his wife with empathic understanding, saying it must be hard for her. For the first time, this was not accompanied by guilt or a sense of deflation. Because he felt understood by and connected to me, he was able to feel strong and secure enough in himself to reach out empathically to his wife. For my part, having participated in co-creating these moments between us I am assured that my selfobject needs for twinship are being met, and my leading edge is in the foreground. This leading edge-leading edge connection in the intersubjective field resulted in the acquisition and solidification of a new self structure for David, a structure which manifests in his increased understanding of his process, his ability to separate from it, and his newfound capacity for empathy for his wife.

Here is an overview of the intersubjective field between David and me as it changed over time. It began in a failed attempt at an idealized bond. It then morphed into a place where both of us felt weak and helpless. Only when I was able to self-reflect and understand my trailing edge dread as it was manifesting in relationship to my patient's trailing edge dread, was I able to find a way to empathize with my patient, allowing our mutual hopes for twinship to emerge and strengthen each of us in the transformed intersubjective field of leading edge hope meeting leading edge hope.

In conclusion, this case illustrates the ways in which the selfobject yearnings, the intersubjective field, and the interaction between the trailing and leading edges of patient and therapist create both impasses and opportunities for transformation. Both David's and my thwarted needs, to merge with an idealized parent, left vulnerabilities in each of us and in the field between us. As I came to realize how these were operating in me, I was able to disentangle myself and find strength in understanding, thereby activating my leading edge. This enabled me to move the relationship towards addressing David's nascent yearning for twinship from within my own sense of twinship with him. As he felt stronger in connection with me, I was further strengthened in my sense of self and both of us could revel in the twinship possibilities now opening up between us.

Note

1 This case was conducted by one of the authors. It is written in first person, but reflects the view of both authors.

Chapter 4

The therapeutic action of Intersubjective Self Psychology, Part I[1]

Peter B. Zimmermann

What is curative in psychotherapy from the perspective of Intersubjective Self Psychology?[2] In answer to this question, two modes of therapeutic action will be differentiated, generated by two different experiences in the therapeutic relationship, the work with the leading edge and the work with the trailing edge. Each mode entails a form of analytic engagement. I begin by introducing several concepts that constitute the clinical language of Intersubjective Self Psychology (ISP).

The patient

Patients come to treatment with their *hopes* and *dreads* (Stephen Mitchell, 1993), and with their *yearnings* and *fears*. These yearnings and dreads may be known to patients and thus conscious, or unconscious, preconscious, repressed, dissociated or disavowed, and thus not known to them.

Patients come to therapy because they *hope* that the therapist can help them. They hope that they can transcend the place where they feel stuck; they *yearn* for a new start. They come to therapy with the hope that they have found in the therapist the person who is going to provide, in the therapeutic relationship, the experiences that they need to be confident to abandon old strategies of self-protection, and pursue new ways of being in and engaging with the world. These experiences have their source in what Kohut (1971, 1977, 1984) discovered as specific, universal modes of engagement with the other required for self development, called selfobject bonds. Self object bonds take hold in the form of selfobject transferences when the patient sees the opportunity for such experiences of engagement in the therapeutic relationship.

The concept of the selfobject transference refers to the emergence in treatment of a specific, enduring sought after relational experience with the analyst that is necessary for the patient's self development to proceed. The selfobject transference is understood as a reinstatement of a needed bond with the therapist for the transformation and growth of the self. This bond had been available to the child to some extent in the original caregiving context but not sufficiently enough to complete self development. The patient continues to yearn for it today.

The selfobject transferences are the prime constellation of what we define as the *generative transference*.[3] The generative transference refers to the dimension of the therapeutic relationship that promotes growth and healing. The generative transference is understood to constitute the *leading edge* in treatment. It entails the establishment of the development-enhancing experiences in the relationship with the analyst that the patient yearns for and needs to reinstate a process that results in the unfolding, consolidation and vitalization of the self experience.

However, as stated earlier, patients come to treatment not only with yearnings and hopes, they also come with their *dreads and fears*. They dread that they are destined to remain mired forever where they feel stuck. They fear that the experience they seek with the therapist will not be available to them, and they fear that they will receive the same faulty response from the therapist that they felt they were met with by the original caregivers, and now, from the world around them. They dread that what will prevail is a miss-attuned or inadequate selfobject experience or worse, a traumatic repetition of the original selfobject failure.

These dreads give rise to the *repetitive transference*, a term introduced by Stolorow, Atwood and Brandchaft (1987) to refer to all that traditionally has been called transference, to set it apart from what we refer to as the generative transference. The repetitive transference is defined as a revival and enactment of an unconscious significant maladaptive and enduring relational pattern from the past in the here and now of the therapeutic relationship. The repetitive transference is the centerpiece of what constitutes the *trailing edge* in treatment.

The trailing edge refers to all the relational patterns that result from the ingrained character structures and all the modes of relating that come into play when the patient anticipates or experiences a repetition of a traumatic experience from the past in the here and now of the therapeutic relationship. The trailing edge includes all the self-protective and restorative measures, the so-called defenses and resistances, that the patient relies on to protect the self experience from further injury and fragmentation.

In summary, the activation of hopes and yearnings characterizes the generative transference which constitutes the leading edge. The activation of dreads and fears characterizes the repetitive transference which constitutes the trailing edge.

The terms leading and trailing edge have been introduced by Kohut, although he never used the terms in his writings. It is Jules Miller (1985), one of his supervisees, who wrote that Kohut used these terms in supervision with him. Marion Tolpin a devoted and gifted student, and colleague of Kohut, was the first psychoanalyst to use these concepts in a paper. She pointed out the importance supporting the 'tendrils of health' in therapy, but used the term 'forward edge' in place of leading edge.

Frank Lachmann (2001) re-introduced trailing and leading edge in his book: *Transforming Aggression*. Since then, forward edge and leading edge have been used interchangeably in the literature. We favor leading edge, as it is Kohut's choice, and it is the natural linguistic partner to trailing edge.

Self disorders

Kohut (1971) initially thought that self disorders come about when missattuned parental responses to the child, lead to faulty or inadequate selfobject experiences. As a result, a patient was thought to be seeking to establish the selfobject bond with the therapist that had been inadequate, insufficient or missing. In other words, in treatment patients would seek out whichever selfobject experience they had NOT adequately received in the original caregiving surround. Faulty mirroring experiences in childhood result in the need for reliable mirroring experiences in therapy; merging experiences with unreliable idealizable figures result in yearnings for a reliable idealizable figure with whom to merge and inadequate twinship experiences result in the search for 'good enough' twinship experiences to restore and maintain the self experience.

In *How Does Analysis Cure?* (1984) his posthumously published book, Kohut proposed a new and more complex way of thinking about self disorders. He introduced the idea of the *compensatory* selfobject experience. He stated that a self disorder comes about if, and only if, after a rupture in the primary selfobject tie, a reliable compensatory selfobject experience is not available or is faulty and fails as well. Any one of the three selfobject transferences can serve as the compensatory selfobject experience based on which self development can proceed and be completed.

Let's illustrate this with a hypothetical example. Let's say a baby's primary self experience is organized around feeling mirrored by her mother. The baby bathes in her mother's joy as the mother administers to her daughter. She is seeing the gleam in her mother's eyes and feels affirmed. At age four however, her little brother is born and the daughter becomes painfully aware that her mother's attention has moved from her to the brother. For the daughter this constitutes a rupture in the mirror selfobject tie with the mother. This could result in a crisis in the daughter's self experience, creating a structural vulnerability in the self that could manifest as a disorder of the self in adulthood.

However, Kohut argues, if at this crucial point in time the father or other parent is available to the daughter as a solidly idealizable figure to merge with, the daughter's self experience or sense of self would not fragment; rather, it would continue to solidify in the merger experience with the idealized figure, and a self disorder would not result. Similarly, if at this point the daughter would start a preschool program and would find a best friend with whom to form a solid twinship tie, a self disorder would not develop either. Either one of these lines of development, the idealizing or twinship experience, would make up, compensate, for the lost mirroring experience around which the self was originally organized.

While there would be certain vulnerabilities in the sense of self, fundamentally, Kohut argues, the self experience would be cohesive enough, depending on the relative strength of the compensatory selfobject experience so that a disorder of the self would not result. If, however, the other parent is absent, and thus a merger with a reliably idealizable figure is not available, or the parents just moved to a new neighborhood so that the daughter also loses her best preschool friend, which would mean that the twinship experience is lost as well, then a compensatory selfobject line would be lost as well. According to Kohut, then and only then, a self disorder would result.

This new conceptualization has far-reaching consequences for how we think about what is curative in therapy and how we go about facilitating a curative process. What are these consequences?

A first consequence is that in treatment patients do *not* necessarily or even primarily seek to revive the primary selfobject tie, the developmental line wherein the original rupture occurred; rather, patients will seek to establish the compensatory selfobject transference bond that will enable the development or consolidation of the self. This is where the patient's hope is found, this constitutes the generative transference, this is the leading edge. The rupture in the primary selfobject bond accounts for the dread of a traumatic repetition that gives rise to the repetitive transference. This constitutes the trailing edge that will manifest in the form of self protective measures and defenses.

This makes it critical that in the initial assessment of the patient, therapists not only seek to establish what the primary selfobject failures were, but also who, if anybody, came through for the patient and what that selfobject experience was. This points to the compensatory selfobject experiences that were most sustaining for the patient. These sustaining experiences will become the yearned-for compensatory selfobject transference that the patient will seek to unfold in the therapeutic relationship with the therapist, the generative transference. This will constitute the leading edge.

Based on the hypothetical example from above, the daughter might have gone through a depressive phase from age 4 to 6, due to the loss of the mirror tie with the mother. The depressive phase lifted when she went into to first grade and again found a best friend from whom she became inseparable all through middle school. A compensatory twinship selfobject tie was established. Only when she started high school, and again felt alienated from her peers because her friend had moved away, did the vulnerability in the underlying self structure become manifest and her sense of self unraveled, causing her to rely on cutting herself or binging and purging to shore up her fragmenting self experience.

This might be the time when her parents suggested that she seek therapy. Once there, she hoped to establish a twinship selfobject transference with the therapist in order to reinstate the compensatory line of development where it was disrupted. However, there might be significant resistances present in the treatment, due to the dread of retraumatization, i.e. abandonment, and thus the dreaded loss of twinship, which would need to be worked through for the leading edge to engage.

A second consequence of Kohut's new formulation of the disorders of the self is that regardless of how traumatic the primary selfobject failure or rupture in the primary selfobject tie, a cohesive, functional, stable self structure and an emotionally positively colored sense of self, continuous in time and space, can still develop, provided there was a reliable and sustaining compensatory selfobject bond available. This means that the central issue in the treatment of self disorders is essentially not how traumatic the primary selfobject failure was, although this plays a significant role in the trailing edge, but rather whether a reliable, stable, 'good enough' compensatory selfobject experience was available and at what point that compensatory selfobject line was derailed or disrupted.

The compensatory selfobject bond could be provided by a sibling or aunt or uncle, a grandparent or teacher or a best friend. In treatment, then, the therapist's work needs to be focused first and foremost on the revival of the compensatory line of development in the transference, and secondarily on the working through of the primary selfobject failure. The primary selfobject failure will come into the therapeutic relationship each time the compensatory selfobject tie is felt to be disrupted by the patient and the repetitive transference is revived, which will require working through. If a treatment is exclusively focused on the patient's trailing edge and the therapist fails to recognize the patient's yearning for the compensatory selfobject bond, the patient will, on an ongoing basis, feel thrust into the traumatic experience of the original selfobject failure that he desperately seeks to extricate himself from precisely with the compensatory selfobject bond.

To summarize, the primary selfobject failure or rupture gives rise to the patient's dreads in the transference and manifests in the repetitive transference, that is the trailing edge. The compensatory selfobject experience is powered by the patient's hopes and yearnings and manifests in the generative transference, that is the leading edge. Leading and trailing edge are in a figure-ground relationship, which means when the leading edge is in the foreground of the analytic relationship and is co-determining the therapeutic situation, the trailing edge is in the background, and vice versa.

Compensatory and defensive structures and strategies

The other clinically relevant differentiation that Kohut (1981) introduced is between *defensive* and *compensatory* structures. Defensive and compensatory structures both serve the same purpose: they protect and maintain the self or shore up a person's vulnerable or fragmenting self experience. The difference is that compensatory structures are capable of undergoing a developmental transformation, and defensive structures are not.

Compensatory structures are able to undergo a process of developmental transformation and become enduring adaptive dimensions of the person's self that enhance and solidify the self experience. They derive from genuine selfobject bonds but also from fulfilling engagements with work, as well as artistic, intellectual or scientific pursuits and hobbies, and other forms of personally meaningful activities such as engagements with literature, music, film, gardening, cooking, sports, humanitarian issues, etc. Involvement in any of these activities may serve a compensatory selfobject function around which the self experience can be organized, and the sense of self can be solidified.

Defensive structures are also manifestations of efforts to shore up, protect or restore the self, but they derive from activities such as drug use, skin cutting, binging and purging, hoarding, compulsive masturbation, sex or love addictions, obsessive-compulsive rumination as well as psychotic preoccupations and delusions, etc. The characteristic feature of defensive strategies is that they do not promote a developmental transformation of the self experience, which means they do not result in the strengthening of self-experience. They only temporarily shore up a fragile or fragmenting self experience and therefore need to be repeated rigidly and indefinitely without bringing about growth and transformation of the self experience. For instance, no matter how many times a person smokes crack after an experience of humiliating failure, or compulsively masturbates, or binges and purges, these activities, while temporarily shoring up a failing sense of self, will not ever result in the growth or transformation of the self experience.

The differentiation between defensive and compensatory allows for the differentiation between pathological and healthy forms of narcissism. In pathological narcissism, in the aftermath of traumatic selfobject failure in the original caregiving surround and due to the absence of a compensatory selfobject line of development, a person relies on connections to others and activities in strictly *defensive* ways that do not enable the development of the self. Instead, these bonds and activities require endless enactment and are rigidly clung to, just like addictions of any sort, gambling, sex, betting.

If these activities and connections to others are not recognized by the therapist as defensive but are thought to be compensatory and responded to as if they were genuine selfobject bonds, and are encouraged to proliferate, they become more entrenched and more rigid, without any transformation of the self taking place. This is the precise opposite of what takes place when a genuine selfobject bonds is engaged.

The pathological narcissistic that Kernberg (1975) describes, who *craves*[4] mirroring, twinship or idealization should not be confused with the narcissistic patient that Kohut has in mind, who *yearns* for a mirror, idealizing or twinship selfobject transference in order to resume development where it was derailed. In the pathological narcissist, no developmental or transformational process is reinstated, because no compensatory line of development was available; rather, a specific narcissistic defense is enacted. Mirroring of defensive grandiosity does not result in the development of empathy (as it does in the mirroring of developmental forms of grandiosity); it results in the entrenchment of haughtiness.

In the language of ISP, defensive narcissistic cravings presented in the form demands, appear as though they are manifestations of the leading edge but are in fact expressions of the trailing edge. They are expressions of defensive maneuvers to protect against the threat of fragmentation stirred by the dread of renewed traumatic selfobject failure. Instead of engaging with them as if they were developmental yearnings they need to interpreted with the defensive function they serve.

When pathological forms of narcissism are not differentiated from developmental forms, defensively maintained narcissistic positions remain unanalyzed. This manifests in more deeply entrenched haughty grandiosity, pathological Mooni-like idealization of cult figures, and sycophantic twinship enactments. Engaging with a patient in ways to promote the unfolding of the selfobject transference bond is only indicated if the selfobject needs are compensatory, meaning emanating from a compensatory selfobject line of development. Pathological forms of narcissism come about precisely because a compensatory selfobject line of development was not available or too unreliable and fraught. This presents the person with too great a threat to the self. As a result, the person has no choice but to rely on the narcissistic defense that fends off the fragmentation of the self.

As is apparent, we contend that there are pathological forms of narcissism that must be differentiated from developmental forms. However, the way an intersubjective self psychologist works with these forms of defensive narcissism is different from traditional or Kernbergian analysis. With an ISP perspective, it is the role and function that the narcissistic defense plays in the maintenance and protection of the self that is interpreted. The therapist, schematically, might say to a pathological narcissist: 'Given that your father was a terrifying figure and you had no sense that he saw anything in you that he valued, I understand why turning to him as a person to look to for guidance felt too dangerous or damaging to you, after your mother sank into a depression and suddenly was emotionally absent, the one person who you felt had championed you, even if it had been for her own needs. As a result, you came to rely on and rigidly cling to an archaic fantasy of yourself as the greatest, infalible human – a genius – that constantly craves to be affirmed as such and at all times demands to be the center of attention.'[5] However, we concur with Kernberg that if defensively maintained narcissistic positions are not analyzed, but treated as if they were compensatory, the entrenchment of the narcissistic defense will result.

To say it colloquially: A therapist can mirror defensive grandiosity, accept a defensive idealization or share in defensive twinship until the cows come home. No developmental line will be reinstated along which self experience will unfold and the self structure will transform. Rather, the pathological narcissistic position will be reinforced.

The therapist

Not only patients come to the treatment situation with hopes and dreads, but so do we as therapists. Like the patient, the therapist brings his hopes and dreads to the therapeutic situation, and those hopes and dreads give rise to the therapist's generative and repetitive transference. Therefore, the therapist's leading and trailing edge codetermine the therapeutic situation.

Therapists also yearn for certain affirming experiences with their patients. We yearn to be seen as capable and effective therapists, as competent listeners and incisive interpreters, as empathic, insightful, smart, caring, and solid therapists. We yearn for these qualities to be validated in order to maintain our sense of self as competent therapists. These needs, in conjunction with more specific personal, selfobject needs – individual therapists may be more organized around grandiosity or idealization or twinship – codetermine our selfobject transference needs and constitute our leading edge.

Ideally, our selfobject needs are on a mature level relative to the patient's needs, based on the fact that we underwent our own analysis and training. This means that our self-experience or sense of self is expected to be sufficiently solidified so we are capable of responding to the patient's selfobject needs and are able to promote the patient's goals and objectives. If our self object needs are on a more mature level, we are not unduly subject to disruption or fragmentation of the self experience when our own selfobject needs are not adequately met in the analytic dyad. This is also one of the reasons why it is important for us as therapists to have in our own lives sources of sustaining selfobject experiences, both personally and professionally, like friends and loved ones, as well as supervisory and peer group support, but also meaningful non-professional engagements with literature, music, recreation, and worthy causes that are commensurate with our needs. Nevertheless, the notion of the therapist's emotional maturity does not hold true in any absolute way, and at a given moment in the therapeutic process the therapist's selfobject needs may be more urgently felt and thus more dominantly shaping the analytic dyad than the patient's selfobject needs, whose selfobject needs on an ongoing basis are permitted to structure the therapeutic relationship.

It is reasonable for the patient to expect that our capacity to understand ourselves in the therapeutic situation is solid enough so that we are in a position to engage optimally with the unfolding repetitive and/or generative transference of the patient and carry out our analytic function without undue interference from our own subjectivity, including our leading edge yearnings.

As therapists, being human or all too human, we also experience our own dreads about the work. We may fear that we will come away from the therapeutic encounter experiencing ourselves in ways that replicate self states that derive from traumatic relational patterns from our own past, leaving us feeling inadequate, overwhelmed, inept, exposed, depressed, enraged, guilty or ashamed. These dreads, when realized, lead to the activation of our repetitive transference patterns in relation to our patients, resulting in disjunctions and disruptions in the therapeutic relationship. This is to say that the therapist's experience is also shaped by his repetitive transference that structures the analytic relationship and constitutes the therapist's trailing edge. This is what traditionally is referred to as the therapist's countertransference. If as a young adult in High School the therapist felt ostracized by his peers, he is likely to struggle to maintain his emotional equilibrium in the therapeutic situation if a patient seeks to establish a twinship transference relationship, since for the therapist this revives the painful experience from his High School years.

The therapeutic situation

Since both therapist and patient bring to the therapeutic situation their respective leading edge hopes and trailing edge dreads, the therapeutic situation is most adequately conceptualized as an *intersubjective field* (Stolorow, Atwood & Brandchaft, 1987) created by the intersection of the emotional, experiential worlds of patient and analyst.

The central claim of the theory of intersubjectivity as developed by Stolorow, Atwood and Brandchaft (1987) is that all psychological phenomena, from the emotionally healthy self states to the most severe forms of disorders of the self, are co-determined by the intersubjective field within which they occur. This captures the fundamental context dependence of all emotional or psychological phenomena (Stolorow & Atwood, 1994).

Consequently, and this intersubjectivity theory's most radical formulation, any self state that either patient or analyst experience in the therapeutic situation cannot be understood apart from the intersubjective context within which it occurs (Stolorow & Atwood, 1994).

In the language of ISP, we conceptualize the therapeutic situation as constituted by the intersection of the leading and trailing edges of the patient emotional world with the leading and trailing edges of the therapist's emotional world. What we seek to analyze and work through (trailing edge), and engage and unfold (leading edge), are generated by this complex intersection and emerge in the therapeutic situation. The therapeutic situation is a bi-directional field of reciprocal mutual influence (Stolorow, 1997), wherein the leading edges and trailing edges of patient and therapist are co-determined, ever shifting in a figure-ground relationship.

What is curative

From the perspective of leading and trailing edge, psychoanalysis as originally conceived by Freud, is a trailing edge theory: it is centered on working through the patient's repetitive transference. The psychoanalytic method is focused on resolving the internal conflicts of the person as they manifest in the transference relationship with the analyst by making what is unconscious (repressed) conscious via insight. Therefore, we can say: the therapeutic action of classical psychoanalysis derives primarily from the work with the trailing edge.

Already at its inception, Freud realized that in order to analyze the neurotic transference, something in addition to the repetitive transference needed to be in place for the analysis to work. The patient had to have what Freud referred to as the 'unobjectionable positive feelings' (Freud, 1912) toward the analyst. Those positive feelings accounted for the fact that the patient, even in the throes of the repetitive transference, would be open to the analyst's interpretations and engage in the process of exploration. The unobjectionable positive feelings toward the analyst formed the basis for what later came to be called the 'working alliance' (Greenson, 1967).

As psychoanalysis began to widen its scope and began to address preoedipal conditions, narcissistic and borderline states, which are what we would call moderate to severe self disorders, working through the negative or repetitive transference came to be understood as the heart of analytic work. Much of the innovation in psychoanalytic theory and practice came from refinements in and amendments to the technique of working with transference. But, it was also in relation to the pre-oedipal conditions that the idea of the analyst as a *new object* (Winnicott, 1965) emerged, which means the analyst as the 'good enough' object (Winnicott, 1955) and thus not the negative transference object.

The preoedipal patient was thought to need something from the analyst, something more than the provision of insight, a new experience, that compensated for what had been missing from the patient's early childhood experience and from the self structure. Without the provision of a new experience with the analyst the patient was thought to remain mired in the negative transference. For this not to occur, the analyst had to be a 'good enough' object.

The notion of the 'good enough' analyst implies that who we are as analysts and how we interact with our patients, rather than how our patients *experience* us as analysts, has an impact on the outcome of treatment and thus co-determines the therapeutic action. Nevertheless, to think about how the analyst could facilitate or promote healthy strivings in the patient and what might be needed from the analyst in the analytic dyad to make that possible, was frowned upon and viewed as diluting the pure gold of analysis with the tin of psychotherapy. At most what was tolerated was the introduction of parameters, wherein the analyst was said to function as an auxiliary ego to the patient's defective one, at least for a time, until said 'parameters' were no longer necessary and thus could be resolved via interpretation. Everything else was seen as providing a 'corrective emotional experience' (Alexander, 1950) and thus was declared as un-analytic. It is hard to understand, rather, we would say, incomprehensible, what the analyst as new object is providing if not a corrective emotional experience. In fact, we argue that even the interpreting analyst is in and of itself already providing a corrective emotional experience in that he is at that moment not reacting to the patient as the original caregivers have.

In traditional psychoanalysis, working with the leading edge, the idea of actively engaging and working with the healthy dimensions of the person, and thinking about how analytic work could promote or strengthen this aspect of the person has been neglected; at best, it has been viewed as an unintended side effect and at worst frowned upon as 'unanalytic.' As stated before, it is the work with the trailing edge that was considered analytic and curative.

Surprisingly, this model of the therapeutic action still largely holds true in self psychology. In *How Does Analysis Cure?* Kohut (1984) goes to great length to describe the therapeutic action as the result of the insight that interpretation provides into the disruption-repair cycle, which means the interpretation of the trailing edge.

What I am proposing here is a reversal: to turn the classic psychoanalytic theory of cure, including Kohut's theory of cure, on its head and say: in ISP, the primary therapeutic action derives from the engagement in and development of the leading edge. Working with the trailing edge, albeit inevitable and necessary, and transformational in its own right, is in the service of our primary objective, which is the unfolding and development of the leading edge.

From the perspective of ISP, a cure is brought about through the systematic engagement and development of the patient's leading edge transference as it unfolds in interaction with the analyst's leading edge. This work inevitably also entails the workthrough of the trailing edge as a necessary step in the process.

The work with the trailing edge is indeed the necessary, albeit not sufficient condition for a curative experience to unfold. The sufficient condition is the work with the leading edge. This model of what is curative implies that there are two different kinds of therapeutic action in the therapeutic context. One type of therapeutic action derives from the experience when the generative selfobject transference is intact and the leading edge is in the foreground, and patients have the experience that they receive the emotional nutrients from the therapeutic context – mirroring, twinship or idealizing – that are needed for self development to proceed. A second type of therapeutic action derives from the analyst's interpretation when the selfobject tie is disrupted, the repetitive transference is activated and the trailing edge is in the foreground. The analyst's interpretations then focus on illuminating the repetitive transference in an effort of working through the disruption, and restore the tie.

Stolorow and Atwood, in their chapter on cure in: *Psychoanalytic Treatment: An Intersubjective Approach* (1987), provide the theoretical formulation to conceptualize the two different forms of therapeutic action. They differentiate analytic work between transforming existing self structures and building new ones. The transformation of existing structure occurs via interpretation of what prevails when the selfobject tie to the analyst is severed, that is when there are ruptures in the intersubjective field. The building of new structures takes place when the selfobject tie to the analyst is intact. That is when the patient has a sustained experience of being met with his selfobject transference yearnings.

The transformation of existing self structures occurs via the interpretation of the repetitive transference. The development of new self structures occurs via the engagement of the generative transference. To reformulate this in the language of leading and trailing edge: The transformation of existing, maladaptive self structures occurs via the interpretation of the trailing edge as it evolves in the intersubjective field in interaction with the analyst's trailing edge. The development of new and healthy self structures occurs via the engagement and unfolding of the leading edge in the intersubjective field as it evolves in interaction with the analyst's leading edge.

In conceptualizing the curative process in this way, we are taking a step that Kohut was not yet able to take himself, at least not conceptually, even though he was clearly there in his clinical work. As mentioned above, when Kohut discussed the curative process, he still focused on the trailing edge and defined what is curative as providing insight and offering interpretations on the rupture in the self-selfobject bond. Yes, such interpretative work was defined as in service of restoring the tie, but Kohut did not yet offer a theoretical explanation for what happens next, when the tie is intact.

If Kohut's conceptualization of what is curative held true it would be incomprehensible why it would be beneficial to have lasting periods when the selfobject bond is intact, since no therapeutic benefit is presumed to derive from this experience. It would therefore be advisable to create as many disruptions as possible, since the therapeutic action is supposed to derive solely from the working through of such disruptions.

Clearly, this is not what we do in treatment – nor did Kohut – nor is it advisable as it would undo the tie that patient and therapist have worked hard to establish and seek to maintain. That is the engagement with the patient's leading edge and is the optimal condition for emotional and structural growth to occur. Kohut could not yet go there in the theoretical formulation of what is curative for fear of being accused that self psychology is promoting the idea of a corrective emotional experience. In his case this would have had significant negative consequences professionally.

The most important self psychological author who transcends the focus on the interpretation of the trailing edge and explicitly addresses the topic of working with the leading edge in the discussion of the therapeutic action is Marian Tolpin in her pioneering paper 'Doing Psychoanalysis of Normal Development' (2002). Tolpin opens her paper by stating that traditional psychoanalysts, with their focus on the trailing edge, 'place[s] unintended iatrogenic limits on therapeutic action because we do not support struggling 'tendrils of health' and facilitate their emergence and growth' (p. 168). She then proceeds to develop ideas on how in psychoanalytic practice we can support 'struggling tendrils of health', the leading edge.

The other author who is important in this context is Howard Bacal who introduced the concept of *optimal responsiveness*. He defined the self psychological stance of the therapist as seeking to be optimally responsive to the patient's evolving selfobject needs. After Bacal, therapists were no longer solely defined in their work by the directive of frustrating the patient's regressive libidinal and aggressive wishes, as Freud proposed, nor by the directive of being 'optimally frustrating', as Kohut suggested, meaning non-traumatically frustrating. Rather, the new guideline for self psychological therapists is to be 'optimally responsive' to the evolving selfobject needs of the patient.[6] Lessem and Orange (1993) noted that the selfobject bond that develops between patient and therapist is a major curative factor.

Even the theory of Intersubjectivity in its current form of intersubjective systems theory, although having clearly spelled out what the therapeutic action is when the tie is intact, is primarily focused on the interpretation of the disruption-repair cycle and disinclined to promote the idea of actively engaging in facilitating the therapeutic process when the tie is intact, that is, when the leading edge is in the foreground. Chris Jeanicke (2015) in his poignant treaty entitled *The Search for a Relational Home; An intersubjective view of therapeutic action* describes, in a gripping and deeply personal way, the therapeutic benefit that derives from working through the therapists and the patients co-created failures. He states: 'it is my contention that in order to conceptualize the notion of cure, we must develop a new perspective on the notion of failure' and he states that 'failure and suffering are integral parts of our subjectivity' (p. 2). And Robert Stolorow, on the back of the same book, writes: 'What is unique about the book is its emphasis on the critical importance of failure, both the patient's and the analyst's in furthering the therapeutic process.'

Working through of failures of patient and therapist indeed represent unique opportunities of transformational experiences for patient and therapist, and are important dimensions of the therapeutic process; but to state this is to keep the focus on the work with the trailing edge. It does not differ from Kohut's strained effort to demonstrate that self psychology is not any different from traditional psychoanalysis in that the therapeutic action was only to derive from the repeated interpretations of the disruptions in the self-selfobject matrix – whether created by the patient or the therapist – and not from the emotionally beneficial experience when the tie is intact and no interpretations are required.

As Intersubjective Self Psychologists, we don't have the constraints that Kohut was confronted with and are free to give the work with the leading edge its proper place in the conceptualization of what is curative. We want to be able to understand and explain what the therapeutic action consists of when the tie is intact! And we want to develop the guidelines that organize our clinical practice when working with the leading edge (see Chapter 8).

When the leading edge is engaged, and the tie is intact, as Stolorow, Atwood and Brandchaft (1987) proposed, structure building takes place. The therapeutic action that results from a sustained experience of engagement of the patient's leading edge with the therapist's leading edge is the development of new psychic structures. This may manifest in the patient's newly developed or increased capacity to organize and regulate affect, develop, and solidify new self states of competence, empathy, humor, wisdom, sorrow, and vitality, and an emergent sense of agency.

These new dimension of the self develop and solidify because the patient has the sustained experience in the intersubjective field of the analyst's *attuned engagement* with the patient's generative transference. We are introducing 'attuned engagement' to differentiate it from optimal responsiveness and highlight that the analyst not only responds but plays an active role in engaging the patient's leading edge experience in the transference. The analyst has to *show up and actively engage with the patient's leading edge yearnings* to generate for the patient a reliable and sustained experience of merger with an idealizable figure or a sustained and reliable experience of mirror or twinship. Such sustained experiences of self-selfobject bonds between patient and therapist provide the developmental opportunities to acquire new self structures and solidify emergent ones.

The longer phases of attuned engagements by the therapist with the patient's leading edge last in uninterrupted ways, the greater the therapeutic action. It is in these periods that patients' selfobject yearnings and hopes are realized. The selfobject transference bonds are intact and the generative transference is unfolding, that facilitate the development and consolidation of the patient's self experience. This is the corrective emotional experience that derives from the work with the leading edge and provides healing.

We now can conceptualize the therapeutic action as consisting of two separate but interrelated processes:

1. Attuned engagement of the generative transference when the therapeutic relationship is intact and;
2. Empathic interpretation of the repetitive transference when the therapeutic relationship is disrupted.

Attuned engagement with the leading edge of the patient when the tie is intact and empathic interpretation of the trailing edge when the tie is disrupted, constitute the therapeutic action of ISP.

It becomes apparent that empathic interpretations of the trailing edge also entail a leading edge experience for the patient, since they are precisely not repetitions, and therefore also result in structure building and vice versa. A sustained experience of feeling met in the leading edge will provide the emotional safety for the patient that allows the therapist to make trailing edge interpretations that will not get rebuffed by the patient or generate ruptures. An example of this might be a 'borderline' patient who may be able to hear and take in an interpretation of their proclivity to rage when the tie is felt to be intact. Yet that same patient would flat out reject the same interpretation when a disruption had occurred, resulting in the intensification of the patient's rage and protective defensiveness.

There are, in principle, four different intersubjective constellations generated by the intersection of leading and trailing edge of patient and therapist, creating different opportunities for therapeutic action for patient and therapist.

I. We have a potential for therapeutic action when the trailing edge of the patient meets up with the leading edge of the therapist. In this case, the therapeutic action lies in the provision of interpretations that address the trailing edge of the patient's experience in the relationship with the analyst. The patient, who is mired in a repetitive transference with the analyst, requires interpretations that illuminate his subjective world, which the therapist is able to offer because she is in a generative transference with the patient and feels on top of her game, practicing her craft. Such interpretations of the patient's trailing edge, where on the mark, result in the transformation of the patient's existing self structures and in the development and consolidation of the therapist's leading edge self experience as the therapist feels effective with his interpretation and feels like she has traction. In the patient, existing self structures are being transformed while in the therapist emergent self structures are being consolidated. This is what therapists and psychoanalysts ideally have done all along.

Patients will feel more hopeful and motivated to change when the analyst's relatively more mature selfobject needs to be empathic, and understanding is expressed in the service of interpreting the patient's trailing edge dreads and her accompanying defensive and self-protective efforts. Such interpretations of the patient's fear and self-protectiveness challenge her negative expectations and encourage hope for the yearned-for engagement from and with the therapist. As a result, the patient feels more confident and motivated and this contributes to the therapist feeling more cohesive and vital in turn.

II. We also have for potential for therapeutic action, although less conventionally so, when the trailing edge of the therapist's transference meets up with the leading edge of the patient's transference. Less conventionally so, because for there to be any therapeutic action, this intersubjective constellation requires the therapist, who is mired in his repetitive transference, to be open to, and accept, the interpretations of his trailing edge by the patient. The patient may be able to offer by virtue of being engaged in her generative transference with the therapist. In this intersubjective constellation, the patient sees that the therapist needs help, because the therapist is enacting his repetitive transference. The patient is able to offer help because she is in a generative transference with the therapist. The patient experiences herself in the role of the therapist and comes to feel valued and values herself for providing to the therapist mired in his trailing edge and thus in the role of the patient. Such interpretations by the patient of the therapist's trailing edge result in the transformation of the therapist's existing structures and entail a consolidation of newly developing or emergent self structures in the patient. Those structures may be the patient's emergent capacity for empathy, insight and self-reflection when earlier she might have felt overwhelmed by the impact of the rupture caused by the therapist's enactment of her railing edge and been thrust into a trailing edge repetitive transference.

In this case, the therapeutic action for the patient results from the experience of being able to offer interpretations of the therapist's trailing edge. This would constitute a leading edge experience and result in a structure building experience for the patient. For the therapist in this situation, the therapeutic action derives from the interpretations the patient provides of the therapist's trailing edge, bringing about a structural transformation of the therapist's self experience.

III. The treatment is most at risk to come to a therapeutic impasse and thus for there not to be any therapeutic action, when the trailing edge of the patient meets up with the trailing edge of the therapist. In this case both parties are caught up in their respective enactments of their repetitive transferences, creating an intersubjective stalemate in the therapeutic relationship. In this case, both patient and therapist are enacting with each other their trailing edge transference dramas and react to each other as if each were the traumatic transference figure from their respective pasts. Both patient and therapist feel profoundly misunderstood by each other and, as Stolorow states, each of them addresses him- or herself to an intersubjective situation that does not exist for the other. Neither patient nor therapist recognize themselves in the way that each of them experiences the other.

These are the classic impasses so often experienced in the treatment of so called borderline patients, and in their starkest form, can be very disconcerting for both parties involved. However, variations of such disjunctive intersubjective constellations occur in most every therapeutic relationship because repetitive transferences of the patient have a strong pull to generate repetitive transferences of the therapist and vice versa.

The productive continuation of these treatments is predicated on either therapist or patient or better yet both parties being able to 'decenter' Stolorow (1984) from their trailing edge self experience of each other and, with the help of the other, analyze and work through the intersubjective constellation. Ulman and Stolorow (1985) have aptly coined this phenomenon 'the transference/countertransference neurosis' that is alive in the intersubjective field, and which more recently Atlas and Aron (2018) have entitled dramatic enactments.[7] When we are able to work our way through such intersubjective impasses (and granted, sometimes we are not) we come to feel not only that we have weathered a storm, but that we have grown, a growth that both speaks to the transformation of existing old structures and the emergence of new ones. This is what Atlas and Aron (2018) mean when they speak of 'generative enactments.'

IV. We have the greatest potential for therapeutic action and for a curative treatment experience when the leading edge of the patient meets up with the leading edge of the therapist. In this facilitating intersubjective context, the yearned-for selfobject experience of the patient matches the yearned-for selfobject experience of the therapist, creating an intersubjective field that is conducive to structure building in patient and therapist. In this case the generative transferences are solid for both parties and self-affirming experiences are shared in both directions, solidifying the self experience of patient and therapist. Every phase in analysis where the work progresses without obvious disruptions but is emotionally alive and deep, is an expression of this fortuitous intersubjective field. This is what most powerfully constitutes a sustained corrective emotional experience, resulting in the acquisition and consolidation of new emergent self structures.

The patient feels more confident and able to make changes when he or she feels that the analyst with understanding, hopefulness and encouragement engages with his newly emergent self experience. In this facilitating intersubjective context, the patient's experience of the matching of his or her longed for selfobject needs, with the therapist's relatively more mature selfobject needs, creates the conditions for the patient's adoption of new models and patterns of self-experience and relating. In this case both participants experience the generative intersubjective field as solid and self-affirming, and as a result both feel their self-experience is enhanced. Every therapeutic relationship, where therapist and patient feel reliably connected and emotionally engaged in the generative transference can be understood as an instance of this type of fortuitous generative intersubjective field.

While for heuristic purposes I have separated these two forms of therapeutic action, in clinical work, both dimensions will always be present in a figure-ground relation. Every structural transformation also entails the development of new structures and every new structure will also entail structural transformations.

In summary, the therapeutic action in ISP comes from two sources, and our attention needs to be focused on both the work with the trailing edge and the work with the leading edge. When the trailing edge is the central theme that is alive in the intersubjective field, the therapeutic intervention required from the therapist is interpretation, i.e. empathic exploration and illumination of the repetitive transference which causes disruptions in the intersubjective field, along with the dreads that are revived and the protective measures that are relied upon to restore or repair the tie that is felt to be ruptured. Such interpretations, from an empathic perspective, result in the transformation of existing structures. This manifests in the ever deepening understanding of the underlying central organizing principles and attendant unconscious fantasies, and the deepening understanding and dissolution of dissociated aspects of the self experience.

The prototype of such an interpretation follows the following model:

> Since you experienced me to be distracted and thought I was contemptuous when you spoke about the anxiety that you felt when thinking about asking your boss for a raise, I understand why you retreated and were consumed with images of disjointed body parts which you tried to deal with by making sure that all the shoes were lined up properly.

Such an interpretation might include a reference to the therapist's own experience, like: 'When you brought up confronting your boss, I felt a twinge of my own anxiety about this, which made me retreat from you and might account for your experience that I felt contempt for you, especially since we have come to understand how helpless you felt in the face of the repeatedly humiliating experience of encountering your father's contempt for you when he was in one of his drunken states.'

When the leading edge is the salient intersubjective dynamic alive in the intersubjective field, the therapist is experienced by the patient as optimally engaged with (his) central selfobject transference yearnings. They are engaged in a mutually generative transference and the therapeutic action is structure building. This is the objective of ISP, and the therapist's goal is the development and maintenance of this curative intersubjective constellation. All forms of engagement by the therapist with the patient during this phase of the treatment are in the service of promoting the maintenance of the leading edge transference. The patient experiences this as the generative intersubjective field conducive to the ever deepening unfolding of his or her leading edge. To do so, the therapist's engagement with the patient's leading edge needs to derive from a detailed and nuanced understanding of the yearned-for generative transference of the patient, and subsequent communications by the therapist need to be in keeping with the understanding of the central self-selfobject experience the patient seeks to maintain in the intersubjective field.

Although interpretations of the trailing edge are important and necessary because they result in the transformation of existing structure, they are nevertheless primarily a means to an end. The end is the unfolding of the leading edge. It is this two-step process of structural transformation via interpretation of the trailing edge/repetitive transference and structure building via attuned engagement with the leading edge/generative transference that constitutes the therapeutic action of ISP and brings about therapeutic transformation, healing, growth and cure.

Psychotherapeutic practice guided by the idea that the work with the leading edge is the goal of therapy, looks fundamentally different not only from analytic work in the classical sense but also from traditional self psychology and the therapeutic work based on intersubjective systems theory. The intersubjective self psychologist is actively seeking to engage and maintain the leading edge transference and develop a generative intersubjective field in order to foster the 'tendrils of health' in the patient.

If we subscribe to this idea, we need to develop our understanding of what constitutes the work with the leading edge much beyond the point where we are today. The whole complex of how to engage with the patient in such a way that promotes the unfolding of the leading edge transference in the intersubjective field, and how to conduct clinical work so as to foster the tendrils of health or emergent self, needs to be explored and articulated more extensively. This will be the topic of Chapter 7.

Notes

1 My thanks go to my colleague Harry Paul, whose friendship of 40 years has provided the context for an ongoing, mutually rewarding clinical dialogue that has fostered my understanding of the significance of the leading edge in treatment, which is the basis for the reconceptualization of the therapeutic action presented in this chapter.
2 For a comprehensive presentation on the topic of the modes of therapeutic action in psychotherapy in general see Martha Stark (1999).
3 Galit Atlas and Lewis Aron (2018) in their book, *Dramatic Dialogue*, introduce the concept of *'generative enactment'*, which is comparable to our term of 'generative transference' in that it refers to a progressive dimension imbedded in the enactment. However, in our formulation the generative transference refers to an intrinsically progressive striving of the patient for the needed experience in the

relationship with the therapist to resume self development, and does not constitute a repetition or enactment.
4 I thank Blethyn Hulton for proposing this terminological differentiation between to crave and to yearn for.
5 For in depth study on how to analyze defense, see Kohut's (1981) chapter on this topic in *How Does Analysis Cure?*
6 Keep in mind that 'optimally responsive', at a particular point in the patient's therapeutic relationship, could mean to be non-traumatically frustrating. In other words, optimally responsive should not be confused with simply accommodating the patient or worse, pathological accommodation, on the part of the therapist.
7 Atlas and Aron also describe the leading edge of patient meeting the leading edge of analyst as enactment. This is what Atwood and Stolorow (1984) label an intersubjective conjunction. Enactment, like intersubjective conjunction entail an unconscious dimension, whereas the intersubjective constellation leading edge of patient and therapist that we describe is actively and consciously in pursuit of the most generative intersubjective field.

Chapter 5

The therapeutic action of Intersubjective Self Psychology, Part 2

The case of Ricky

Aviva Rohde[1]

In this chapter I will demonstrate the fundamental principles of Intersubjective Self Psychological treatment by means of a discussion of my four year treatment of Ricky. Rather than following the case in a strictly chronological manner, I will focus instead on moments in the treatment which illustrate the ideas that are central to Intersubjective Self Psychology (ISP) and which collectively tell the story of Ricky's experience of transformation and growth in therapy. After I describe the struggles which brought Ricky to treatment I will discuss the generative and repetitive themes, and the leading and trailing edge transferences which emerged over time. Because this treatment was conducted from the perspective of ISP I will also discuss the interplay of Ricky's leading and trailing edges with my own as they emerged in the therapeutic relationship. Taken together these selected themes will paint a picture of Ricky's transformation, from depressive despair and reactive acting out to reflective self-awareness, thoughtful self-care, and a cohesive sense of self. This transformation will demonstrate the value of working from an Intersubjective Self Psychological perspective.

Introduction to Ricky

The voice on the phone requesting a consultation sounded sullen, miserable, forced. He didn't need to tell me that he wanted no part of coming to therapy. It was obvious. To say nothing of what he told me: He'd had an argument with a co-worker during a work shift and punched him in frustration. As a result his employer mandated psychotherapy if he intended to maintain his employment. Showing up for therapy seemed quite the long shot.

Not only was I surprised when the bell rang right on time, but I was stunned to open the door to find a well-scrubbed young man dressed in a suit and tie and dress shoes. I was even more surprised when he strode into my office, tossed off his jacket and tie, kicked off his shoes, and opened our therapy with the following challenge: "Guess where I've just been?" Of course I had no idea and said so. "Court," he said. "The damn cop thought

I ran the red light – which I didn't, of course! – and then he nailed me on weed possession. Today was the court date to answer the charges." Since he was off and running I simply climbed aboard. "How did it go?" I asked. "No big deal. All I have to do is stay out of trouble and then my record will be cleared." That was my introduction to Ricky, 24-year-old college dropout who had a knack for getting into trouble.

Ricky's first-day bravado masked a significant and long-standing depression. He'd spend long days hiding out in his room, missing commitments, risking being fired. He was either sleepless or given to excessive oversleeping, irritable and reactive when challenged or silent and withdrawn. He could be punishingly self-denigrating or brash and boastful. Though he never made a suicide attempt, the thought of suicide came to him frequently. He drank often and excessively.

Ricky presents with myriad contradictions. On the one hand, he seems much younger than his age: he dresses in the casual and disregarding manner of a junior high school kid late for school (his first-day suit notwithstanding), he slumps or fidgets in the chair, and speaks with the audacious language of a rebellious wiseacre. He has the emotional vocabulary of a pre-adolescent. On the other hand, he is quick-witted and sharp, smart beyond his years. His fund of knowledge and fluency of ideas reflect a natural brilliance and an unusually well-developed capacity for abstract thinking. He absorbs information easily and hungrily, recalls details and nuance like no one else I know, synthesizes ideas with an astuteness of purpose and direction, and does all this in rapid time. The dichotomy between his raw lack of emotional development and his fine-tuned intellect is apparent in every session.

History

Ricky is the second of three sons of professional parents. His mother is a practical woman, long on competence, short on patience, compassion, or attention. Most times when mother comes up it is in the context of Ricky reporting an episode of mother's exasperation that Ricky is too coarse, too harsh. I sense that mother feels embarrassed by Ricky's gritty presentation, which runs counter to the more traditional style of the family. I have an image of mother throwing up her hands at the impossibility of curtailing Ricky's reactivity and argumentativeness with his brothers. Despite mother's chronic impatience, Ricky calls her in the middle of the night when despair envelops him, hoping for a receptive ear, a calming response. Unfortunately, Ricky's depression wears his mother out, or worse, it angers her. Ricky's father is a more even-tempered parent, but is emotionally naïve and clueless about the responsibilities of parenting. Ricky rarely turns to him.

Ricky was a challenging kid. He pushed limits, was provocative and brazen; he never saw the wisdom in holding back what he thought. He played rough, got detention, broke bones. He had little respect for adults who prioritized discipline over substance and as a result he alienated them. At the same time, he was deeply involved in all that moved him – literature, music, sports. And he excelled at all he took up. So while he was challenging, he was also appealing to those who appreciated his curiosity and broad-ranging awareness. From those he regarded as people of substance he extracted admiration.

Treatment

Working from an Intersubjective Self Psychological perspective I asked myself to understand Ricky's selfobject needs, respond to his hopes in the form of his leading edge, and interpret his dreads in the form of his trailing edge, as they emerged in the transference. All the while I paid attention to my own experience and considered the relationship between his experience and mine. What was my impact on the field between us and thus on his self experience? What was his impact on the field between us and thus on my self experience? These were the guiding questions that framed our work.

Ricky's trailing edge

Ricky's trailing edge was apparent from the start. The fight with the co-worker that brought him into treatment was not readily resolved and led to additional physical altercations between them. The co-worker would taunt and Ricky would lash out. Or the manager would express doubt about Ricky's ability to maintain calm and he'd explode in rage. Not surprisingly he lost the job. This pattern persisted in new situations. The holes in Ricky's growing up experience left him feeling grievously unrecognized and frighteningly unmoored; he was unable to regulate strong emotions, unable to self-soothe. Helpless to despair, anxiety, and reactive rage, he would turn to alcohol to numb distress, which only complicated his experience by facilitating impulsive or aggressive action. Ricky's experience of pervasive selfobject failure led to symptomatic expression of depression and dyscontrol, Ricky's trailing edge in need of interpretation.

Selfobject themes

Explicit exploration of the trailing edge often enough took a back seat to a meandering journey through a narrative of Ricky's daily life. It was in the early wandering that we discovered and developed the yearned for selfobject ties of mirroring, twinship, and idealization that characterized the treatment over the years. I will take them up one at a time.

Mirror theme

The typical session with Ricky involves a recitation that winds from events with friends or work, to thoughts about current events, books read, stories about others. Sometimes he gripes about a problematic interaction he's experienced. He never asks for comment or advice. He needs just enough in the way of an affirmative nod or mmm-hmm to keep going. And if he finds his way to the natural end of a tale he finds something else to share with me. He is sometimes animated, other times sullen. Occasionally at the end of a session he'll hint at a conversation about the presenting issues – the provocative fights and aggression that brought him to therapy or the underlying depression. But these hints are rarely elaborated upon. In general, they feel like updates about the situation, rather than invitations to explore their meaning.

Early on, though I felt that Ricky was meaningfully engaged with me, it was unclear what he was looking for in therapy, what he hoped to find in me, or what he might be getting out of our talks. Asking questions about his emotions was useless. Exploring more deeply the events and ideas he spoke of never seemed possible. I resigned myself to responding as naturally as possible and hoping to understand more down the road. It continued to surprise me that Ricky came to session after session, with not a hint of the reluctance I thought might have been there at the outset. I was aware that my confusion created a nagging doubt in me about what I was doing and also made me feel at somewhat removed from Ricky. For those reasons I decided to ask him how the sessions were going for him, even though I felt that this question introduced a potentially awkward shift in the nature of our dialogue. The awkwardness that I introduced was confirmed by the expression on Ricky's face that looked to me like, "Duh, that's a stupid question." He said simply, "I always feel better after I talk to you."

Perhaps it was a stupid question, but his answer was a good and clarifying one. Ricky was looking for and finding with me an engaged receiver for his experience; he found in me a mirroring selfobject. The experience of being heard, of finding a willing, non-critical ear with me was restorative to Ricky's self-experience. With me he could delve into tales of his unhappy, complicated life, take pride in sharing his copious knowledge and flexible intellect, and experience the relief of expressing anger and frustration. In all these ways he could trust that I would receive him exactly as he is. As I thought about his mother's impatience and casual criticism – what Ricky surely experiences as mother's disregard, her unwillingness to be open to Ricky as he is – and father's emotional absence – leaving Ricky feeling invisible – I understood that the experience of being regarded, listened to, and accepted without question in therapy is a central progressive force for Ricky. This mirror experience – Ricky's yearning to trust in the possibility of being seen and appreciated – was organizing for him and constituted the leading edge that moved the treatment forward.

Twinship theme

Ricky often spoke of food and drink in vivid detail. He'd speak of $4 pitchers of specific brands of beer at a specific beer garden or he would come rushing into the office not just having stopped for a quick breakfast but reporting on the double Big Mac with salty fries that he'd just wolfed down. Once after visiting his hometown he made mention of his favorite pizzeria, Nick's Brick Oven. "Right," I said, "the one at the intersection of Route 9 and Millbrook, where they serve those little garlic knots in an oversized orange mug." "How did you know?" he asked, of course. I told him that I worked at a summer camp near where he grew up and loved that pizzeria too. He was intrigued and our conversation turned to various places we knew in common and the differences between my adolescence of yesteryear and his more recent childhood. Then he asked: "Why didn't you tell me before now that you knew my hometown so well?" I was struck by the pointedness of his question. Privately, I had been aware of feeling cautious and restrained with Ricky because I didn't understand well what was happening in his therapy. I had been unthinkingly following the advice handed down through the psychoanalytic ages: If you are not sure what to say, don't say anything at all. The spontaneity of my comment caught me as much by surprise as it did Ricky and came in part from my own as yet unarticulated need to feel actively engaged in the conversation. I told him of the connection because *I* wanted to share my delight in Nick's with him. So when Ricky asked me why I'd never before said that I knew his hometown I said, "I suppose I was following some psychoanalytic rule of neutrality, but in the moment I just wanted to tell you that I love Nick's as you do." Ricky scoffed at the notion of any kind of psychoanalytic rule or standard – he thought that was preposterous. Not only that, but Ricky was alert to and made anxious by anything that felt inauthentic. He regarded my earlier reticence as artificial and rightly objected to it. My later spontaneity and more natural human reaction were a relief to him, a communication that we together could be direct, honest, human to human with each other. And I recognized that not only did he feel enhanced by the shared connection, I did too. We both felt my greater ease as facilitating a twinship experience between us.

Over time our twinship grew to incorporate a range of themes: place, food, current events. It even allowed us to appreciate differences between us. For example, we have on-going playful references to Ricky being edgy and daring to my nerdy and moderate. Or we return over and over again to his loving gummy candies and my disgust of the same. In all these ways the twinship provides for us a neutral free space of shared, non-conflictual enjoyment where sameness is humanizing and difference opens up a feeling of play. Given the ways Ricky felt alienated in his family, the opportunity for experienced alikeness with me gives him a feeling of quiet belonging he hadn't known before. And like the mirror transference above, the twinship constituted an aspect of the leading edge – a hope that human connection would provide a pathway for growth – that laid the groundwork for cure. While the twinship was not the central and most transformative selfobject experience in the treatment, it was a necessary backdrop to the other more transformative selfobject experiences.

Idealization theme

Early in the treatment the following interaction occurred. Ricky was chronicling for me the adventures of a recent weekend night, an occasion that included friends, beer, shots, and a late night drive to the 7–11. My response was instinctive.

"You drove drunk?"

"Yeah, sure, I guess," he responded. "But it was two in the morning. No one was on the road then."

"No matter. You were drinking and driving. Don't ever do that again."

Ricky was silent for a moment, a little surprised perhaps. Then he said, "You're right. I won't do that again. Ever. I promise."

While I can't know for sure, I believe that he has kept to his word and has never again gotten behind the wheel of a car after drinking.

At this point in the treatment we were still new to each other. I did not have clarity about what might have characterized our transference tie. Neither did I have confidence that I had the emotional traction with Ricky to support my directive to him. Looking back I believe that I intuitively felt the importance of the natural responding that we've seen is central to both his mirror and twinship yearnings in the transference relationship with me. But at the moment all I was aware of was my responsibility to speak plainly and with all the authority of one who knows better. Ricky's response was telling. His initial adolescent-like protest faded quickly into a readiness to be guided, contained, structured. Unable to rely on his parents for guidance and direction, Ricky flailed. In contrast, he was eager to experience me as a knowing and concerned parent, a parent on whom he could rely for guidance. Experiencing me as a knowing and responsible mother he welcomed the clarity and authenticity of my assertion. This was the first hint of the idealization that I came to understand as the primary selfobject yearning, the selfobject tie that would ultimately emerge as the primary need for development. Ricky's hunger to use me as an idealizing guide was a leading edge itching to emerge.

My trailing edge

It was important also that I recognize and work through my own vulnerabilities, activated in the treatment with Ricky. The archaic quality of much of

Ricky's relating to me – the way Ricky conducted something of a monologue, rarely making room for a response from me – risked leaving me feeling distant from him. There are consistent themes in my responses to Ricky – risk that I would be less authentic and retreat into reticence out of a lack of clarity about Ricky's selfobject needs. Conversely, there was risk that out of my yearning to be seen I would be overly active in an effort to assert my presence. My comments in each of the selfobject themes (mirror, twinship, and idealization), helpful as they ultimately were, might have been influenced in part by my own need to fight off passivity, my trailing edge in the treatment with Ricky, activated when I feared becoming invisible in the intersubjective field. I asked myself to pay careful and active attention to my tendency to retreat or my defense against the same. Staying engaged, which most often involved silent but active listening required fighting off the tendency to fall into passivity.

The greatest risk in the treatment would be the possibility that Ricky's trailing edge would be met by my own. If Ricky's vulnerability to feel unrecognized, alone, or unsupported was met by my own vulnerability to withdraw or be less than authentic he would feel abandoned to his most anxious, depressed self and feel he had no choice but to lash out or retreat. My awareness of this risk served as a constant reminder to stay present, stay close to Ricky's experience, and err on the side of thoughtful engagement rather than caution.

My leading edge

On the other hand, if I could meet Ricky's trailing edge in the transference with my leading edge – the experience of self in which a sense of confidence, internal calm, and fundamental humanity combine to facilitate an empathic, attuned, and transformative response – we would have the potential to heal his long-standing pain and move the treatment forward. Ricky's yearning for a maternal transference to me as a steady, reliable, and interested mother opened up for me an explicit awareness of a maternal feeling I had for Ricky. The more I was able to access my own ideal of maternal calm, the more I could hear Ricky's long tales with openness and curiosity, take pride in his newfound commitment to be successful in the work world, share myself more freely, and step in firmly and with authority when needed. The more I could access my own sense of maternal patience, guidance, and love, the more authentic I could be with Ricky. This was my leading edge.

Over time, as the selfobject ties became more reliable and as I was better attuned to my own leading edge, interpretation of Ricky's trailing edge became possible. For example, when a difficult argument with his brothers led to another shame-filled retreat into depression, I could interpret the rupture in Ricky's mirror experience. I might say something like, "When your brothers excluded you from their hiking trip it felt like all those times you were left out before. Of course you felt you had no choice but to retreat." My interpretation signaled my acceptance of his experience, a correction from the criticism he had received from his mother, in addition to allowing me to articulate his symptomatic response. Or when Ricky lost his temper at his new boss when he was given extra responsibility but inadequate training I could interpret the rupture in the idealization. "You'd so hoped that your boss would be the mentor you could count on that it was hard to contain your anger when he failed you." Again, in empathizing with Ricky's underlying yearning I was freer to comment as well on his angry experience.

Ricky's leading edge

Fortunately, Ricky's leading edge was always apparent to me. For all the difficult moments in Ricky's life, his sincerity, and his striving to be an honorable person in the world at large and in the relationship with me as well were always guiding forces in the treatment. Sometimes discussion led him to express hopeless outrage. Other times he would be sullen and only after gentle prodding would he reveal that there had been another contentious argument. Occasionally his silence would yield only after persistent urging for him to open up and he would reveal that he had once again lost his temper and spilled a torrent of hateful invective at someone he cares about, or even struck out again. While he was often too ashamed to share the content with me, he was always clear that his expression of anger was outsized and destructive. At these moments he hated himself, so filled he was with shame, that he could barely make eye contact with me. "I fucked up again," he would say.

Ricky knew all too well that he had to mend his ways. Because of this I did not need to address the physical aggression directly. Instead I could tell him that I understood how hard he was trying to be his best self, how earnest he was in feeling guilty that he had hurt someone he cares about, and how difficult it was to feel in control of painful emotions given renewed experiences of grievous misunderstanding, alienation, or despair. Through all of Ricky's suffering, he was always sincere about wanting to do better. This was his leading edge, a leading edge that was both impressive and moving to me.

Treatment progresses

Treatment progressed and over time, with Ricky's mirror and twinship experiences in the foreground of the intersubjective field and engaged with my leading edge maternal affection for Ricky, his self-experience consolidated and things improved in his life. Ricky secured an entry-level job in a field of interest, a job that had the potential to become a launching pad for a satisfying career. He began a new relationship which, while rocky, did not involve physical aggression. And in general, the emotional and interpersonal crises became less frequent. I believe that these developments were the outgrowth of Ricky's previously derailed development being put back on track. Feeling himself to be recognized and understood in the mirror transference, and feeling the shared humanity of the twinship transference Ricky began the process of transformation from less to more mature forms of self-experience and interpersonal relatedness.

At the same time, the deepest layers of trouble remained. While Ricky had developed a good measure of self-control and became less vulnerable to lashing out at others, either physically or verbally, his depressive despair was too often close at hand, leaving him vulnerable to inner lack of control, rage, and binge drinking. More was needed. It was at this point that the following episode occurred.

Ricky was talking, as he often did, of social experiences during the growing up years. Long afternoons spent watching TV in friends' basements, hanging out in neighborhood backyards. Often enough these conversations included talk of connections with his friends' parents. I was always struck by the sense that Ricky had incredible skills making conversation with adults and being admired and responded to by them in return. Thinking of the impatience and lack of attention Ricky experienced at home with his parents, I said, "It must have felt great to have the attention and respect of your friends' parents." Ricky agreed, but with a shrug of his shoulders. He went on to explain:

"Of course they loved me – I always brought a bottle of wine when I came over."

"I don't understand," I said. "I thought we were talking about playdates when you were 8, 9, 10 years old?"

"Yes, we are," he said. "My parents wanted me to be a good guest so they always sent me to friends' houses with a gift for the parents. The gift was always a bottle of wine."

I was shocked and said so. "I thought the standard for a playdate was you go to a friend's house, have hot dogs and cupcakes, and say thank you to the parents when you leave. Period."

Ricky's response was telling: "Obviously, *you* know that because you're a good mother."[2]

Here was a clear statement of what was emerging as the primary selfobject theme – idealization, and specifically, idealization along the maternal line. Ricky allowed himself to express an awareness of a maternal transference, a yearning for a selfobject transference in which he'd receive the mothering guidance of one who knows better. Given the failures in maternal idealization which left Ricky vulnerable to overwhelming despair, the potential to merge into the stronger, wiser, more confident embrace of a maternal figure who guides and sets a standard of safety was deeply relieving to Ricky. Here was a fortuitous moment in the treatment: Ricky's selfobject longing for a trustworthy, reliable maternal figure was matched by my own selfobject longing in the intersubjective field to be experienced as a competent maternal figure, reliably present for his dissociated affect states. The intersubjective field became a safe context within which Ricky could begin to articulate jumbled affects states and tolerate the anxiety this entailed for him. He began to feel held in the transference relationship with me as the idealizable figure who was reliably present for his needed merger experience.

The treatment opened up more fully as a result. For example, the toughness that was the typical top layer of talk began to soften into revealing areas of timidity and vulnerability. Ricky began using words to describe emotions – words like anxious, angry, scared, hurt. Most significantly, he started cautiously daring himself to say directly to me, "Something happened that I need to talk about." Knowing these areas of vulnerability and knowing that Ricky's willingness to share them came from implicit trust in me, I felt a growing tenderness for Ricky, a tenderness that felt maternal. This facilitated not just Ricky's idealization and the development of my leading edge, but was the necessary foundation that made it possible to weather and benefit from the crisis which followed.

Crisis

The crisis occurred over the weekend, and I learned first of it by text: "I completely screwed up," he said. After a night out with friends, Ricky awoke in a hospital emergency room and was told that he was dropped off by a cab driver who didn't have his address. Realizing that he had blacked out and did not have memory after the first few drinks, he was alarmed, sickened, and deeply ashamed. We stayed in touch by text until his next session, keeping track of how he was feeling, making certain he was safe, noting feelings to be addressed when we would next meet.

In the sessions that followed, Ricky began talking explicitly about his depression. He was overcome with sadness, felt alone and without resources, and confused about his relationship to alcohol. He spoke of his mother's impatience with his depression, his discovery that his friends were not people he could talk to. He was overcome with tears and then berated himself for being melodramatic, he spoke of realizing that he presents a false version of himself to the world and hides his authentic self away. In all these discussions I responded with a quiet welcome of his openness, an acknowledgement of his distress, and an expression of my conviction that we would find our way through to a better day.

This was a painful episode for Ricky and our conversations did not readily take the pain away. But it ushered in a period in the therapy in which

Ricky began communicating more plainly and earnestly about his despair and underlying affect, using words to describe feelings, and appealing directly to our relationship for comfort and understanding. While the content of these conversations focused mostly on acknowledgement of Ricky's experience and in so doing addressed the need for mirroring, the backdrop to these conversations was his yearning to have me be the idealized receiver of his dysphoric affect. I believe that it was Ricky's leading edge idealization, newly exposed and available for use, in active combination with my leading edge maternal response, that allowed Ricky to reveal a much deeper layer of emotions than we had known together before. Trusting in our tie and experiencing me as the calm and steadily engaged receiver of his despair, he began to develop the capacity to self-regulate and self-soothe. For my own part, feeling Ricky's leading edge trust in me and the benefit that accrued therein, I felt affirmed in my own leading edge yearning to be an available maternal presence to Ricky. Leading edge meets leading edge and we are both enriched.

Resolution of the crisis

Three significant shifts happened in the weeks and months after the crisis. First, Ricky made the decision to go attend AA. He was surprised and relieved to discover others in the meetings who received him warmly, were like-minded, and admirable. While his AA attendance has been sporadic and he is ambivalent about addressing the meaning of his relationship to alcohol, he has cut back his use considerably and actively feels the benefit for his health. After a recent social gathering at a pool hall he texted me, "My game is so much better sober!"

Second, Ricky started a new and healthy relationship in which he has made a commitment to be his best self. He opens up to his partner when he's distressed, pushes himself to express himself verbally about his emotional experience. He expects of himself that he be open to his partner's experience, no matter how difficult that might be. He appreciates that his partner is more moderate than he is regarding alcohol. Most notably he's been open with me about his tender feelings, his pleasure in being kind and generous, and his pride in addressing challenging moments with maturity and patience.

Third, he returned to college to complete the studies he'd left behind. In my leading edge maternal feeling, I am inordinately proud of Ricky.

Ricky and I continue to have lots of work ahead. We will continue to pay dedicated attention to Ricky's generative selfobject experiences and his leading and trailing edges, emerging in the context of my own. This is the intersubjective field we have created which has opened up a world of possibilities for Ricky: A world in which he feels recognized in all his individuality, feels a sense of kinship with those who are important to him, and benefits from the sustained experience in the therapeutic relationship of the merger with me as an idealizable maternal figure from whom he can acquire the ability to regulate difficult emotions, soothe himself, and talk about it all.

Notes

1 Grateful thanks to Dr. Peter Zimmermann, whose clinical wisdom informs my work every day. And a special shout out to Ricky, who has taught me more than he could imagine.
2 Incidentally, the revelation of Ricky's parents' inappropriate use of alcohol as a playdate gift opened up a discussion of the glorification of alcohol in the family and the ways reasonable standards for alcohol use were not taught to Ricky. This later became an important building block in successfully addressing Ricky's excessive drinking.

Chapter 6

Working with the trailing edge
Resolving the fear of repetition

George Hagman and Susanne M. Weil

In this chapter we will discuss the understanding and treatment of the trailing edge in Intersubjective Self Psychology (ISP). As the reader will learn in the next chapter we believe that the primary driver of therapeutic change is the intact selfobject tie, in which patient and analyst are in sync, as both experience the tie between them as meeting selfobject needs resulting in sustained and productive collaboration referred to as the leading edge. However, ISP recognizes that frequently the trailing edge, the resurgence of fears of retraumatization and subsequence defenses, predominates and must be addressed in order to set the conditions for the expression of hope, and the realization of long sequestered selfobject longings. For example, there comes a point for some patients in psychoanalytic therapy when they experience the treatment as a threat. Often this occurs early on when the vulnerability so necessary to the process feels dangerous to them. Rather than risk a relationship with the analyst they demur, disengage and assume a "resistant" stance. The analyst response to the expression of the trailing edge transference is crucial. That being said the activation of the analyst's fears of repetitive trauma may initiate a disjunction in the treatment relationship, disrupting the clinical process, and perhaps resulting in an impasse as the analyst's trailing edge and the patient's trailing edge become locked in an unproductive, perhaps destructive cycle. This chapter will explore this form of intersubjective disjunction characterized by the interaction of the patient's and the analyst's fears of failure and hidden longings for success; in other words when the patient's trailing edge meets the analyst's trailing edge. We will show how with specific analytic relationships these reciprocally interacting needs and dreads may contribute to the development of treatment impasses as well as opportunities for effective interpretation and therapeutic change.

Consistent with ISP as a whole, this chapter builds on the groundbreaking paper by Bacal and Thomson (1996) in which they argue for the psychological similarity between patients and analysts, and in particular they emphasize the importance of recognizing and accepting the analyst's selfobject needs in the unfolding dynamics of the treatment. They write:

The analyst's self is ordinarily sustained in his work by ongoing selfobject responses of the analysand, and his or her analytic function may be substantially interfered with (i.e. countertransference reactions occur) when these selfobject needs are significantly frustrated. The therapeutic function is enhanced as a result of his lessened requirement to protect himself against the awareness of these needs.

(Bacal & Thomson, 1996)

From this perspective we recognize that there is an ubiquitous, creative tension, which is active throughout treatment, between selfobject needs, and their frustration, both within the psychological life of the analyst, as well as the patient. This dynamic relationship is an important part of the evolving intersubjective field of the psychoanalytic relationship. The analyst's ability to recognize this tension, and make use of it, may either enhance the process, or impede it.

It is recognized that patients long for renewal, but frequently fear the repetition of failure. These generative and repetitive dimensions of the transference (Stolorow & Atwood, 1992), also described as the trailing and leading edge (Tolpin, 2002), are ubiquitous and powerful aspects of clinical work. In fact, in agreement with Bacal and Thomson (1996) we will argue that the repetitive and generative dimensions characterize both the patient and the analyst's contribution to the treatment relationship. In light of this we will show how the analyst's desire for selfobject experience may evoke selfobject yearnings in the patient that paradoxically stimulate the patient's dread of repetition and the activation of powerful fantasies of retraumatization with concomitant self-protective responses. These "defensive" responses may in fact be self-actualizing, feeling out the analyst's needs and vulnerabilities with disguised hope. However, the analyst may misread these responses. Faced with a patient whom he or she believes is entrenched and "resistant", the analyst experiences the repetition of earlier failures (rejection, abandonment, abuse, and most important, shame) and resorts to his or her own self-protective strategies. In this way the well-meaning and positively motivated analyst becomes locked in struggle or a state of hopeless resignation with the "resistant", avoidant patient; in this way an impasse occurs.

The leading edge and the trailing edge

The leading edge of the transference is primarily organized around longings for selfobject experience. However, the patient's relative openness to the selfobject tie is based on the degree of security or risk which he or she feels. In many cases the hope of the leading edge and the dread of the trailing edge are linked, as the expression of leading edge strivings becomes tied to the pull of trailing edge fears and anxieties. One of our patients described this as "the rubber band effect" – as he reaches out and seeks generative goals he feels suddenly snapped back by old fears and expectations of failure. Repetition replaces renewal; the leading edge is inhibited and controlled by trailing edge pessimism and fear. In this co-constructed enactment, the emergence of selfobject needs stimulates the dreads of the trailing edge, which inhibits the progressive strivings that threaten traumatic repetition. On the other hand, hope may gain strength from hope, as the patient's leading edge meets the analyst's leading edge, amplifying the dyad's positive strivings (see the following chapter for an extended discussion of such an intact selfobject tie). The bottom line is that neither dimension of the transference and countertransference can be understood without attending to the other. In fact, both dimensions gain their content and power from the other. Fear arises from longing, desire is powered by the hope to escape the dreaded repetition (Ornstein, 1974, 1991). Clinically we see how the patient's fear may evolve from their needs and longings while the analyst, his or her more mature self-object needs in check, recognizes and engages with the patient's trailing edge. Another, more abstract way to imagine this is to visualize a tension arc between the two edges of the transference, neither pole can be activated without an accompanying change in the other. An increase in longings and strivings is accompanied by an intensification of dread and defense; the fear of failure stimulates a desire for reparation and renewal. One or the other becomes foreground or background as the patient's and analyst's relative experience of safety or danger oscillates. Optimally the balance shifts as the confluence of analyst's hopes and patient's hopes tips the balance towards growth and self-actualization.

In the next sections we will review the basic components of intersubjective self psychological theory as a prelude to a discussion of our understanding and treatment of the transference's repetitive dimensions, the trailing edge. We will show how all of us, more or less, struggle with fears of the repetition of past traumas and/or relational failures and on the other hand, the desire for restorative, selfobject experiences. And we organize our relationships according to these two powerful sets of fantasies, which in instances of close relationships (such as in psychoanalysis) these different propensities for transference, interact, affect each other and reciprocally organize into unique new configurations. At times, these new configurations may lead to impasse. However, if understood and addressed by the analyst such impasses may also be opportunities for creative change and clinical progress.

Returning to intersubjectivity

As we have discussed in earlier chapters, ISP is a field theory or systems theory that seeks to comprehend psychological phenomena not as products of isolated intrapsychic mechanisms and fixed intrapsychic structures, but as forming at the interface of reciprocally interacting worlds of experience (Stolorow et al., 1987).

> The principal components of subjectivity are the organizing principles, whether automatic and rigid, or reflective and flexible. These principles, often unconscious, are the emotional conclusions a person has drawn from lifelong experience of the emotional environment, especially the complex mutual connections with early caregivers. Until these principles become available for conscious reflection, and until new emotional experience leads a person to envision and expect new forms of emotional connection, these old inferences will thematize the sense of self. This sense of self includes convictions about the relational consequences of possible forms of being.
> (Orange et al., 1997)

A central area in which any person comes to organize experience is in relationship with important, intimate others, in which we engage each other according to the thematic structures of our personal subjective worlds. This is not unilateral but a dyadic, dynamic intersubjective process of mutual construction. From a dynamic systems perspective these structures or patterns of meaning are *emergent* from "the self-organizing processes of the continuously active living system (the clinical relationship). These emergent structure formations develop from the intercoordination or cooperative interaction of their elements or subsystems as they coalesce into self-organized patterns" (Orange et al., 1997, p. 75). In psychoanalytic terms we and our patients co-construct a transference matrix which becomes a microcosm of important aspects of the patient's psychological life, the analysis of which provides a focal point around which the patterns dominating the patient's existence can be clarified, understood, and thereby transformed (Orange et al., 1997).

The co-constructed organizing principles, which make up the intersubjective field are the source of both health and pathology in the clinical relationship. The transference dimensions, which are most important in this regard, are described by Stolorow and Atwood (1992) as the *selfobject dimension* and the *repetitive dimensions*. As to the former dimension each of us yearns for our partner to provide selfobject experiences that may have been missing or insufficient during the formative years. In the latter, which is the source of conflict and resistance, we expect and fear a repetition of early experiences of failure. These two dimensions continually oscillate between the experiential foreground and background of a cotransferential matrix in concert with the varying attunement to each other's emotional states and needs. For example, when the analyst is experienced as malattuned, foreshadowing a traumatic repetition of early developmental failure, the conflictual and resistive dimension is brought to the foreground, and the patient's selfobject longings may go into hiding. On the other hand, when the analyst is able to accurately understand the patient's experience of the failure and the meaning it held for them, the selfobject dimension becomes restored and strengthened and the conflictual/defensive/self-protective dimension tends to recede into the background.

In other words, the stability of the intersubjective field is variable. Most of the people who seek treatment experience themselves as trapped in patterns of interaction and meaning which may appear (even to the analyst) as inevitable, hardwired, and intractable. These organizing principles of their subjective world are themselves unconscious, in which case the patient and analyst are unaware of their role in creating the transference. In fact, it is almost invariably the case that the patient assumes that their experience of the analyst is objectively "true." Given this unawareness, the strong unconscious, sustaining motivations, and despite the often-desperate desire for change expressed by the patient, the transference "may be of such strength and stability that only severe perturbations can disrupt them" (Thelen & Smith, 1994, p. 61). Ideally the disruptive power of the analyst comes from his or her offer to the patient of an opportunity for the mobilization of the selfobject transference which has remained hidden due to the traumatic, repetitive experiences of the patient's relationships. Recognizing the patient's vulnerabilities, the analyst through the communication of understanding and because of his or her attunement to the affective experience of the patient offers an opportunity for selfobject experience – however, this does not mean the patient is ready for it, or more specifically, prepared to experience the fantasies and feelings associated with the emergence of selfobject longings. Given the amount of distress and failure in the patient's relational history, the intensity of the longing for a selfobject bond can be quite strong. With this in mind, the analyst attends to the patient's unfolding experience of the clinical relationship (his or her longings, vulnerabilities, fears, and self-protections), as it is manifest in the coconstructed subjective field. However, a frequent challenge for the analyst is the tolerance, management, and use of their own responses to the patient's enactments and affect states. That being said, often the analyst's own fears and defenses are activated, at times derailing the treatment process.

It is important to note that all meaningful relationships become organized around mutually evoked transference patterns. What makes the intersubjective field in psychoanalysis different is its therapeutic structure and function. The initial conditions for therapeutic action are unique to psychoanalytic treatments. The person coming to treatment is a "patient" seeking some type of helpful service which he or she hopes will decrease psychological distress and increase happiness and well being. This role involves emotional vulnerability distinctly different from most other relationships. Seeking to meet this need, the analyst offers to provide a service to the patient, which hopefully, will reduce the patient's distress, provide opportunity for the satisfaction of developmental needs, increasing the probability of well-being. However, on another level the analyst also seeks some type of psychological benefit, which in his or her case involves the fulfillment of selfobject needs by means of enactment of the role of therapist. Not surprisingly many analysts fear failure and shameful incompetence, especially if they themselves have histories of selfobject failure and relational trauma. The tension between these two poles or edges of the analyst's experience is played out in the treatment. In addition, there is a dynamic tension between the needs and fears of the analyst and those of the patient characterized by conjunction and disjunction. However, it is ultimately and fatefully the tilt towards the patient's experience and needs which is crucial. Both parties bring to these roles a lifetime of personal experience which will determine how they organize themselves in relation to the other. Right from the start each party begins to interact and react to each other, organizing their subjective experiences according to past models and new adaptations. In many instances, and perhaps at times in all treatments, it is the repetitive dimension of the transference with accompanying trailing edge defenses and self-protective tactics, which is evoked (either for the patient, or for the analyst, or perhaps both) leading to a state of disjunction, which must be addressed for the therapeutic opportunities to become realized.

In the following case report regarding the treatment of Tom by one of us, Susanne Weil, we will provide an example of such a disjunction. The treatment relationship described demonstrates how as self-psychologists we are often seeking connection with our patients, as well as opportunities to be helpfully empathic and immersed in our patient's experience. Often, especially during the early phases of work with traumatized or neglected patients, such as Tom, our needs come up against the patient's feelings of vulnerability and strategies of self-protection. Paradoxically the techniques, which we may associate with good practice, are experienced by the patient as threats, or at least as empathic failures – or both. In these instances, the patient is not resistant, or reluctant, but legitimately threatened by the possibility that our needs may dominate and retraumatization will occur. How we manage and negotiate the complex ramifications of this disjunction determines the success or failure of treatment.

Tom

Tom was a 50-year-old married father of two young kids. He was seeking therapy because he could no longer stand the vicious cycles of fighting with his wife, which often resulted in his filing divorce papers, or packing up and going to a hotel. He was unable to withstand the separation and quickly returned home. Tom became tearful as he described their horrible fights and told me, surprisingly, that the last time he had cried was while watching *Good Will Hunting*. I felt encouraged that he had access to his feelings and hoped that I would be Robin Williams – healing Tom and being healed as well.

He described a harsh, colorless history as the son of an alcoholic teacher who came home from school, sat at his garage workbench and ritually drank five beers. He would eat dinner silently and go to bed. If you got in his way you were the target of his fierce contempt. His mother was unstable and prone to screaming/crying fits and leaving home for days at a time. Upon return, she would buy Tom off with candy and deny her frightening behavior. Nothing was ever, ever talked about. Tom was estranged from his parents and sister.

I asked Tom how he felt growing up in this surround had affected him. He said he didn't know how to be with people: he was rude, challenging, and fights with everyone. He said, "I am surprised I got this far without someone really hurting me." He then lamented how different things might be, had he learned how to have relationships. Again, I felt encouraged by his ability to reflect and tell him that growing up without experiencing recognition, stability or trust would make welcoming others into your life very frightening. I wondered what that might mean for us but I held out hope that our relationship might be transforming in some way.

In our sessions, Tom was intensely focused on the discord with his wife. A pattern in their relationship that could easily destabilize him centered on his taking up an issue with her, her denying any culpability, his driving her to recognize his truth in the matter and her intractable denial of his experience. This would result in rageful attacks and his wife becoming confirmed in her belief that Tom has an anger problem, or worse was crazy. He invariably labeled this repeated experience with her, "unfair." There were no other words for it. In Tom's world she should not be allowed to do something if he can't do the same. He wanted symmetry. I visualized a little boy protesting to his parents that something is unfair and being ignored.

I empathized with the awful feelings of not being responded to and being shut down. I said that I could imagine when this happened in his family he would freeze as a way not to be overwhelmed by the pain of his parents' cruelty. Or, the other side of that coin would be to invite a fight to show how he could bravely endure any abuse they doled out. "Yes", he said, "but what do I do?" It became clear that Tom did not want to explore the effects of his past on his relational difficulties with his wife. He had constructed a narrative about his family and it was now fixed. He wanted straight up concrete intervention from me.

Here I neglected to heed one of his central organizing principles: if I opened up and expressed how I felt, something would go horribly bad.

My longings to heal Will Hunting collided with Tom's deep anxiety about closeness. A disjunction occurred and the field shifted.

In the ensuing weeks, I imagined myself as a giant crowbar trying to lift out feelings situated in his body (he described having a lot of muscle pain and tension leading up to his explosive behavior). I encouraged him to talk about the pain of being demonized by his wife. She had a serious cancer that required constant management. I further suggested that their fights might be a way to keep distance from the pain of losing her. He consistently replied, "I don't care." I was struck by this coldness but understood the potential for dissociation. In addition to all of Tom's early relational trauma, he was a survivor of 9/11.

Although I am aware of signs of Tom's past trauma, I felt a strong urge to help him feel valued. My own trauma history (which I later share with him), of being threatened with abandonment as a child, activated me to go into overdrive with Tom in an attempt to prevent another such loss. I pressed on and began to see him on Saturday when he was in crisis with his wife. I agreed to lower my fee despite the fact that he worked for a hedge fund and did well. I suggested concrete strategies to engage his wife, even role-played with him. After each of these conversations he said, "Look, I am an engineer, you have to tell me what to do." When I suggested that I have been doing just that (at least in my mind), he countered that it is hopeless. I felt stiff armed and angry. Chaos ensued and instead of trusting myself to be in this cacophonous world with him, I felt the need to control it or, if that didn't work, to distance myself from him and the growing fear of abandonment. This took the form of pathologizing. In an attempt to make sense of the upheaval, I searched for labels. I imagined Tom as a case of PTSD and dissociation, or that he suffered from disorganized attachment, or maybe he was on the autism spectrum. I even pasted "dry drunk" on him.

I recognized that we have moved into the repetitive dimension of the transference, yet despite this "insight", I couldn't manage my feelings of urgency that he must avoid another marital battle. I was gripped by anxiety that a woman with life threatening cancer and two innocent children would be further harmed by Tom's need to restore himself. My fear became entangled with the overpowering pressure I felt from the constant refrains of "what do I do?" and the ensuing ineptitude. My dread of being left alone with such vulnerable feelings, as I was as a child whose family was becoming unhinged by loss and grief (my repetitive dimension) was overwhelming and caused me to miss the opening he good-naturedly provided. "I feel like I am frustrating you", he said with surprising self–awareness. "NO", I bark at him, "I AM JUST TRYING TO UNDERSTAND YOU." At that moment, my need for self-protection left me blind to Tom's bid for connection, further solidifying our disjunction.

Tom told me he had it with his wife and was going to tell the kids that he was leaving. I knew he was not ready to make such a move and I became terrified that he was weaponizing his children. I clamored on about how devastating this would be to his family, but he has shut me out. I asked him if he would be comfortable with my sharing something from my own life with him. He looked alarmed and asked if I should be doing this. I said that I think so but only if he was agreeable. He nodded. Then I began to tell him my story of the threat of abandonment by one of my parents when I was a young child, the same age as his older son. My parents had just lost an infant son, and I a brother, and on that day they had a heated argument. It was during that argument that my overwhelmed father said he was leaving (which he didn't). That moment has been seared into my being and is forever a part of me. I have known no terror greater than this, I told Tom. He said nothing.

Despite my thinking that he was too vulnerable and too dissociated to make use of a relational interpretation, I offered the idea that he is enacting with me, in a more muted way, what might go on with others: being provocative and recalcitrant as a way of closing down the prospect of intimate connection.

My desperation to reach him continued. I suggested that when he is disrupted he loses access to verbal articulation of his feelings so he threatens his wife with abandonment that serves to activate her anxiety. She would know how he felt. And, finally, so did I. Tom resonated with this and shared that leading up to their going to social events which they often must do because she runs a large company, he experienced a deep dread that something was going to go very wrong. Unable to express this anxiety and enlist his wife as a source of comfort, he threatened to leave her on her own. I told him that I thought what he most needed in those moments was connection not separation. I understood, I said, that he did not yet trust a tender touch and was always protecting himself, preparing to be slammed. After saying this, I sensed that he heard me and I imagined the intersubjective field shifting. Tom picked up on it too and told me how much he longed to feel comfortable and at ease. I felt that we experienced a moment of conjunction; a re-ordering and we went on.

I don't know all the forces that were interacting between Tom and me that enabled us to momentarily shift into a more stable state. What allowed me to let go? What allowed Tom to calm down? There are endless possibilities. What IS important, however, is that as systems-informed analysts, we continually must challenge ourselves to stay open, curious, flexible, respectful and to rigorously embrace uncertainty.

Discussion

The focus of an Intersubjective Self Psychological Treatment such as with Tom is the subjective experience of the patient in the context of a treatment relationship with us, the therapist. All transactions between patient and analyst are in terms of feelings, fantasies, meanings, etc. Subjective experience is always in flux, ambiguous, complex, and context sensitive. Of course this can feel like conducting a treatment on shifting sands (Stolorow et al., 1987). Patients and analysts seek to concretize treatment processes, systematize understandings, and reify relational metaphors which provide the feeling of substance and reliability in an ultimately unknowable and chaotic subjective reality. Vulnerable people may organize their experience around fearful patterns, forged in early life, in an effort to anticipate and protect against the repetition of trauma. For example, patients like Tom want "to be told what to do." to protect against the terror of intimate connection. As an engineer, he imagined that a "straight up, concrete intervention" would meet his needs without the risk of opening up and risking retraumatization. On the other hand, the analyst, prepared and ready (perhaps longing) to address the patient's feelings and fantasies, feels put off, even rejected, reduced to the role of adviser. Thus, as we saw in the case report, the withdrawal of Tom's responsiveness precipitated a reaction in Susanne that interfered with her therapeutic function, activating her countertransference (Bacal & Thomson, 1996). As a result, a disjunction erupted in which Susanne's fantasies and longings to heal came up against Tom's fear of being cared for. Susanne's report of her struggle to cope with and perhaps make use of her part of the transference, vividly captures the work that the ISP clinician engages in at the trailing edge.

For this type of disjunction to be resolved interpretations must include both dimensions of the transference and countertransference, especially the way in which both are mutually determined and interdependent. After much struggle Susanne and Tom find a moment of recognition in which a balance between fear and need, between enactment and interpretation is found. Susanne succinctly expresses the difficult struggle within Tom between longing for connection and understanding, and the dread vulnerability which necessitates the need to defend and reject. After a long struggle to find a way to "be" his therapist, she is able to put aside her own desperate need for confirmation and emotional resonance, so as to articulate Tom's crushing dilemma. Paradoxically Tom's confirmation of the rightness of Susanne's interpretation is the moment of connection which she has sought for so strenuously. But it was only when she had relinquished her personal needs in favor of clinical understanding, that she finally succeeds. They go on.

Conclusion

While it is inevitable that the analyst experiences his or her own selfobject needs in the course of any treatment, in the end these must be of a mature nature if the patient is to fully benefit. Rather than the gratification of mirroring, idealization or twinship, the analyst must satisfy mature selfobject needs through the skillful and effective practice of his or her professional craft; in other words, the experience of being a good enough analyst. The achievement of such a role necessitates the cultivation of an intellectual and emotional stance, which allows for the intertwining of empathy, objective assessment, and self-awareness. As Susanne notes in her work with Tom, if we are to recognize and manage these types of impasses and disjunctions between our patients and ourselves we must be vigilant and radically self-reflective. Our motivations are always more complex, uncertain, and perhaps even opaque to us. Hence we should never take ourselves at face value. We recognize that much of what we are dealing with are appearances and far more ambiguous and complex than we know. We hold our understandings gently and often quietly. Interpretations may for a time be provisional because it is highly probable that when we think we understand, we are in fact wrong, or at least only partially aware. On the other hand, there may be a need, as with Susanne and Tom at the close of her report, when uncertainty suddenly shifts and we find ourselves making clear statements of understanding, even confronting the patient, hoping (perhaps in desperation) that it is what the patient needs and has become able to make use of us. Hence the clinical process of Intersubjective Self Psychological Treatment is ever evolving, emergent, and open to possibilities. While we strive to understand our patients but may not fully understand what they are trying to achieve in any given moment, it is crucial that we maintain our interest, curiosity, flexibility and respect for his or her subjective experience. Ultimately we must recognize the legitimacy of the ways he or she organizes and maintains a meaningful and valued sense of self. An analyst who is responsive to the patient's longings, who recognizes and is attuned to the patient's vulnerabilities, who appreciates what the patient fears and hopes for, who respects the need for self-protection even while challenging the patient to take a risk, and who identifies and mobilizes the inherent strengths and resourcefulness of the patient, will be an analyst whom the patient can trust and make use of in the pursuit of change.

Chapter 7

Working with the leading edge
When the selfobject tie is intact

Harry Paul, Peter B. Zimmermann, and George Hagman

In this chapter we explore the *intact selfobject tie* and how it supports and promotes the leading edge of self-development in Intersubjective Self Psychological treatment. By intact selfobject tie we mean the shared experience in the analytic relationship during which the selfobject transference and selfobject countertransference of patient and analyst remain in sync, and disruptions in the tie, due to failures in empathic attunement, are minimal or absent. The sustained, intact selfobject tie in the therapeutic relationship allows for the expression of the leading edge strivings of both participants which come to dominate the intersubjective field. Finally, we will demonstrate by means of an in depth case discussion how to promote and sustain the intact selfobject tie, the leading edge, and curative agent of ISP treatment

Not only have self psychologists, following Kohut's lead, neglected to conceptualize the transformative/curative nature of the intact selfobject tie between patient and analyst, but in addition, they have failed to recognize the legitimate transformative effect of leading edge transference interpretations. Instead self psychologists have emphasized the importance of the empathic rupture/repair sequence, and the interpretation of the trailing edge dimensions of the transference (the patient's deficits, fears and defenses as expressed in relationship with the analyst). While we fully recognize the importance of the interpretative work with the trailing edge, we believe that as a result of this focus on pathology and disruption, even self psychologists have failed to adequately address the critical growth promoting role served by intact leading edge interpretations, formulated out of an active discussion of the on-going selfobject relationship. A discussion initiated, we might add, by either patient or analyst. We will demonstrate how and why transference based interpretations of the intact selfobject relationship can actively contribute to successful treatment by broadening and deepening therapeutic collaboration.

Freudian psychoanalysis emphasized interpretation in making conscious what was unconscious. And, it was argued that the power of reason over the unruly *Id* was the basis for cure. Interpretations were thought to address transference distortions leading to greater awareness and the expansion of rationality. Technically the work of analysis was the exploration of primitive desires and the patient's mechanisms of defense – in other words of the patient's pathology. Later, still following Freud, others recognized the importance of non-pathological aspects of the analytic relationship, using terms like "therapeutic alliance", "working alliance", or "real relationship", but then saw no need to interpret any aspect of these ties because they were preanalytic and extra transferential and thus had no value in relation to growth or structure. These positive dimensions of transference were considered simply an important background support for the real work, the interpretation of unconscious fantasy, defense, and resistance, which we, building on Marianne Tolpin's work (2002), call the trailing edge of transference. Kohut's original concepts such as optimal frustration or the idea that the building of psychic structure only occurred after a moment of empathic failure are ideas that were grounded in classical psychoanalytic thinking. Even after the selfobject transference bond and selfobject experience were recognized as the linchpin of the entire therapeutic endeavor, Kohut and his followers still viewed them as extra analytic and as only a necessary but clinically neutral requirement for an effective analysis.

Consistent with the classical analytic treatment models, Kohut believed that self psychological cure was based on a two part system: phase one involved understanding and phase two explanation. Self psychology's contribution to the theory of cure has been that for growth to occur (e.g. self-structure building) there must be a reactivation of thwarted developmental needs in the form of the selfobject transference (Kohut, 1984, p. 100). The analyst's role was to resolve the obstacles to the emergence of these selfobject longings by means of the understanding conveyed through his or her interpretations. However, even after the successful expression of selfobject needs, Kohut believed that self-structure building only occurred via optimal frustration of those mobilized selfobject needs which is supposed to result in transmuting internalization. He concluded, in his last published book that psychoanalytic cure can only occur when there is rupture in the patient therapist connection accompanied by what he called *optimal frustration* (non-traumatic frustration of selfobject needs), and only when the patient can assume the analyst's function can he or she begin to heal and ultimately, after this process is repeated many times, can a cure be attained. Therefore, the selfobject transference was seen by Kohut as the necessary but not sufficient component of the curative process. Consistent with his classical psychoanalytic training, Kohut still saw the analyst's interpretation as the sufficient condition, specifically the interpretation of the patient's experience of the disruption of the selfobject tie. This is when transmuting internalization was thought to occur, as the patient takes in the analyst's interpretive function as a part of his or her own self structure.

In her groundbreaking papers, *Compensatory Structures: Pathways to the Restoration of the Self* (Tolpin, 1997a) and *Doing Psychoanalysis of Normal Development: Forward Edge Transferences* (Tolpin, 2002), the Self Psychologist,

Marian Tolpin, despite her recognition of the importance of corrective experience, still believed that personal development proceeded from disrupted, optimally frustrating experiences.

On the other hand, it was with the seminal work of Howard Bacal (1985) that psychoanalytically informed self psychologists began to speak about *optimal responsiveness* which was defined as the analyst's on-going affectively toned understanding of the patient. Bacal elaborated on this idea from a specifically self psychological perspective by associating the analyst's *optimal responsiveness* with the patient's *corrective selfobject experience* of the analytic relationship (Bacal, 1990). Leaving behind the concepts of optimal frustration and transmuting internalization, Bacal declared that personal growth occurs as a result of the ongoing emotional tie between patient and analyst. However, neither Bacal nor Tolpin considered the clinical value of the *sustained and undisrupted* selfobject experience in and of itself, nor did they conceptualize the therapeutic power of the interpretation of the intact and undisrupted selfobject transference.

In agreement with Bacal and building on the work of Tolpin, we believe that it is the analyst's responsiveness and empathic attunement during the sustained experience of an intact selfobject tie, which provides the therapeutic context within which the analyst and patient are enabled to engage in dynamic and *generative* clinical work. It is during this period that the patient experiences a durable sense of safety and heightened engagement with the analyst, as a result of which he or she can make more effective use of the psychological and pragmatic resources which the analyst makes available to him or her. It is this period of sustained and vital collaboration between patient and analyst that is the focus of this chapter.

In summary, we are challenging the traditional self psychological idea that the analysis of the therapeutic relationship only occurs when the tie is disrupted. We would like to offer an important addition to the theory of ISP: that transference interpretations offered when the selfobject tie (the leading edge) is intact have an equally important psychotherapeutic function as trailing edge interpretations, and constitute an important area of exploration and elaboration with a patient. Just because treatment is proceeding well does not mean that analysing and making use of this positive emotional dimension can't contribute to the treatment process. It is our contention that shining the analytic light on intact leading edge experiences between patient and therapist widens and broadens our understanding of the psychotherapeutic process.

The intact selfobject tie: the leading edge of the transference

Kohut often referred to the sustaining role of selfobject experience as a type of psychological oxygen, necessary for survival and growth. The selfobject tie being intact or the treatment being organized around the leading edges of patient and analyst, means that both patient and therapist are receiving the steady flow of cognitive/emotional oxygen that allows both persons to breathe, and thus live, in accordance with their personal design. Realistically, this flow may be disrupted; however, in a well functioning analytic relationship the inevitable ups and downs and instances of less than ideal attuned responsiveness from the selfobject milieu all lie in the non-traumatic range. That being said, we argue that these failures are not primarily responsible for therapeutic change, in other words the patient does not grow stronger because there are tiny, even if non-traumatic interruptions of the metaphorical airflow – although how these disruptions are analyzed when they occur is essential to the positive transformation of self experience, as Kohut has demonstrated. Any living organism grows optimally when there is an uninterrupted, steady provision of oxygen. Psychologically, the mirror experience, the merger experience with an idealized figure, and the twinship experience are examples of specific sources of this psychological oxygen.

In other words, over time, even in the best of conditions self experience is subject to ongoing fluctuations and micro disruptions in the intersubjective field. Thus, the reliability of the selfobject experience is at all times contingent on the proper attunement by the caregiver and later on by the analyst whose responsive management and empathic interpretations of the micro disruptions that constitute the adjustments that keep those disruptions in the nontraumatic range.

When the selfobject tie is intact a developmental line is reinstated and there is a consolidation of fragile or tenuously established self states as well as the discovery and unfolding of new self states or dimensions of self experience. As a result, the patient can begin to engage with the analyst and subsequently with the world and initiate actions that result in the actualization of the self in accordance with his/her ambitions, capacities and ideals, reflecting a renewed or emergent design/vision of him or herself. The person has the needed and longed for self-selfobject experience in a sustained way that is the requirement for the development of a healthy and solid sense of self, which manifests in the renewed capacity for love and work, and for self-reflection and self-agency, meaning the capacity to take thoughtful action on their own behalf, which all of us need in order to realize who we are and yearn to be. We believe that this leads to the consolidation of an on-going healthy sense of self and the development of psychic structure.

In addition, we assert the continued importance of the three major selfobject transferences identified by Kohut in the healthy elaboration and growth of the sense of self. As in development, the reliable experience of merger with the idealizable therapist results in the development of an improved capacity for affect regulation, as well as a reduction in distressful affects such as anxiety and depression. The connection with a mirroring selfobject leads to enhanced self-esteem, confidence and vitality. And the experience of twinship results in the development and consolidation of a sense of identity and trust in oneself. In these instances when the selfobject transference is sustained over time, self experience stabilizes. Strengthened by a more established sense of self, of self-agency, and of trust in self and others, the person engages the world with more confidence, vitality and resourcefulness, actively and creatively negotiating their path, actualizing their program of action, and further solidifying their sense of themselves as competent, lovable and desirable, etc. ... In the end, the experience of leading edge work also includes the optimal or good enough response to the inevitable disruptions in the patient's self experience. If a person suffers a setback, a disappointment, an experience of failure or a limitation, all of which constitute disruptions of the narcissistic balance, emotional equilibrium and sense of self, the attunement of the analyst at these moment takes the form of work at the leading edge. In other words, an intact selfobject tie does not mean that disruptions do not happen; it means that the attuned responsiveness from the analyst remains available, consistent and durable. That is the healing experience – that is what enables the growth and transformation of the self.

The therapeutic situation

As patient and therapist, we view the therapeutic situation through the lense of our subjective worlds by which we organize our experience of each other, investing the relationship with our personal meanings (Stolorow et al., 1987). Our subjective world comprises the sum total of who we are as a person. It is composed of our consciousness with all its facets: cognitive and linguistic abilities, knowledge, experience, memory; as well as our unconscious world with all its dimensions: fantasy life, dream world, preconscious organizing principles, repressed and dissociated experiences and memories. It also includes our emotions and affect states: joy, sorrow, desire, anger, despair, elation, pride, ambition, shame, guilt, and anxiety, as well as our yearnings and hopes, and our fears and dreads. Finally, our subjective world includes our character structure, temperament, genetic predisposition, biological makeup, and physical constitution. All these different dimensions compose our unique subjectivity by means of which we experience ourselves and the world with which we are engaged.

In the therapeutic situation the subjective worlds of patient and therapist come together, generating a unique, complex "intersubjective field" (Atwood & Stolorow, 1984), and each participant's experience of the therapeutic relationship is shaped by the unique dynamics of this interaction.

However, as unique and idiosyncratic as they may be, the meanings which we construct according to our subjective worlds have to do justice to reality as we encounter it. This is where we depart from Stolorow's theory of intersubjectivity, as he held a view which sees no necessary correspondence between the subjective world and the world at hand (Stolorow et al., 1999), while we claim that there *is* one objective world that has to be comprehended and known. Our subjective worlds have to adequately capture and organize our experience of external reality and our place in it, in order for us to be able to navigate the world successfully – or, as the saying goes, saber-toothed tigers would long ago have devoured us. In other words, we can only go so far in believing that tigers are fuzzy cute little things before that worldview proves lethal. The higher the degree of "object-adequacy" of our subjective worlds, the greater our capacity to successfully manage our reality which includes the interpersonal world.

In other words, against the postmodern trend, which privileges subjectivity at the expense of objectivity, we do not let go of the claim that our subjective worlds have to correspond with an objective world – however complex and provisional any such claim proves to be. This means that in order for us to survive and make a life, in the pursuit of love and work, our subjectivities and those of our patients have to be organized in such a way that they are able to do justice to the reality at hand.

Where this link is severed and all we have is subjective worlds, ungrounded in reality, we can no longer speak of facts, truth and objectivity, and in regards to clinical knowledge, we can no longer be sure if therapeutic change is moving the patient closer to a psychotic world-view or to an object-adequate adaptation corresponding to the world in which he or she lives.

The work of therapy, therefore, is to transform and develop the subjective world of the patient so that it does justice to the reality we inhabit, which allows the patient to navigate the world more successfully. This point of view inevitably requires that the subjective world of the therapist in principle has a higher degree of object adequacy than the patient's subjective world – even if at any given moment the reverse may be true. In the therapeutic dialogue between patient and therapist, we always are faced with this dilemma, which is why we aim to create the capacity to decenter from "the central organizing principles" (Stolorow et al., 1987) of our patients and ourselves. This makes it possible for us to be aware of how we organize our subjective worlds and the resulting experience we have of them. As is evident, the idea of decentering from our subjective world itself implies the existence of an objective world. In fact, when we "decenter" from our experience, we temporarily treat our own subjectivity as part of the objective world, treating it as a phenomena whose meaning it is important to decipher and manage. The development of the patient's capacity to decenter, and reflect on his or her experience, is one of the major accomplishments of psychotherapy, as it is also at the heart of the therapist's skill.

In ISP we have divided the therapeutic process of transforming and developing the patient's subjective world into working with the trailing edge and working with the leading edge of the patient's subjective world. The leading edge consists of the patient's hopes and yearnings and constitutes the patient's generative transference, the bond the patient needs with the therapist in order to complete self development. The trailing edge comprises the patient's fears and dreads and constitutes the patient's repetitive transference, which manifests in the patient's defensive and self-protective adaptations and character structure, which is what needs to be worked through and transformed in order to restore self development.

Leading edge hopes and trailing edge dreads are what patients bring to the therapeutic relationship. And what holds true for the patient is also true for us as therapists. We too bring our leading edge yearnings and hopes, and our trailing edge fears and dreads to the therapeutic situation. And it is the intersection of the leading edge and the trailing edge of patient and therapist that constitute the heart of the clinical intersubjective field; for it is within the therapeutic situation that we work through and transform the patients dreads and welcome the emergence of healthy yearnings, as they unfold in interaction with *our* dreads and yearnings.

None of this happens by itself, like water running down a mountain toward the ocean; rather, such effort requires an active therapist, who, with an awareness of his/her own leading edge yearnings and trailing edge dreads, engages the patient, working to understand and work through his/her dreads and fears as they evolve in relation to him/herself, the therapist, while *guiding* the therapeutic process so as to facilitate the unfolding of the patient's leading edge. All our therapeutic interventions and provisions are offered in the service of this goal. This goal does not come about without effort, even struggle. Working through the frears and dreads of the trailing edge requires effort and skill, as does working with and facilitating the unfolding of the leading edge yearnings and hopes.

The therapeutic tool for working through and resolving the repetitive trailing edge transference is *interpretation*. Optimally, this results in the transformation of the subjective world of the patient. We offer interpretations in the service of illuminating and transforming what has proven to be maladaptive for the patient. We might say:

> Given that my inquiry into your relationship with your girlfriend felt demeaning and reminded you of your father's criticism of your relationships, I understand that you want to withdraw from me because you felt the need to protect yourself from me.

This interpretation of the trailing edge aims to dissolve the defensive adaptation that is central to the patient's subjective world and has limited this patient's capacity to engage with people for fear of criticism. Our interpretations aim to transform this particular existing structure of self experience, which, if active, gets in the way of expressing the yearnings and hopes of the leading edge.

On the other hand, the therapeutic tool for working with the leading edge is *optimal responsiveness* (Bacal, 1985) or, as *we* have come to call it, *attuned engagement,* during which the therapist actively engages the patient in such a way as to accurately understand and respond to his/her selfobject needs, thereby providing the patient with an opportunity to have these needs met, and as a result facilitating the patient's developmental growth. In other words, as therapists we are not only responding, we are actively participating in the intersubjective field in keeping with our understanding of the salient selfobject transference yearnings of the patient. We *show up* for the selfobject transference, engaging the patient's yearning and needs. This is what allows for the activation and unfolding of the leading edge.

The revival, unfolding and maintenance of the leading edge via optimal and phase appropriate attuned engagement, results in the structuralization, integration and cohesion of the evolving subjective world of the patient. Hence, when we engage with the patient's leading edge, all our efforts aim to deepen and maintain it. While interpretations of the trailing edge aim to dissolve the repetitive transference and seek to bring about a structural transformation of the existing self experience, attuned engagement with the leading edge aims to deepen the established selfobject transference in order to create an emotional environment that facilitates the development and consolidation of new self experience. The success of any psychotherapy therefore depends on these two steps: 1) working through of the trailing edge transference, and 2) facilitating the unfolding of the leading edge transference. While working through the trailing edge often constitutes the necessary condition, it is never sufficient for the therapeutic work of ISP. The sufficient condition for cure in ISP is the unfolding of the leading edge (see Chapter 3).

In light of this, we offer the following interpretive guidelines:

1. Interpreting the trailing edge: When the trailing edge is in the foreground, the patient experiences the therapy, and the therapist as a threat to his or her self experience. Rather than expecting to get help, the patient fears a repetition of past traumas in the here and now of the therapeutic relationship. As a result, self-protective measures in the form of defenses are activated as a protection against the dreaded repetition of a traumatic experience. Therefore, the emergence of the trailing edge *always* requires interpretation as the patient is under the sway of the repetitive transference, which dominates his/her experience of the therapist. If the trailing edge is left uninterpreted, it will result in the enactment of the repetitive transference and in the entrenchment

of defenses. At best nothing transformational will take place nor anything curative, and at worst this will result in the disruption of the tie with the therapist, threatening the treatment.

The trailing edge may manifest noisily, in the form of florid enactments and repetitive patterns, accompanied by complaints, protests, accusations, anger, and rage at the therapist, or more insidiously, in the obsequious and unacknowledged way of pathological accommodation. Both adaptations, as they are defensive, preclude a genuine therepeutic engagement. The therapist, therefore, must interpret these trailing edge fears and work to resolve the repetitive transference. It is this working through process that brings about a structural transformation in the self experience, and the conditions for the emergence of the leading edge.

In addition, the working through of the trailing edge in turn will allow for the genuine selfobject yearnings to emerge and for the establishment and development of the yearned for selfobject transference. Only then will the leading edge move into the foreground.

At this point patients begin to experience the treatment and the relationship with the therapist as an opportunity to establish the longed for bond, the selfobject transference or generative transference, which facilitates the acquisition of new structures and results in the growth and development of the self. This process requires the therapist's attuned engagement with the leading edge.

2. Attuned engagement with the leading edge: When the leading edge has taken center stage in the treatment, the result is unfolding "tendrils of hope" (Tolpin, 2002) for which the therapist must show up. This means that the patient has the experience that his/her selfobject yearnings are met with the requisite optimal engagement from the therapist. The sustained experience by the patient that her/his leading edge transference yearnings are met, facilitates the acquisition of new self structures and the consolidation of self experience.

What does the therapeutic work with the leading edge consist of? When the leading edge is engaged, the patient feels that he/she is receiving the emotional nutrients needed for emotional growth, psychological development, and self-consolidation. Thus, all our therapeutic responses and modes of engaging aim to maintain the needed leading edge experience of the patient. Interpretations of the leading edge bond, unlike trailing edge interpretations, are not a requirement as it is the experience of the bond itself that is curative. They are not advisable early on in the treatment as they tend to make the patient self conscious of his/her connection with the therapist. In fact, a premature interpretation of the leading edge, as in: "You are feeling alive today because you feel that I delight in your expansive display of your potential" may make the patient feel self conscious or even ashamed, thus provoking anxieties and fears related to the emergence of selfobject needs, and are therefore, paradoxically, weakening the selfobject tie. Thus, decisions regarding the timing of interpretations of the leading edge must be made with an awareness of the particular patient's vulnerability to repetitive fears vis-a-vis the activation of selfobject needs. What is required is for the therapist to understand what the leading edge transference is for each patient. Only if we understand the selfobject yearnings *and* vulnerabilites, which characterize the patient's leading edge transference as it unfolds in interaction with the therapist, can we know how to respond with optimal, attuned engagement. This awareness safeguards and promotes the patient's curative and growth-producing experience in the therapeutic situation.

However, interpretations of the leading edge are indicated, especially in the middle and later phases of treatment, as they often strengthen the patient's experience of the therapist's attuned engagement, thereby solidifying the generative intersubjective field. Once actively engaged, the generative transference constitutes the emotional context that promotes psychological growth and the building and consolidating of new self structures. In well-established treatments, where a solid, shared leading edge transference/countertransference prevails in the intersubjective field between patient and therapist, interpretations of the leading edge may help to further strengthen the selfobject tie, as such interpretations convey to the patient that the therapist is committed to *showing up* for the patient selfobject yearnings. Finally, often the patient initiates a discussion of the leading edge, which may be a marker of further engagement, increased self-awareness, greater empathy for self and other, and an indication of a decreasing vulnerability to shame and humiliation.

To summarize, interpretations are indicated if they support the establishment and/or maintenance of the leading edge or promote its expression in the therapeutic relationship. Interpretations of the leading edge are contraindicated if they create self-consciousness and shame over the need for the selfobject tie. This is to say that the decision to actively focus on and articulate the yearnings in the leading edge is a clinical one. It is determined, as all questions pertaining to our practice, by the patient's potential response at a given moment in time.

The following clinical report is an example of work with the leading edge when the selfobject tie remains intact.

Michael

Michael is a 70-year-old man who has been in treatment for five years. He has struggled with a non-clinical depression for most of his adult life. He had been married for 45 years until five years ago when his wife died from complications of alcoholism. It was at this point that he entered three times a week therapy.

Although his wife struggled with her alcoholism for most of her adult life, she and Michael were deeply committed to each other. He ran his own business and legal practice. Michael and one assistant were the only employees, given his many fears about being a "boss", a role he perceived as overwhelmingly difficult. He was often gone during the week, visiting clients, returning home for weekends to find his wife drunk. Earlier in their marriage, she had had a brief sexual liaison. Michael has been never been able to perform sexually, either before or during his marriage.

Michael is 5 ft 8 and at the beginning of the treatment he weighed 220 pounds. Presently, he weighs 200 pounds. When he graduated college, in 1969 from an Ivy League college and law school, he weighed less than 180 pounds. He has been extremely successful by any standard. When traveling for his job, Michael was the consummate professional, very friendly and extremely competent. He prides himself on his social skills. For example he would choose the same restaurants to frequent on business or when at home, getting to know every waiter and owner. However, if you asked him to list the friends that he has made over the last 50 years he would be hard pressed, except for a few clients and his personal banker. Though not aware as it was happening, he now understands that he gained weight over the years, to be less attractive to women. He could not perform sexually, and he did not want to be in a situation in which he was expected to assert himself in any way. To say yes or no, was excruciating, in any personal situation, including saying no to a woman. Therefore, he opted out of almost all relationships with men or women, unless the relationships were transactional. Business partners, waiters or owners of restaurants were the only safe places to be "out" with himself.

He describes a situation in his business life, in which he believes that he was the person he wishes he could be in his personal life. In accompanying a potential client to Kennedy Airport, he and the client had not yet closed the deal and as they arrived at the airport and they were talking about the client's upcoming trip to San Francisco, Michael, quite spontaneously, said, "I'll jump on the plane with you, we can have dinner in San Francisco and continue to talk". He closed the deal, but most importantly he felt alive and vital – the man he wished he could be.

Michael began treatment soon after his wife passed away. At that time, he was depressed, depleted, complained of having very little energy and was often teary in the session. Michael's wife had managed almost every part of his life, because in forums other than the professional, he was exquisitely vulnerable to injury, shame, anxiety, and depletion. When she died he became immobilized. The initial months of the therapy were often occupied with his self criticism and self contempt for not saving her life. His sense of himself was that if something in his life went awry, it must have been his fault. In the case of his wife and her alcoholism, he should have been able to help her more. A concurring thought was "why wasn't I important enough or didn't I matter enough to her that she stop drinking?"

Almost every time these two issues came up, he preceded their discussion with, "I know that I shouldn't feel this way, but". His concern was that I would in some way join him in his self criticism. In this initial phase of the therapy, I helped him to see that not only did I not believe that he was responsible for his wife's alcoholism, but I also felt that his feelings were valid. And, we needed to understand why he felt the way he did. His self-blaming had historical roots, I suggested. If he could have empathy for himself (something he admitted was in short supply) he would feel less in the wrong, less guilty for having these feelings.

Self doubt and self examination were perfectly understandable questions, but to be trapped in a web of self-criticism was neither fair nor helpful to him, I said. Michael said that it helped him when I shared my similar feelings and questions. He then felt more normal. I believe that it was at these moments that a twinship dimension of the transference began to unfold. For the most part, however, the generative leading edge of the idealizing selfobject transference fantasy was in the foreground.

I noticed in the last paragraph, I wrote "we needed to understand". In working with the intersubjective context, I often use words like "we" to communicate to the patient that "we" are in this work together.

In the early months of the therapy, Michael often missed one out of every ten or so sessions, saying that he was too tired. This was his code for feeling depleted, and that it would be better for him to sleep. He was also overwhelmed with guilt and self blame for his wife's death. Our meetings were usually at 8:00 AM. He would retreat from life by staying in bed; eating his meals in the bed so that newspapers, pizza boxes, and other remnants would clutter the bed and his environs. I don't mean this as an occasional retreat to bed to relax, but a systematic escape from life, and his feelings – a form of self protection by which he tried to maintain a precarious self-cohesion. Interactions with anyone were psychologically perilous. He had relied on this strategy for almost his entire adult life.

When he first started missing sessions, I questioned myself, wondering what I had or had not done. Was his missing sessions a reflection of a disruption in the intersubjective field caused by an empathic failure, in which he had to distance himself from us? Had he felt injured by something that I said or did not say in the session? I became aware of the strength of my countertransference. Would the intensity of my vulnerability and my anxiety drive me to chase after him when he missed sessions, or become critical of him? However, I quickly appreciated that these misses were almost always not due to an empathic failure, rather they reflected Michael's difficulty in dealing with any relationships without his wife, including me. If my self-esteem remained steady, I could then help him understand why he felt the way he did, as well as his need to sleep in. If I didn't retreat to a trailing edge for me, that is needing him to mirror me, then the intersubjective focus was on his trailing edge and understanding what he was afraid of. Michael had no idea what he was escaping from, and did not know what he felt, just that he needed to retreat and find comfort and solace in his aloneness. He would say, "I am just tired". *I told* him that I understood that he *felt* caught in a terrible cycle, that he did not understand his need to escape, even as he criticized and raged at himself for the behavior, thus becoming further depleted and withdrawn. I pointed out that this was neither fair nor empathic to himself, but something "we" could understand.

I held firmly onto the idea that Michael was very invested in the treatment and in our relationship. Appreciating the power of the trailing edge, I told Michael that I understood why he needed to miss the sessions, and isolate himself. I told him that I understood that he felt so bad and vulnerable that he needed to avoid everyone, including me because he was convinced that our conversations would only reflect what he was feeling about himself, which would only make him feel worse. He feared that eventually I too would share his hopelessness about himself. How could I feel anything different? He felt worthless and feared that if we spoke, I could only affirm what he already felt or perhaps, that I would say something to him which would make him feel worse. I explained that with all of this in mind, I understood why he needed to retreat.

He slowly came to understand that I accepted his need to be alone, and he was relieved that I was not angry at him. At first, he denied that his need to sleep in was related to the anxiety about being seen, even by me. I wouldn't do that to him he at first protested, but he came to understand that the impact of engaging anyone, was rooted in his past with his father. Again, I stated, he came by his fears honestly, and that I understood why he needed to be secluded, even from me. He came to understand, that although his feelings were not logical, his fear of me was directly related to his father's abusiveness, and the terror and confusion he almost always felt in his father's presence. All of this composed Michael's trailing edge, which was often in the foreground in the first year of treatment. Michael experienced his father as only critical of him and if he dared to assert himself in any way his father was unrelentingly punitive. His mother offered no protection. Overwhelmed by the burden of bringing up three children, she was passive in the face of his father's hostility.

Helping him understand his own behaviors, and letting him know that "we" could understand them together, was enormously relieving to him. I told him that he could never understand himself alone, but when he dared to open up in the therapy, taking a risk with me, he had the opportunity to feel differently. He felt better after almost every session, he began to say.

In between sessions, when he would lapse back into states of self contempt and psychological paralysis, usually triggered by an external event that we could not understand, two interpretive stances were most helpful to him. Firstly, that his feelings made sense, being so ingrained in him that they felt inescapable, and secondly, though he almost always felt good when he left a session, I told him that our new shared understanding did not yet have enough power to counteract his old "bed" feelings, however soon they would. I hoped that the process that "we" were engaged in would unfold organically, I told him.

The "we" and "us" is the power of the leading edge, in this case the generative idealizing selfobject transference. which was slowing occupying more and more space in Michael's psychic experience. It has also occurred to me that occasionally the "we" reflected the twinship, with an older brother. Michael was startled that he could actually begin to understand what he was feeling and he would frequently remark after I said something to him, "Oh, I have never thought about it that way", or "that's a great way to say that", or "Oh, that's exactly right". Of course, to me this mirrored my sense of myself as a competent therapist and my leading edge and increasingly affirmed the idealizing selfobject transference fantasy that was the dominant dimension between us.

In the context of these discussions, Michael reported a dream of his maternal grandfather and his compassion and his belief in Michael as a person and a professional. Michael and I spoke about his grandfather's relationship as a life saver and as a template for the successful business connections he was to develop. I also interpreted to him that his grandfather was with us in the room and that it was the foundation for the relationship that he and I were developing. Michael agreed.

Michael accepted the discussion of our relationship without shame or humiliation. He admitted that he needed "us" to help him manage his feelings about himself. I spoke to him about the comfort of "us" being able to understand what he felt. He associated that he often felt this way in the comfort of his relationship with his wife, when she wasn't drinking, and knowing that we could find that same place was comforting to him.

Discussion

During the first year of the therapy, Michael might begin a session and I could feel after five, ten minutes or so, that he was exhausted and struggling. A number of times, I asked him if he wanted to stop because he felt tired. More than once, he accepted my offer that we interrupt and end the session. Upon further discussion of these moments, Michael would either describe that he didn't know he was that tired before the session started, or he said that he would push himself to talk. After every time we interrupted a session, he would thank me for initiating the end of the session.

Our discussion revealed that asserting himself, or as we have come to say, "to be in the equation", was very difficult for him. Again, it was revealed that it was difficult to both trust himself and what he felt and to also assert himself with me or others. "Being in the equation" has become part of the language between us, when Michael speaks about asserting himself. "Being in the equation" reflects the developing "we" of the leading edge.

The early missed sessions exemplified the trailing edge, Michael's fears and anxieties. However, over the last few years when Michael has missed a session, I have come to believe that these misses exemplified not the trailing edge, but the leading edge. Michael would say with both some relief and pride, that he knew that if he needed to miss a session, that he was free to do so, and he knew that I would agree. In the most recent misses, Michael declared (and I accepted) that his misses were now more a part of his "being in the equation", reflected the "we" of our relationship and that they were examples of him asserting himself. If one accepts that either the leading or the trailing edge, is in the foreground or background, in these examples, Michael asserting himself and missing a session mostly exemplified his trust in me as an idealized selfobject, the leading edge moving into the foreground. He knew that I would understand, and that I would fully accept his self-assertion.

As part of the unfolding idealized selfobject transference, Michael said that he was amazed that I could understand what he felt and needed. He was coming to rely on me and my understanding of him. He also said that he appreciated my different perspective on what he was feeling or regarding any situation he was facing. A conversation of the comfort in the "we" of our conversations, often was connected with the "we" in his relationship with his wife or his grandfather. I said to him that when he felt the "we" in all of these relationships, including ours, that he was at his best and felt more free to express and assert himself. This constitutes an instance where the interpretation of the leading edge resulted in the solidification of the leading edge, manifested in his developing sense of agency.

In all of these discussions of the idealizing selfobject transference, either initiated by him or me, Michael increasingly felt more relaxed and self assured. A discussion of our relationship affirmed for him that the comfort and security he felt, was real. This was something that we both felt, and speaking about it concretized and affirmed his experience. We now had a shared fantasy in that we both understood how important our relationship had become to his well being. A shared fantasy of the importance of the idealizing selfobject transference became the cornerstone of the treatment.

In the course of talking about how good it felt to be understood by me, Michael told me that he had unsuccessfully tried treatment when he was 30 years old. The analyst had him lying on the couch, in a once a week treatment and Michael's experience of this was that the therapist barely said a word. In fact, he thought that the therapist had been asleep, in more than one session. In the course of this discussion, Michael said that he appreciated that I was talkative and involved. Again, in this conversation, I responded that I thought that he was at his best when he felt connected to another, meaningful person, and that in the *prior* treatment there was no "we". I noted how the therapist had a responsibility in helping the patient create a good working relationship. He had always blamed himself for that earlier treatment failure, and was relieved to think that it was not all his fault, like his wife's alcoholism was not his responsibility.

During the third year of the treatment, as he was lamenting his loneliness and his fear of never meeting a sexual partner, I said to him that perhaps with the right partner – the right "we" – that his sexual issues would not be the obstacles that he always had felt them to be. Again, saying "I never thought about it like that", he began to consider that with the right person, "they" will work it out. This still has enormous terror and shame associated with it, but being able to talk about it has freed him up to join Match.com and he has even had a few dates with women.

Presently, if he isn't ready to face someone, or feels badly about an interaction with a man or woman, I reassure him that we could understand what was happening. Over and over again, I have told him that when his self-esteem was in the right place, he will feel able to do what he wants to do, and that this would unfold organically. This has helped him to empathize with himself instead of attacking himself, at times when he has felt unsure or unable to approach another person.

Recently, Michael was on an airplane, listening to the people behind him. He recognized one of them as a musician in a band and he found their music on YouTube. What he really wanted to do at that moment, was to play the musicians music on youtube and then engage him in a conversation. Michael believed that if he heard his music, the musician would engage him. At that moment, he began to feel tired and he did not go to youtube and didn't play the music and never engaged the musician. Before he even came to the appointment which was later that day, Michael realized that although he failed to engage the musician, the incident did not lead to a round of humiliation and critical self attack. He regretted not being able to be more assertive, but he realized that he had not been flooded with overwhelming shame. Now in session, as he thought about the situation, he realized that in the past he would have never been able to remember what happened, let alone process it. He said that in the context of our talking and with the treatment as a facilitator, he was pleased that he was now able to reflect on himself, his feelings and motivations, even though he had not engaged the musician.

More recently, Michael began a session talking about his feeling good and accomplishing what he wanted to get done in the last 3–4 days. He was able to go to the hospital and sign up for a preventive heart program. He had his workout with his trainer (he hired a trainer for a three times a week workout), for which he had bought new sneakers. Afterward he treated himself to an enjoyable lunch. At lunch he said that he had become annoyed at the owner/friend of a restaurant who had not treated him well. What was most important to him was that he had been assertive, spoke about what he wanted to say, and that it just came out spontaneously. For Michael, this was completely affirming of what he and I had been talking about – that when he was ready to assert himself, he would do so. Adopting an empathic stance towards himself, when he couldn't assert himself, yielded the hopeful results he wanted: he could now "be in the equation". This recognition has deepened the leading edge and the idealizing selfobject transference.

This therapy has affirmed for me the power of actively engaging the leading edge, particularly when it is not disturbed. Self psychology, has always articulated that interpretation of the transference was only initiated by the therapist after an empathic failure and a disruption in the transference. This case demonstrates that a discussion of the tie, either initiated by the therapist or the patient, has enhanced the work and the leading edge of self development. even when the leading edge and in this case, the idealizing transference, was firmly in place. Michael was aware, albeit first only unconsciously, that he was at his best when he felt connected to a trusted other, and he has come to consciously understand the power of a deeply felt relationship. Including leading edge interpretations in the therapeutic discussion has anchored both of us in the intersubjective dimension of the analytic work and broadened and deepened the relationship for both of us.

Section 2

Clinical applications

Chapter 8

Melancholia revisited

Depression and its treatment from the perspective of Intersubjective Self Psychology

Peter B. Zimmermann

I will begin this chapter with an examination of melancholia (or depression)[1] and its treatment from the perspective of Intersubjective Self Psychology. I will begin with a discussion of Freud's 1917 seminal work *Mourning and Melancholia*. Based on this early formulation, I will offer a reconceptualization of melancholia from the perspective of Intersubjective Self Psychology (ISP).

I will show how depression is the emotional reaction to the felt loss of the self. When confronted with the loss of a significant other or an important engagement with the world, what is felt to be lost is the selfobject function that the person or activity served in the maintenance of the depressed person's self-experience. The consequence of felt loss of the needed selfobject function is the loss of the self. What results is despair. I will then provide a description of the treatment guidelines that follow from this conceptualization of depression. I will illustrate my thesis by discussing the treatment of Adam, a profoundly depressed and suicidal young man who I worked with early in my career. Adam taught me one of the most important lessons about depression and its treatment: The depressed patient yearns for his despair to be understood, and most importantly in the clinical context, that the despair makes sense to *me,* his therapist. The experience of being understood and received with the depression provides the context of attuned engagement with the therapist that permits the depressed patient to begin the mourning process.

My theoretical starting point is Freud's (1917) paper on *Mourning and Melancholia*. In that seminal work, Freud examines the difference between the experience of the mourner and the melancholic, concluding that the mourner is grieving the loss of the person, while the melancholic suffers from a loss in regard to the *ego.* Freud notes that the single most differentiating factor between melancholia and mourning is what he terms a "disturbance of self-regard". He views this disturbance as a characteristic of melancholia but absent from mourning. He states: "In mourning it is the world which has become poor and empty; in melancholia it is the ego itself" (SE, XIV, p. 246), and then adds the following important sentence: "the analogy with mourning led us to conclude that he [the patient] had suffered a loss in regard to an object; what he [the melancholic patient] tells us points to a loss in regard to his ego" (p. 247). Freud concludes that if this were true, psychoanalysis would be "faced with a contradiction, that presents a problem, which is hard to solve" (p. 247). His seminal paper, of course, is his attempt to solve this conundrum and culminates in the haunting phrase: "Thus the shadow of the object fell upon the ego and the latter could henceforth be judged by a special agency, as though it were an object, the forsaken object"[2] (p. 249).

Clinically most important, Freud advised that therapists should not question the veracity of the depressed person's experience of the felt loss in regard to their ego; on the contrary, "we must confirm ... [the patient's] statement, for he must surely be right in some way and be describing something that is *as it seems to him to be*" (p. 246). A few paragraphs later, Freud continues:

> The essential thing, therefore, is not whether the melancholic's distressing self-denigration is correct, in the sense that his self-criticism agrees with the opinion of other people. The point must rather be that he is giving a correct description of his psychological situation. He has lost his self-respect and *he must have good reasons for this.*
>
> (p. 247, italics added)

Freud says that to understand the patient's melancholia we must understand it from within the patient's experiential world. We must accept that the patient's depressive mood *makes sense,* which means that there are "good reasons" for it, reasons that the therapist and the patient can come to understand.

Freud is thereby strongly advocating for what is referred to as *the introspective viewpoint of empathy,* which Kohut (1959) identified as the observational stance of psychoanalysis and restored to its proper place in his study of narcissism. This is in contrast to the extrospective perspective of biological psychiatry that declares the patient's depressive reaction as inappropriate or disproportionate to the circumstances, and devoid of any meaning, the result of a biochemical imbalance in the brain. Freud unequivocally states that we need to understand the depressive reaction from within the patient's own frame of reference, and that from within this frame of reference their experience makes sense. This is how we come to understand the patient's depression.

Freud's comments about the melancholic patient have an uncanny similarity with a central idea that Kohut articulates in his psychology of the self with regard to the narcissistic patient. Kohut argues that to understand narcissistic patients, we must explore their experience from within their own frame of reference.

In this context it is relevant to note that Freud wrote *Mourning and Melancholia* in 1917, shortly after he had written *On Narcissism* (1914). This speaks to Freud's developing awareness of a relationship between narcissism and melancholia. In *Mourning and Melancholia* Freud stated that "the disposition to fall ill with melancholia lies in the preponderance of the narcissistic type of object-choice" even if that theory "has not yet been confirmed by observation" (p. 250).

Since there is a relationship between narcissism and melancholia it makes sense to rethink this link and the "preponderance of the narcissistic type of object choice" within the framework of ISP.

I start with self psychology. Contained in Kohut's (1977) *Restoration of the Self* is a theory of depression, which he termed *empty depression*, where shame and humiliation are the dominant affects.[3] Kohut noted that,

> on the one hand, there are people who, despite the absence of neurotic symptoms, inhibitions or conflicts lead joyless and fruitless lives and curse their very existence. On the other hand, there are people, who, though plagued by serious neurotic problems, lead meaningful lives and derive a sense of well being and fulfillment from their lives.
> (pp. 242–243)

He argued that it is the state of the self – its cohesion, structural stability and emotional vitality – that accounts for this difference. While an analysis may be successful in eradicating neurotic symptoms and inhibitions, Kohut claimed that if the self pathology remains unaddressed, the patient will remain unfulfilled, joyless and without vitality,[4] and her life will lack a sense of meaning and direction: in short, the person will remain depressed.

Kohut's most important contribution to our understanding of the human condition is his insight that people look to others not only as objects of love and hate, which was Freud's discovery, but also as *selfobjects*, whose empathic responses we need for the development and maintenance of the self. We experience the selfobject as a part of ourselves. The object as selfobject provides psychic functions that the person is not yet able to perform for herself, but are essential for the development and maintenance of a cohesive, positively colored and empowered sense of self. For a person to acquire a firm and resilient self, Kohut (1984) stated that we require an empathic selfobject environment – an environment that,

> firstly, responds to his need to have his self confirmed by the glow of the parental pleasure, by the gleam in the parents' eyes (mirroring need); secondly, that responds to his need to merge into the reassuring security and strength of a powerful adult (idealizing need); and, thirdly, that responds to his need for an experience of essential alikeness, to feel human among humans (twinship need).
> (p. 194)

These are the three selfobject experiences that Kohut identified as essential in the development of a self. If these selfobject experiences are missing or inadequate, the person's self organization will remain fragile and vulnerable to narcissistic injuries and fragmentation.

In the depressed person, the ability to regulate the emotional equilibrium and the sense of agency is fundamentally compromised. The depressed person has a profound sense that she is utterly helpless to change how she feels or bring about any change in her life.

To the degree that the selfobject milieu has been unempathic during development and our mirroring, idealizing and twinship needs were not adequately met or were traumatically rejected by the caregivers, we will not have had the experiences we need to gradually acquire the self structures necessary to regulate our self experience. As a result, we will remain dependent on external sources to regulate our self experience, our emotional equilibrium. We will lack what Kohut (1984) described as "a sustaining sense of self and motivating ambitions, a sustaining relationship to internal ideals that provide guidance, and a sustaining relationship to his or her talents and skills" (p. 203). What results is a fragile, fragmentation-prone self that is dependent on external provision of vital selfobject functions.

This is the core self experience of the depressed person: a profound sense of dependence on a person or activity to provide the desperately needed selfobject experience to maintain the self, in particular the sense of agency, but that person or activity is felt to be irretrievably lost. Because the essential selfobject experience is felt to be unrecoverable, the depressed patient experiences deep despair. The depressed person's experience is that an important dimension of the self is missing. This is the difference between mourning and melancholia that Freud identified.

In mourning, the sense of self regard is felt to be recoverable; in melancholia it is experienced as irretrievably lost. From the perspective of self psychology this means that in melancholia the sense of self is profoundly affected in ways that in mourning it is not. What accounts for this? In its most succinct form I propose the following formulation:

Mourning is the emotional response to the loss of the object as object. Melancholia is the emotional response to the loss of the object as selfobject.[5] And since the loss of the object as selfobject results in the loss of the self, melancholia is the emotional response to the loss of self. Therefore, we can say: Mourning is the emotional response to the loss of the object. Melancholia is the emotional response to the loss of the self.

In mourning the person experiences the loss of other as other. In melancholia the person experiences the loss of other as a loss of a dimension of him- or herself. In mourning, the grief and sorrow are about the loss of the object that feels lost and thus the world feels like an empty place. In melancholia, grief and sorrow become despair and humiliation, because with the loss of the needed selfobject tie, the self feels irretrievably lost. Thus, the self feels like an empty place. Shame and humiliation result because of the sense of helplessness that permeates the self experience. The depleted, empty self is shameful to the person.

The more fundamentally the lost object served an essential selfobject function for the person grappling with the loss – that is, played a constitutive role in the patient's self experience – the stronger the depressive reaction because of the experience of the loss of the self and thus the feelings of despair, shame and humiliation. If pure mourning existed, the person would miss the other only as other. But since all significant involvements with another entail a selfobject dimension, the loss of that other will also always entail despair. This holds true, exquisitely so, for the love object, as the love object always provides an essential selfobject experience. This means that with the loss of the love object the person's self experience is inevitably also profoundly impacted, and a depressive reaction is an inexorable part of the mourning experience of the love object. The severity of the depressive reaction is a function of the centrality of the selfobject function that the love object played in the maintenance of the self experience of the person. In other words, the more the person was reliant on the tie with the loved one for the maintenance of the self, the stronger the depressive reaction in the face of the loss of the loved one.

Under optimal circumstances a person is gradually able to recover the self, which means regain a cohesive self experience, through the mourning process. Optimal circumstances are those where 1) a receiver is available for the sorrow, hopelessness and despair generated by the loss. The experience of an empathic receiver enables the mourning process; and where 2) ultimately new forms of selfobject engagement are available through involvement with others or activities that restore essential selfobject functions, and provide the self experience with a renewed sense of possibility.

In protracted mourning this is what proves difficult, because the lost selfobject was central and constitutive to the mourner's self experience. Very often the person whose loss is mourned is also the person who was most essential, not only in providing the needed selfobject experience, but also in providing the understanding and accepting receiver for the experience of loss and the attendant emotions generated by the loss. This again holds most definitely true for the love object.

It is not only engagement with others but also with activities, e.g., work and play, interacting with nature or ideas or causes, that can be constitutive to a person's self experience, like the pursuit of a hobby, a sportive activity, engagement with art, music, literature, etc. Any of these activities may also play a central selfobject function. The loss of such engagement, either because the selfobject experience is no longer available or the person is unable to engage in it, can also result in the experience of the loss of the self and lead to despair, shame, hopelessness and helplessness and a sense of humiliation.

The experience of helplessness is a key characteristic of depression. It reflects the loss of a sense of agency, the capacity to take action on one's own behalf. One of the hallmarks of depression is the fact that the person experiences herself in an unbearably painful and humiliating predicament, the depression itself, that she is unable to do anything about. The depression itself confronts the person with the lack of a sense of agency, and thus the sense of humiliation and shame that is so characteristic of depression.

A sense of agency derives from the experience of being able to take action on one's own behalf, as an independent center of initiative. The belief that the person can shape her life in accordance with her ambitions, her ideals and her talents and skills and give it the desired meaning, brings about a sense of well being and vitality. This derives from the earliest experiences of a responsive selfobject milieu.

A baby will feel she has an impact on her environment when she can bring about the response that she needs. When she articulates her needs – initially in the form of crying or later on through the verbalization of her needs – and the caregiving surround proves responsive, the baby's sense of agency will gradually develop and she will have a sense that she can take action on her own behalf. Conversely, if the baby feels unable to elicit the needed response from the environment, due to an unresponsive selfobject milieu, her sense of agency will be poorly developed, if established at all. She will, on an ongoing basis, feel entirely dependent on other people to initiate action on her behalf. When later in life, the other who performs this central selfobject function is absent or lost, that person is not experiencing the loss of the object but the loss of the needed selfobject experience. More archaic selfobject needs will emerge as well as the risk of fragmentation and disintegration anxiety and the accompanying affects of terror and despair. Despair, hopelessness and helplessness are to melancholia what grief and sorrow are to mourning.[6]

In every relationship, the bond with the love object has an object dimension as well as a selfobject dimension, which coexist in a figure-ground relation. In a person inclined toward depression, the selfobject bond is the primary tie to the other and thus is "figure". This means the selfobject bond is the most salient dimension in his or her relation to the other. In case of the loss of that other, the selfobject bond is felt to be lost, resulting in the loss of the self and depression. In mourning, the object dimension is primary, is figure, and the selfobject dimension is ground, operating more quietly in the background. In case of object loss, the tremors will be felt there in the selfobject dimension of experience, but no traumatic disruption of the selfobject bond will have been felt to occur. No fragmentation of the self experience will ensue and no protracted loss of the self will take place. The emotional response will be grief and sorrow as described by George Hagman (1995, 2017) in his conceptualization of the mourning process.

The treatment of depression

The treatment of melancholia, as formulated in the framework of ISP, consists of two key steps. The first step is to provide the context in the therapeutic situation within which the patient feels his experience of loss is understood. The depressed patient yearns to feel that his sense of loss makes sense and that his depression is understandable to his therapist. The melancholic patient yearns to have his depression understood in the context of its meaning for him or her. This constitutes what in the framework of ISP we have defined as the leading edge of the patient's transference yearning.

Depressed patients frequently do not yet know themselves what accounts for their depression or where it comes from, and their dread is that they won't have an engaged receiver in the therapist for their experience of despair. In other words, they are afraid that not only are they beyond help, but that the therapist can also not possibly understand why they are feeling this way, and may experience them as a burden. This dread may have been confirmed, from the patient's perspective, by prior unsuccessful therapy or by the response from family and friends who have been worn down by the patient's depression. The dread is that they are beyond hope and a burden to the therapist. The hope and yearning, however buried and tenuous, is that they have found in the therapist an attuned, engaged receiver who comes to understand what the patient feels is amiss or comes to discover it with the patient.

Once depressed patients feel understood with the reasons for their depression, once they feel they have an attuned and engaged receiver for their experience, i.e., a responsive intersubjective context, they yearn to express their sorrow and despair and trust that they will be received. This will enable the mourning process. When a depressed patient's eyes well up with tears for the first time in the therapist's office, it is indicative that a mourning process has been initiated, and the working through of the depression has begun. As therapists we provide a safe environment for the patient. This allows for the depth of despair to be revealed and for the patient to feel that she has an emotional home for the totality of her emotions.

The second step emerges, many months or even years later, when the patient shows a renewed desire to seek an engagement with the therapist that provides the selfobject experience that permits the emergence of the "tendrils of health" (Tolpin, 2009) and the consolidation of self development. This consists of establishing a context of attuned engagement that enables the vitalization of the self, that ceased when the original loss occurred.

If a person's sense of self as worthwhile, competent, and able to take action on his or her own behalf, develops and solidifies in a "context of attuned responsiveness" (Stolorow & Atwood, 1992), or as we say, "context of attuned engagement", then it follows that the single most important task in treating the depressed patient is to establish a context of attuned responsiveness in the therapeutic situation. This will permit the restoration of the patient's self experience and result in the development of a sense of agency. This is what the patient yearns for in the second phase of the treatment of depression. This entails two seemingly contradictory commitments from the therapist. First: the commitment that the therapist show up for the selfobject experience engagement that the patient needs to regain the self. Second, that the therapist shows understanding and patience for where the patient feels unable to take action on his or her own behalf.

In treatment, it is the second step that the therapist needs to address first: To provide a context of attuned engagement with the patient's depressive affect. This context of attuned engagement facilitates the working through process of his depression. Once the depressed patient feels received with his despair and experiences the therapist as holding out a context within which he is able to come to understand the reasons for his depression, and feel understood with his experience and the accompanying affect, the mourning process is initiated. It is the experience of an attuned receiver that permits the initiation of the mourning process. In this phase the therapist conveys to her patients that, given what they feel they have lost, the experience of despair is comprehensible, makes sense. Only when this is the case, can depressed patients begin to come to terms with what they experience they lost, and only then may they ultimately be able to seek what might make their life meaningful and worthwhile again or make it possible to bring themselves to their existing life in new and meaningful ways. This is what it means to establish a context of attuned engagement which facilitates the patient's recovery process from depression.

What follows is a dramatic example from my own practice of a depressed patient's urgent need to be *understood* by me with the reasons for his depression. Early in my psychoanalytic career, Adam, a 20-year-old young man came to see me one year after he had been released from the hospital following a suicide attempt. When he came to see me he was again profoundly depressed and preoccupied with suicidal thoughts. For several weeks he teetered on the edge of living or dying. Feeling deeply concerned and anxious, I found myself desperately trying to find reasons for why he should go on living. The more I tried, the more hopeless and suicidal Adam became. I argued that he was still young and would have a chance to discover what else he might want to do with his life. I offered interpretations of how he turned his rage at the parents against himself. I told that, yes, his parents would be sorry if he killed himself, but he would be dead – but all to no avail. Adam was in complete despair because, clearly, I failed to understand how meaningless his life felt to him. After each session (I saw him multiple times a week) Adam left feeling more suicidal, and more despairing – as was I – until he did end up in an emergency room where he was admitted to the psychiatric ward. He was medicated and held for several weeks before he was again released into my care.

When Adam resumed his therapy, I was finally calm enough to actually be able to listen to him and really understand the reasons for his depression, rather than trying to convince him of reasons to live. Ever since he was a little boy, he had wanted to become a professional baseball player, but his parents, it turns out, had stopped taking him to little league games when he was 8 years old. He felt they destroyed his chance at a professional career in baseball. He had not swung a bat since and now was excruciatingly painfully aware that his dream of becoming a baseball player was not ever going to come true. He was overcome with a profound sense of hopelessness and humiliation since this also meant that he was not ever going to overcome his station in life and feel human among humans and equal with his peers.

Adam's depression for the first time somewhat relented and his acute suicidal preoccupation disappeared, almost instantly, once I had reorganized my therapeutic stance and dared to say to him:

> Given the fact that you had always wanted to become a baseball player and here you are, now 20 years old, having to come to terms that this won't be the case, and all the hopes for a future that you can embrace are dashed, I understand that life does not feel worth living.

I said this with great trepidation, and with even greater desperation because did this not mean that I concurred that he should kill himself? And yet, to my surprise, the very opposite happened. Adam for the first time seemed to feel less suicidal. Why? Adam felt truly understood by me.

In retrospect it seems so simple, but it made all the difference. The idea of becoming a professional baseball player had served a central selfobject function all through his deprived childhood. It was how he was going to become a normal American man. When it became clear that this goal was not going to be realized, Adam sank into a suicidal depression. Once Adam felt that I understood his reasons for why he was feeling depressed and did not want to live, we for the first time made a real connection. Adam now felt that he had a receiver for his experience. This allowed him to fully voice the despair he was feeling and believe that I understood it.

What ensued was a five year treatment with significant ups and downs in our relationship as we continued to struggle with Adam's despair about his life. But Adam's suicidality disappeared for good. We were now on the same page. The experience of feeling understood and feeling that his despair had an attuned receiver in me, gradually permitted Adam to come to terms with his profound sense of loss, begin the process of mourning with me by sharing his sorrow and despair. His yearning for being understood with the reasons for his depression was a manifestation of the generative transferences and constituted the leading edge of Adam's relationship with me.

Once the depressed patient feels understood with the reasons for the despair, the yearning will be for an attuned engagement with the depressive affect that is walled up in the patient. The first step consists of arriving at an understanding of the depression. The second step consists in providing the depressed patient with an attuned home for the dysphoric affect. Having a receiver for the patient's despair who is not overwhelmed or impatient constitutes the core curative experience in the treatment of depression. It is the depressed patient's deepest yearning to have a steady and emotionally available receiver for the depressive affect. This is the new experience the patient needs for the mourning processing to unfold. It can last for months and months before a renewed sense of hope emerges and may resurface any time a setback occurs even if the patient has already found a new path along which to consolidate or realize the self.

What follows is an example of the depression lifting and making room for mourning because the patient felt she had found an attuned receiver who engaged with her depressive mood.

Sandy is a 45-year-old woman who had called me in an acute state of depression because of a sudden traumatic experience in her life. Her 15-year-old daughter was hospitalized following a drug overdose. When my patient came in for her first appointment, she told me with great shame, how she felt like such a failure as a mother. This time around I was sure of what was needed from me. I replied that I understood: "If our children are not doing well, we as parents can't help but feel that we have failed". With this, the flood gates opened and Sandy sobbed and sobbed. Then and for many subsequent sessions, Sandy told me the story of her failures as a mother and the shame and guilt she felt, all along sobbing deeply, while I was quietly and patiently listening.

I learned that ten years earlier, after her divorce from her husband, Sandy had made a suicide attempt, which had left her partially paralyzed. Life had been a real struggle ever since then. Given this knowledge, I replied that there appeared to be a lot to feel despondent about and that I was there for her to share her woes with me. I again added that I understood her shame and anguish and that I wanted to come to know and understand all her despair. This resulted in more tears and sorrow over weeks and weeks of her treatment. Gradually and increasingly, Sandy came to trust that I was not judging her and that her depression was not too much for me and that I did not need her to move on or "get over it". She came to trust that I would stay with her and her depression however long she needed me to be there with her. This was Sandy's leading edge yearning: to have a sustained experience wherein she felt received and accepted with her profound sorrow, grief and despair.

Over the course of the years that I have seen Sandy, as with Adam, there have been profound emotional upheavals in her life, her self states, and in the therapy. But with the experience of the connection with me as the attuned receiver of her upsets and depressive states, she was able to hold onto herself, and make a life for herself. Any setback in her struggle, and a struggle it was, would trigger profound depressive reactions. At such points Sandy would call for an emergency session, or a moment of contact, to ensure that she had not lost me as an attuned receiver of her depression. Since this occurred many times over the years that I have seen her, any recurrence of her depression would revive her dread that *now* she had become a burden to me, that *now* I was disgusted and fed up, and would want to rid myself of her.

I have learned to interpret this over the years by saying: I understand that you fear that I have lost my patience with you and your depression, and you fear that I don't want to be bothered by you anymore. During a more recent setback, when her new romantic relationship appeared to fail, she reached out to me feeling acutely depressed and terrified of my reaction. She was afraid to let on just how discouraged and hopeless she was again feeling.

I calmly stated that she needn't worry, I was not overwhelmed nor fed up, nor had I lost my patience but instead invited her to tell me her story. Sandy again began to sob deeply, almost heaving, while telling me what she was going through. By the end of the session, I felt confident that the experience of having an attuned receiver had led to the consolidation of our connection. I felt confident that Sandy felt capable of taking on her life again even though she was deeply sad that the relationship had not worked out. The analysis of the meanings that the traumatic experience had revived for Sandy followed in subsequent sessions.

Once Sandy felt she had a reliable receiver for her depression, and had mourned all the ways she felt she had failed, the focus of the treatment gradually shifted to the establishment of the needed selfobject experience with me. This tie allowed her to begin to develop her sense of agency. She increasingly felt that she could master the challenges that her daughter presented her with and therefore that she was a "good enough" mother.

A developmental process was reinstated in the therapeutic context that ultimately led to the internalization of the calming and soothing function that previously I had performed, leading to self regulatory competence and to a restoration of the sense of herself as worthwhile and as an independent center of initiative.

When a patient has acquired the sense of being able to take action on her own behalf, she is once again able to begin to give her life the desired meaning and actively pursue her goals. The depression will have lifted. Since a person's sense of being able to take action on her own behalf derives from the experience of a responsive selfobject milieu, the therapeutic situation represents a perfectly suited context for the revival of the needed experience. The patient is able to elicit the needed response in the selfobject transference relationship with the therapist that is commensurate with her developmental needs.

As the leading edge yearnings of the patient are realized in the selfobject transference relationship, the therapeutic situation becomes a generative intersubjective field resulting in transformation and growth of the self experience. The depression will recede and make room for the consolidation of the self. However, the depression will recur or intensify when the patient experiences this bond to be disrupted. Such disruptions in the context of attuned engagement are the inevitable accompaniment of treatment. The working through of these disruptions, along with the sustained experience of the intact connection with the therapist, are necessary for the recovery from depression and the regaining of the self.

As Stolorow, Atwood and Brandchaft (1987) pointed out,

> the analyst's task is to *analyze* the ups and downs of the analytic discourse, including the inevitable derailments, from the perspective of the patient's experience and explore the impact they are having on the patient's sense of self and the early traumatic experiences they revive.
>
> (pp. 13–14)

In other words, the therapist needs to address how the patient's depression in treatment intensifies or recedes, contingent on how the patient experiences the therapist in the transference and the meanings these experiences assume for the patient, and what they revive from his past.

Derailments in the context of attuned engagement are inevitable and unavoidable. The responsibility of the therapist is to analyze and explore these experiences from the patient's perspective. Through such analysis the therapist restores the transference bond and establishes a context of attuned responsiveness that allows for the mourning process and the restoration of self development. Prolonged disruptions of the context of attuned responsiveness that are not understood by the therapist lead to an entrenchment of the patient's depression and greatly intensify the risk of suicide. The depressed patient's dread in the transference that her need to be received and responded to in the way she needs will be met with the same faulty responsiveness she received from the original caregiving surround, will lead to powerful resistances, and an intensification of the depression. Such resistances are evoked by experiences in the treatment that to the depressed patient signal the lack of attuned engagement and availability on the part of the therapist. Depressed patients, who already feel worthless and ashamed, will be inclined to hear the slightest comment or gesture by the therapist that lends itself to this end as a confirmation of their worst fear, i.e. that the therapist concurs with their sense of hopelessness. This leads to further feelings of despair and humiliation. In particular, anything that smacks of impatience on the part of the therapist, will be "proof" to the depressed patient, that the therapist is fed up, and could result in the patient withdrawing further and getting more depressed.

In the treatment of the depressed patient, there is the potential for a dangerous counter-therapeutic spiral based on the therapist's counter-transference reaction to the patient's sense of helplessness and hopelessness. The spiral may appear in the following way. The patient feels despairing and hopeless and thus turns to the therapist. The therapist, with the wish to ameliorate the patient's suffering and the urgent need to fend off his own sense of helplessness, is drawn into offering suggestions about how the patient could help herself. The patient in turn experiences these "well-meant" suggestions as additional pressure to do what she does not feel up to, to begin with. As a result she feels even more depressed, because she now is also worried about disappointing the therapist, and fearing that the therapist will give up on her. This intensification of the depression threatens to lead to an even greater sense of helplessness in the therapist, which he will fend off by becoming more active, and thereby perpetuating the vicious cycle, until the patient may finally make a dramatic suicidal gesture or in some other way express that this is all too much.

The therapeutic stance, when we are confronted with a patient in an acute state of depression, is to engage the patient with her experience, to listen and explore what from the patient's perspective is lost, and then convey that, given what we learned, the patient's despair is understandable, makes sense. *The task is not to do something in an attempt to change what the patient is experiencing, but to engage the patient with what she is experiencing.* Such empathic understanding helps establish the transference bond, the connection, the context of attuned responsiveness, wherein the patient experiences herself understood and received with her experience. This bond is the lifeline in the treatment of depression. As long as the lifeline is intact, the treatment of the depressed patient can proceed and the risk of suicide is contained. If at any point during the treatment of a depressed patient the therapist feels that the bond is broken or lost, or if the therapist does not feel that he was able to establish an emotional bond after a particular session, *then he must do something*; then he must intervene, for the risk of suicide is great. The interventions may range from advising the patient to come in for an emergency session, or contacting the partner, friend or family or advising the patient to go to the ER or calling 911.

The single most difficult countertransference problem in dealing with depression is the therapist's own sense of helplessness, hopelessness, futility and despair in the face of the patient's depression, and the resulting urge to *do* something about it. In addition to the careful explorations of our own emotional reactions that is characteristic of our dealing with any countertransference reaction, I believe this particular problem requires additional provisions. We need to have in our own life a sustaining selfobject milieu that is commensurate with our yearnings and needs. Without such an attuned and responsive emotional home – whatever that may be for a given therapist – we have no business believing that we could hold out a leading edge experience to our depressed patients.

Notes

1 I will use the terms melancholia and depression interchangeably as the most important clinical manifestations in both are the same: they are both mood disorders characterized by negative affect states, rumination, suicidal preoccupations and anhedonia.
2 This formulation, the special agency that judges the ego, became the basis for the concept of the superego.
3 What shame and humiliation are to Kohut's empty depression, guilt and self incriminations are to Freud's guilty depression.
4 Andrew Solomon wrote in an article about his recovery from his own depression: "The opposite of depression is not happiness but vitality, and my life, as I write this, is vital, even when it is sad."
5 On the difference between object and selfobject see also Tolpin (1986). With regard to the role of the selfobject in the mourning process in children see Shane and Shane (1990).
6 In everyday language it has become customary to use sad and depressed as equivalent, but they are not. Sadness is the affect that accompanies mourning; the affect that is characteristic of melancholia is despair, hopelessness and helplessness and ultimately the absence of any affect, a state of emptiness, a catatonic state.

Chapter 9

Addiction
An intersubjective self psychological perspective

Harry Paul[1]

Psychoanalysis has had a long but not terribly successful history of treating addictions, burdened by the tenets of classical theory that espoused that all addictions evolved from an early masturbation fixation, and informed by classical technique that focused on the importance of historical understanding, and did not have the tools for effectively treating addicts.

Patients were too often left to fend for themselves in long treatments, often worse off than before they began the therapeutic process because they remained addicted throughout the therapy. Early psychoanalytic pioneers like Rado (1933), described addiction "as a narcissistic disorder that artificially maintains self-regard" and Simmel (1948) described addiction as rooted in fantasy. And, though they both had begun to understand the addict's experience, as clinicians they were still burdened by treatment principles that stigmatize addicts as untreatable, or very difficult to treat because narcissistic patients were thought not to develop a "real" transference. Furthermore and most importantly, addicts endured a treatment focus on what ISP refers to as the trailing edge, as if that alone would be enough to initiate and sustain abstinence leading to sobriety. That is, addicts were not offered an opportunity to engage in the hopeful leading edge transference experiences that the ISP model we are proposing affords them. In our model, the focus is on the generative transferences, the leading edge and hope as the facilitator of psychic growth. The establishment and maintenance of the needed leading edge transference with the therapist takes the place of the illusory fantasy fueled by the addiction.

For addicts this means the capacity to have an addiction-free life. Once engaged in the therapy and the therapeutic process, and experiencing the leading edge tie as providing the necessary therapeutic nutrients, through the power of the shared selfobject experience, addicts can have a successful treatment experience that is transformational. The developmental process reinstituted through the leading edge of the transference, results in the acquisition of the missing psychic structure that the addict attempted to repetitively replace with his or her substance of choice. Patient and therapist attempt to maintain a successful treatment that affords both the experience of "living in the leading edge". The sustained engagement of the longed for and needed generative selfobject transferences, instead of the narcissistic fantasy, constitutes the therapeutic bond with the therapist that provides the missing structure. This is in stark contrast to the classical notion that the patient is being "gratified" in the treatment. Instead, the patient is taking in, through the leading edge of the selfobject transference, the necessary psychic structure missing from the original parental selfobject context.

In the 2006 book, co-authored with Richard Ulman, we proposed that at the heart of an addiction lies the "Narcissus Complex". Narcissus, according to Greek mythology starved to death because he became transfixed by his own image. By combining the myth of Narcissus with Lewis Carroll's *Alice in Wonderland* (1865), we hypothesized that the addict is lost in an addictive wonderland, or narcissistic fantasies, and that these fantasies are so powerful that, like Narcissus, the addict becomes dissociated and oblivious to his physical and psychological well being. Critical to the Narcissus myth and also to the understanding of an addiction is that Narcissus loses himself in a pool of water, an inanimate object, and he uses and abuses this pool of water, as the addict does in choosing his drug of choice.

Under the influence of these intoxicating fantasies, addicts are convinced that they control others and things, megalomaniacally, only later realizing that they are destroying themselves. The story of Mickey Mouse in the Sorcerer's Apprentice depicts a cautionary addictive tale in which Mickey is seduced by the magic of the Sorcerer's broom and like the addict becomes lost in a megalomaniacal fantasy literally and figuratively drowning in the illusions of his power.

This model of addiction is composed of four parts, the first being "what" is an addiction or the phenomenology of addiction, second the etiology and pathogenesis of addiction, third the typology of addiction, that is that there are different types of addicts who have an addictive personality, and lastly how to treat an addiction. I will discuss all but the typology of addiction, which if the reader is interested, is discussed in great detail in *Narcissus in Wonderland*.

As stated earlier, all aspects of this theory and treatment of addiction share basic understandings with the tenets of ISP. However, ISP goes beyond these ideas, particularly focusing on the broader notion of generative transferences, and the significance of the leading edge in the treatment process and that growth is promoted in the leading edge of the transference and not only in the analysis of ruptures as originally proposed by Kohut.

Addiction is rooted in the use and abuse of what we (Ulman & Paul, 2006) call addictive trigger mechanisms, or ATM's, such as alcohol, drugs, food sex, which provide ersatz or fake selfobject experiences, in the place of the psychic structure that the addict never metabolized as a child, because of the inability of caregivers to provide enough real human selfobject experiences. It is the limited unavailability of a human selfobject experience that leaves the child prone to addiction. Unable to modulate self-esteem from the inside, and not having had good enough experiences with caregivers to provide selfobject experiences leading to psychic structure, the addict uses ATM's to activate these fake selfobject fantasies that only temporarily enable him or her to feel more cohesive and whole, unfortunately only leading to more ATM abuse. They are fake selfobject fantasies, no structure building can occur and they must be relied on indefinitely to establish a sense of narcissistic equilibrium. All addiction then involves the fixation to an archaic narcissistic fantasy. The use and abuse of ATMs, animate or inanimate things and activities involves the unconscious reliving of these early childhood fantasies, providing dissociation and anesthetization from dysphoric cognitions and affect states, as part of a trance or fugue like state. These selfobject-like fantasies, involving idealization, mirroring and twinship, provide only a temporary fix for the real selfobject experiences for which the addict yearns.

ATM's temporarily alleviate these dysphoric affect states because the archaic narcissistic fantasies, idealizing mirroring, and twinship and moods of narcissistic bliss mimic anti anxiety, antidepressant, and humanizing selfobject experiences. The selection, use and abuse by an addict of a particular agent is dependent on the specific psychoactive effect of a specific ATM. The addict whose early developmental failures were primarily in the area of idealization, is in search for a merger with a calming, soothing sedating experience, providing antianxiety functions. The addict whose caregivers failed him or her in providing sufficient mirroring selfobject experiences and requisite psychic structure is in search for antidepressant uppers, and these addictive experiences trigger an uplifting exhibitionism before fake mirroring selfobjects. Thirdly, the addict who calls on an ATM to act in the service of a twinship selfobject experience, unconsciously fantasizes an experience with an alter ego twin in which one feels joined by a companion, providing the experience of feeling more human, or humanization. Lastly, the use of ATM's triggers a megalomaniacal fantasy, an illusion that the addict is in complete control of their environment. That is, by ingesting something or using something or someone, they maintain the illusion that they can control everything and everyone around them. Pop a pill, have a drink, use a person, and so on, the addict believes that they are the master of the universe. A critical part of the treatment process involves the therapist creating an environment in which the patient has the illusion of controlling the treatment process, which mimics their experience of control while using their ATM of choice. In the course of that process, the therapist shows up as a reliable selfobject figure with whom the addict risks, dares and revives the longed for selfobject experience that results in the acquisition of permanent self structure, and is no longer reliant on illusion and fantasy.

There are four criteria that differentiate real selfobjects, generative transferences, from the fake, ersatz selfobjects. First, real selfobjects are transformative which continue to support the healthy unfolding of the self throughout life. Ersatz selfobjects are deformative leading to destructive and deadly experiences that threaten the integrity of the self. Second, real selfobjects are evolutionary in advancing from early childhood forms to mature selfobject relations. Ersatz self objects are devolutionary and they remain stunted in primitive experiences. Third, real self objects provide life-sustaining experiences, while ATM's are degenerative. And, lastly, real selfobject experiences are rehabilitative and restore a healthy sense of self, while fake self objects are debilitative and only weaken the self.

Next, our (Ulman & Paul, 2006) understanding of the etiology of addiction unfolds in three specific developmental phases. In Phase I, the pre addictive child, like all other children invests a caregiver with healthy and necessary life sustaining selfobject needs. In Phase II, a child invests some of the selfobject experience associated with caregivers for the nonhuman selfobject experience of magically endowed things and activities, like a blanket. As the child grows, caregivers are no longer able to provide all the necessary healthy selfobject experiences and these roles are given over to the nonhuman world. The child anthropomorphizes things and activities and endows them with semi-human qualities and they then become healthy transitional selfobjects. Next, in a healthy environment, the child maintains connectedness to transitional selfobjects, and at the same time continues to engage in relationships that are more and more emotionally intimate, developing the psychic structure necessary to live a full and generative life, with the support of others and healthy (and they are by definition, as opposed to ATM's which are unhealthy) transitional selfobjects. Addicts, suffer from a developmental arrest that finds expression in their limited ability to engage in emotionally intimate selfobject experiences with other people, all a result of their limited healthy selfobject experiences with the caregivers of their childhood.

Through the lens of ISP, caregivers, emotionally burdened themselves in their own trailing edge, cannot provide the necessary leading edge experiences for their children to create the necessary psychological structure. The developmental arrest involving addiction pushes the pre addictive child off into defensive constellations which are far afield from the leading edge experiences of a more healthy child. These leading edge experiences necessary for growth become buried and unavailable for hoped for psychological growth, because reliable selfobjects and sustaining selfobject experiences are not sufficiently available.

The child who becomes an addict and no longer primarily relies on human caregivers, then moves away from the human world and begins to over invest and overly rely on things and activities. Such a child too often feels used or ignored more than related to as a person by caregivers and becomes developmentally arrested in the world of the nonhuman. This becomes a crystallization point for later psychopathology. Human selfobject experiences are more and more unavailable, and seen as less and less reliable when they are experienced, leaving the child more hopeless and despairing. The combination of the overuse of things and activities, the experience of being used and not related to as a child sufficiently and not experiencing sufficient real selfobject experiences predisposes one to a future of addiction.

Mark, who became drug addicted and alcoholic, remembered that as a child he would attach a vacuum cleaner to his penis to stimulate masturbation, relying on a non human machine, a concretization of what was missing, a reliable human selfobject experience, not an uncommon experience for an addict. Joe, an alcoholic, injured a finger as a child. When his father was told the cost of repairing the finger, he asked the doctor whether it was cheaper to fix or cut off Joe's finger. Empathy was replaced by his father's treatment of him as a nonhuman entity and Joe's memory of this childhood moment recalls his experience of not being fully regarded as a human being.

Lastly, the treatment of addiction is focused on the fantasy promoting nature of the psychoanalytic process. The first step in treatment involves making abstinence a goal in which the addict is weaned off the ATM of their choice, so that healthy selfobject fantasies of the treatment, the generative leading edge transference experiences can eventually replace the functions of the patients' ATM's. If the addict remains addicted to his ATM of choice and the corresponding fantasies temporarily provided, the selfobject nutrients of the therapist do not have an opportunity to replace the functions of the ATM's and there is no opportunity for the leading edge of the transference to impact the psyche of the patient. This was the mistake of early psychoanalysts, who did not make abstinence an important goal. Patients were expected to learn more about themselves and their pasts, which analysts mistakenly believed would lead to therapeutic progress. The focus of ISP and the Narcissus model is the shared fantasy providing reliable and sustained mirroring, idealization or humanizing experiences, where the inevitable ruptures and relapses which are on an ongoing basis occurring between the patient and the therapist are worked through without blaming the patient. In such an experience, the addict first fantasies about the therapist as a transference version of a combination of a transitional selfobject and a human selfobject. ISP alters this model of the treatment of addiction by focusing not just on the ruptures, as Kohut did before us, but on the importance of the ongoing generative transference fantasy and the attuned engagement of the therapist, both of which lead to the healthy self-esteem. The power of the leading edge transference experiences gives the addict patient hope from their dreadful experiences of their past.

The more addicted and dissociated the addict, the more the initial transference with the therapist is structured by a recapitulation of the transitional selfobject, and less by the human selfobject experiences of their past. However, the initial leading edge transference, as experienced by the addict, is mostly structured by the analyst's humanness and his or her attunement to the leading edge, providing the addict the formative psychological nutrients, which he or she has missed. This is a significant change to the initial theory and treatment approach initially proposed in *Narcissus in Wonderland*. It is the power of the leading edge human qualities of the transitional selfobject that the addict first experiences in treatment which then progresses to a full fledged human selfobject experience. It is a combination of the process of the rupture/repair cycle, and the felt presence of the generative leading edge transference that propels the treatment process, and the therapist is gradually experienced as being more and more reliably human. Such a transference experience entails the provision of anti-anxiety or pacifying idealization, antidepressant mirroring or shame relieving twinship. This induces a healthy therapeutic dissociation and in such a fantasy the therapy and the therapist become a fantasized dispensary. This leading edge transference provides the addicted patient new life and the capacity to live free of fake alternatives, and opens the door to more intimate human relationships.[2]

Roberta, a 37-year-old woman has been in treatment for almost three years. The treatment began as a couples therapy and Roberta and her wife, Sharon had been recommended to me by a colleague who was also a friend of Roberta's and her wife's. Neither had ever been in treatment before and they had been married for ten years. They arrived in New York from California just a year before they started treatment. They came seeking help because increasingly over the years the arguments that peppered their relationship were becoming protracted and interfered with what they otherwise both felt was a good relationship. Roberta's response to these arguments was to withdraw and not talk to Sharon for days at a time.

Earlier in their relationship, they engaged in an "open" relationship, in which sex with other partners was acceptable, if it did not involve an emotional connection and if it was done openly and honestly. However, when they decided to marry, they had pledged to each other that this flirting and sex outside the relationship would cease. Twice, in the past five years, Roberta's trysts were discovered by Sharon. They were both concerned that this would continue and lead to the breakup of their family. They are a strikingly beautiful and elegant couple, and when they arrived for their first appointment I was aware that their appearance and good looks were exceedingly important to both of them. They looked like they could have appeared on the cover of a magazine with the underlying article in the publication touting the success of this professional couple, both lawyers from a prestigious Ivy League school, managing their careers and their two children.

Roberta[3] was also a formerly nationally ranked collegiate athlete and only because of a career ending injury did she not qualify for the US national team in her sport. Athletics have always been critically important to her and to her well being. Her mastery in her sport of choice, on the one hand, contributed greatly to her self esteem and overall sense of well-being, but on the other hand it also contributed to her sense of her grandiosity, which fueled her addiction and megalomania. And, a factor that has significantly contributed to this treatment is that her vision of herself as an athlete and my own sense of myself and the role of athletics for me fueled a shared fantasy and constituted an essential part of the leading edge of the therapy, which I will discuss in more detail. As a young woman immediately following school, Roberta's legal career had been on an upward trajectory. At the age of 27 she was a partner in an entertainment industry related business that she had started and then walked away from with a few million dollars. She then started a new business, which though successful had her out of town 4–5 days every week. She left that job and her stake in that company, as she found it increasingly painful to be away from her growing family. She was also very aware that being a successful gay woman in this business, put tremendous pressure on her relationship with Sharon. Trust issues related to both of their flirtations in the past, was part of what led them to my office in the first place. As I was to learn, her relationships with her children are extremely important to her, and being away so much was reminiscent of her father's frequent absences in her own childhood, which she did not want to replicate, especially for her youngest child, a son who is disabled.

The thought of her being unavailable for this child for days at a time was intolerable, and so she left the business and for a period of a few years stayed home to be more available for her youngest son. Roberta also revealed that the time spent away from her wife and children led to numerous encounters with other women, some of which led to sex, but often these encounters led to extended dinners in which she would wine and dine and flirt for hours. If there was a sexual experience, she rarely saw the woman more than a few times.

For her, the excitement was in the experience of meeting a random woman at a bar after work in a strange city and winning her over.

She knew she was playing with fire, but she could not help herself, and had no idea why. She said that winning them over made her feel special and that it instantaneously led to a high. Later in the treatment, she would liken it to a runner's high. And, as the treatment unfolded she came to acknowledge that she craved feeling loved. Besides being more available for her youngest son, another reason she left her job was, she believed, was to curtail her involvement with other women. As she was to understand, this was only a geographical cure, as her interest in engaging women soon returned a few months after she stopped working.

For the last eight years, Roberta has been a serial entrepreneur. As an attorney, she has been able to remain engaged in some of the deals which had fueled her early success, but for the most part, she remained inactive. However, two of these businesses have failed and the one that remains, has been somewhat successful but she does not regard this as an accomplishment. Her wife, on the other hand, has worked for two law firms for over the last ten years, and she recently became a partner. Though immensely proud of her and very supportive, when she compares herself to Sharon she feels like a failure. Over the last five years, in the morning when her partner leaves at 8:00 AM to go to work, she has been responsible for their children, dressing, feeding and dropping them off at school or daycare. This also involves her taking and dropping off her youngest disabled son to a speciality school a half hour from their home. She is by all measures a great Mom, and although she has struggled personally and professionally, Roberta cares for her children with a smile and great pleasure. Part of the struggle between Roberta and Sharon, is that she doesn't want Sharon to take what she does for granted. Roberta understands Sharon's pressures at work and supports her but she also wants Sharon to be more appreciative of what she does, in support of the family. As we have come to understand, she has been desperate to be seen and mirrored and affirmed as worthwhile.

All of this, the business failures, her sense of herself as only Mom, has led her to become increasingly depleted and leaving her with little tolerance for her partner. She can forget to call her during the day, or not be able to make a pick-up at night because of a work commitment, and Roberta would sulk, be angry and withdraw from her. The arguments between them often take the following course. Roberta would become offended and hurt by her feeling slighted by Sharon, and she would then either stop talking to her and withdraw or they would have an all night discussion, unable to work out the issues. From Roberta's perspective the problems kept persisting without a solution. Sharon too often felt that she was failing Roberta and often felt like she was not a good enough wife, because Roberta was always disappointed.

During one of the early sessions, as we were discussing her history she told a story, the discussion of which led to a critical shift in the therapy. Roberta grew up in California in a privileged family life. One afternoon at the age of six, as she was riding in the car with her mother, all of a sudden the car stopped, and she demanded that Roberta get out. Roberta had been complaining and was upset and not listening to her mother. Roberta was abandoned at the side of the road. She recalls not having any idea where she was or what she should do. Five minutes later, her mother drove back, picked her up, and told her that she was teaching her a lesson. From now on, her mother said, she would not disobey her. Roberta told the story as one would talk about an everyday ride in the country. It seemed, she said, that her mother was talking to her and she hadn't listened to her, and the consequence was she was thrown out of the car for bad behavior. The manner in which Roberta told the story was for me completely out of sync with the terror I knew that a 6-year-old girl would feel after having been left at the side of the road and abandoned by her mother. She remembered the actual incident but what she remembered more was her mother and father repeating the story many times as an example of something funny and one of the stories that were part of the family lore. I asked her what she felt about the story, and more pointedly reflected that the tone in which she told the story was dissonant with what that child must have felt.

Roberta was quite thoughtful and open to my question, and she began to talk about the story and how badly she felt each time her parents would recall it and she didn't know why she was laughing. She was profoundly impacted by my questioning her story and how she felt about it. At first, she denied that she felt anything, but by the end of the session she was quite upset. She called in between the next session and said that she and her wife had discussed it and she asked if it would be ok if I saw her alone for a few sessions. She explained to Sharon that she needed to see me first if they were to make progress. I agreed and it is almost three years later and I have not seen Sharon since. Sharon has found her own individual therapist and Roberta and I meet twice a week. Roberta came back the next session eager to talk about the car incident and many more family moments where how she should feel was so different from what she actually felt. In rethinking these moments she realized that she often would hide what she felt. To own that she was terrified or frightened was unacceptable in her family. Her mother, she reported, was rarely present, and her father who was more available emotionally, could not accept her truth. She has described her mother as not empathic with any of her children, her brother or herself.

I often felt in the beginning months of the therapy that, Roberta spoke, using the language of music, in staccato bursts, that often her articulation of a story involved some kind of shortened burst of words, somewhat disconnected. In the early months of the therapy I did wonder whether I could follow her or understand her. These dots and dashes of words and sentences after a few months led to more and more continuity in her speech (legato, to use a musical term). Her sentences were more connected and she was much easier to follow and understand.

This change in her style of communicating with me, I believe was the result of a deshaming process that occurred in the early months of the therapy and a result of Roberta and I engaging the leading edge, that is, her wish for an idealizing selfobject transference fantasy. In the context of an idealizing transference fantasy, Roberta revealed that although she and Sharon were happy, the relationship had begun with lies. She explained that through the first six months of their relationship, she had also been dating many women, who had also expected to have a future with her. She then revealed that this had happened more than once, that is, that ten years before she met her wife she had dated more than one woman at a time. In that situation, the two women also believed that they were the only ones she was seeing. As Roberta was free associating about her history of dating, she also revealed to herself and to me, that there was rarely a time since she was in middle school when she was without a girlfriend. As I described earlier, she also revealed that there had been short flirtations with other women since she married. She reported that she liked to flirt and feel a woman's interest in her. The flirting, she reported was more important than a sexual liaison, most of the time. If there was sex, the most significant part of the experience was that the woman experience her as a great lover, who thought she was great and special. She and her wife had an active sexual life that she enjoyed. Sex for sex's sake had little interest for her, she reported, and she had no interest in excessive masturbation or pornography. It was at this point that I understood that Roberta's addiction was not to sex but to love, to the fantasy elicited by the company of women who showed a powerful interest in her, and that winning over their interest counteracted her depletion and elicited grandiose fantasies of herself. Being special, feeling that she mattered, and was loved, was most important to her. This became more and more clear as the idealizing transference fantasy unfolded, initially by my "omniscience" and knowing what she felt about being abandoned. I was not the passive and absent father who failed her, but interested in her feelings.

In the course of discussing her serial need for a girlfriend, I used the language 'shame bound', in referring to her need to always have a female by her side, and how she felt about herself. She came back for the next session, and something was different. Over the course of the prior few weeks, I had felt more and more connected to her. There had been more continuity to her speech, and I was feeling increasingly connected to her. Something had shifted. I asked her if something was wrong because I could feel that she was uncomfortable, but I was not sure why. Slowly through that session, though initially not able to talk freely about what she felt, Roberta said that she was upset with me because I had used the language 'shame bound' in describing her. In exploring what she felt, she first said that she was upset with me. However, what she slowly came to realize was that she didn't like the word 'shame' because it meant weakness and that she didn't want to be seen as weak. The problem was not, she said, in my use of the word 'shame', but that she was worried about what I thought of her. It became obvious that the trailing edge had to be discussed, and we did so. Roberta dreaded that talking about her shame or vulnerability was seen by me as a weakness. When she felt that, unlike her father, I was interested in what she felt, had empathy for her and her experience as a little girl, the yearning for an idealizing transference experience was realized:the leading edge. We spoke further about the shame she felt about seeing her own need for women, and I spoke about the courage it took to look at her own humanness and to talk about these issues. Deshaming and becoming more aware of her vulnerability went hand in hand with the idealizing transference fantasy and formed the initial strand of the leading edge.

Roberta's increasing ability to talk and reveal herself, occurred in an intersubjective context that supported the leading edge, that is the developing idealizing transference fantasy. The idealizing transference also developed in the context of particular moments, when I explored with her, certain behaviors that kept repeating. For example, when I questioned her use of time, like her commitment to cook a four course meal over a busy weekend, she would become thoughtful and realize that she was doing these projects not only because she could, but because she hoped she would be regarded by her wife as a super housekeeper and chef. However, after cooking an artfully prepared meal, she never received enough appreciation, felt more distant from Sharon, and they were more likely to get into an argument. Roberta was an accomplished chef, who after law school had attended and graduated from a prestigious cooking school. Using her cooking skills to garner attention and praise had been an effective tool when she was single, but as a mother these superhuman meals did not have their intended effect, and when I was able to point this out to her, she was grateful, which again helped to strengthen the idealization. Or, at other times, in an effort to be super mom, she could cook dinner, decide to schedule numerous nighttime activities that she thought they would all enjoy, only to again be depleted herself by the end of the evening. She was thankful when I questioned these activities and helped her realize that they were failing attempts to make herself feel better. We also explored that being with her family, not doing for them, was most important, an idea that she did not fully understand. More than once, after such conversations she remarked, "This was helpful". All of these moments encapsulated the unfolding idealizing selfobject transference. The more the idealizing transference unfolded, the less shame, and the less staccato was in our conversations.

Within the first six months of the treatment Roberta was discussing vacation plans and mentioned that vacations were very different than it used to be earlier in her life. I asked what she meant and she then proceeded to tell me about some of the adventures she had taken, all of which she now believes were important and thrilling, but, as she now understands, they were overdetermined. Adventurous vacations involving her superior athletic fitness, or skydiving and jumping out of airplanes, or paragliding were extremely important to her and a measure of her superior athletic ability. The sporting activity that she had competed on at an Olympic level, she also gave up because she believed that it was potentially too dangerous. She admits to taking risks that she would no longer take today, and that the thrill of the risk was a way for her to go away or to dissociate. However, after her second child was born, she decided that these activities were much too dangerous and she stopped herself from engaging in these behaviors.

She often came to our appointment fresh from a work out in the gym or from a quick run in Central Park in New York. Through the first three months of the therapy, if she discussed her own workout which sometimes involved running I wondered about telling her about my own interest in running, but it just didn't seem the right time. I had my own reluctance to talk about running, actually because I feel so good about my own running that I wondered if I would be pushing it on her, instead of offering a twinship experience.

My own running schedule, usually involves running three times a week, a long run on Sunday and two shorter runs during the week, often before work. It had crossed my mind that I might encounter her running in the park. One morning, as I was running in Central Park, all of a sudden alongside of me is Roberta, about to pass me. We looked at each other, both with smiles on our faces as we unexpectedly encountered each other. For a few minutes, we spoke and then she went on, each of us committed to our own workout. The next day, she came in and said that she didn't know that I ran too, and she was eager to ask about my running and workout schedule. So, I had my permission to talk about our common interest, for her what had been a passion earlier in her life and for me a hobby that has led to a great deal of self satisfaction and pleasure. Roberta wanted to know all about my running. I also think that she felt free to ask because if she had asked me before and the answer had been that I didn't exercise, she might have been disappointed. However, by seeing me run, she didn't have to take that risk. I also did believe, however, that the treatment was on enough of a right track that it would have been a tolerable disappointment even if the answer was no. I told her that I did run, that I ran three times a week and that it was my principle exercise. I also then told her that I had run in the last two New York City marathons, and this began a conversation about running and exercise and working out that continues today.

We talk about running technique, strategies, clothing, all things running which solidifies and affirms what I believe has been an unfolding twinship transference fantasy with me, as the idealized father figure. Though she had been an award winning athlete, her father himself had taken no interest in joining her, but he had only enjoyed her exercise for the personal satisfaction it gave him to have a daughter competing at such a high level. It became his and not hers and he had no interest in joining her in the enjoyment. Over the course of the last five years I have continued to run four of the last five NYC marathons during which she followed my progress on race day and we speak not just of the good times but of the injuries and disappointments. Acknowledging my own vulnerabilities without shame, taking care of myself after an injury, waiting to run again only when healthy, accepting slower times as I have gotten older, are all important parts of these conversations. And, twice, we have stopped to talk for a few minutes in Central Park, as both of us were out for a Sunday run in the park. And, recently when I was taking a walk in between patients, Roberta happened to be walking in the street and she approached me. She was accompanied by a woman whom I recognized was an elite runner. To my great surprise, she introduced me as her therapist and fellow runner, all of this reflecting the solidity of the leading edge and how the issues surrounding shame and vulnerability had been worked through.

In a recent session, Roberta revealed that when she asked why I run she was also asking if I am running away from feelings as she has, or am I like her father who time after time in private life has flown too close to the sun and ended in business failure, because he has a proclivity to risk, that ends up in failure. Her father, a physician, has participated in one bad business deal after another. In the course of talking to Roberta about running I have talked about pushing the limits and my awareness of this and at the same time I am older and not running a 3:30 marathon but am just satisfied in finishing, as I told her, before the truck has to pick me up. My pleasure in finishing or talking about the pleasure and satisfaction of just competing with myself and no one else offers her my own measured grandiosity, neither expecting too much but being pleased with what I can accomplish. Over the course of watching her father practice medicine, she has seen him squander large amounts of money, and at the same time she believed that as a teenager she knew that her father was likely having affairs and was overly sexualized. It was also revealed in the course of the therapy that Roberta's mother had been involved in a 20 year affair. This was revealed to Roberta by her father and never discussed by her mother with her. It was no surprise to Roberta considering her mother's absence in her life. I understand that when either she or I initiate a conversation about exercise, that our common interests in these activities are part and parcel of the leading edge of the twinship, and that their conversation concretizes that we think and have common interests and feelings about these activities, that all lead to an increasing sense of well being and greater sense of ourselves, an experience which is an antidote to her father's unbridled grandiosity and mother's absence.

I have been aware that at no time in the course of this ongoing three year treatment, has the intersubjective field between us become sexualized. I questioned myself wondering if I was in denial or repressing sexual feelings for her, but I have concluded that this is not an active or difficult issue between us. Roberta came out as a young teenager with little conflict and difficulty because her parents and friends quickly embraced her, and she has only felt increasingly sure of herself as a lesbian. I experience her as a woman struggling with an addiction, and though I do care about her, these feelings have not become sexualized.

Roberta has spoken to me about two occasions in the first two years of the treatment in which she was tempted to engage women out of a sense of depletion, once while away on a business trip and the other situation with the mother of one of her daughters' friends. In both circumstances, she came to sessions and spoke about feeling vulnerable to what was happening and how our relationship helped her to manage her feelings. In one situation, while on a two week business trip, she spoke of the loneliness and distance she felt from Sharon and her family, but that our talking and preparing her for the trip, and actually talking during the trip, as I had suggested, had helped her feel less alone, that her merger with me as an idealized figure was strong enough to help sustain her. As we also came to understand, Roberta had been coping with a knee injury, that was severely limiting her physical activity. Exercise, often a source of healthy self-esteem, was not available to her, which had also contributed to her depletion.

Roberta told me that my suggesting that we talk meant that I was interested in her because I understood, she suspected, that being on a trip away from her wife and family, would leave her vulnerable to feeling lonely. She experienced me as the father, a compensatory selfobject experience, who is interested in her well being, unlike her father who was grandiose, self involved, or overinvolved in her early athletic prowess. Women could be used by Roberta to counteract the depletion she often felt, but of course, this was only a defensive maneuver, which did not lead to healthy self-esteem. Roberta said, that when she felt stronger and when women didn't even come to mind, she understood that, to coin her term, she was building "core strength", the term for becoming stronger on the inside, which helped her feel better about herself. In this way, I reminded her of her physical trainer, who was a part of her athletic team, the entourage involved in her early athletic career. The trainer, who spent four or five years with her as a coach on her team, cared about her as a person, and she felt seen by him. I proposed and she agreed that the early relationship with this trainer, was the precursor to our relationship, and in both cases she feels that we care and see her as a person. This notion of "core strength" is also an expression that we have used over and over again in discussing how good she feels about herself.

Recently, a housekeeper employed by Sharon and Roberta, began to show her attention that she felt was uncomfortable, but welcomed. She understood what this meant and she was tempted to play in this dangerous game with her. Early in the therapy, I suggested that she play out in her mind acting out with someone, what she would feel, what that would look like, thinking through those difficult moments that she was sure to face in dealing with an impulsive need. She spoke about how using this idea both brought me to mind, and that when she thought about how she would feel if she accepted the housekeeper's invitation, it lost its luster and the fantasy, she said lost its power. She resisted and has since talked to Sharon about what she felt and they let this employee go. In this way, Roberta took comfort in the idealized merger experience with me, the leading edge of her transference experience.

In the course of talking about these moments, Roberta revealed again that it was not so much the sex that she became desperate for, but the feeling of a woman being interested in her, that she mattered a great deal to her and she would do almost anything to be with her. Yes, she said, this could be expressed sexually but most importantly, what she needed was to feel that she was special and mattered, and always on a woman's mind. She free associated at that moment and remembered going to the beach, not far from her childhood home in California, sitting on the beach with her girlfriend at the time, who she believed she cared for. However, during the course of that afternoon, she found herself staring at a number of other girls, and she remembered questioning herself, as to why she would be doing this, since she was also sitting with someone she cared about. She realized that she needed more of something that at the time she did not understand. She sometimes dated multiple women simultaneously but she didn't understand why, and it made her feel that there was something dreadfully wrong with her. These women became interchangeable and it scared her that she would never really fall in love.

There have been two principal moments when a therapeutic disjunction occurred in which the leading edge receded. In the first situation, Roberta was traveling to the west coast on business. As she prepared to leave, we talked about the difficult moments in which she would be tempted to "hook" up with a woman. This instance occurred after the sixth or seventh month of the treatment. On this particular trip, she was going to a city that was nearby an old girlfriend who in the past she had often looked up. We spoke directly about how she might be tempted to "hook up" with this woman, and that although being with her felt very real, it was essentially the fantasy speaking to her. I made it clear, I thought, that even though we were talking about this situation, that the temptation to call her might still be powerful.

Roberta initially told me that the trip went well and that she had not been tempted to call her former girlfriend. We met for a few times, and at the end of the second session after her return, she said to me, that she needed to tell me something, and I looked at her and asked if she had seen her former girlfriend while away. Increasingly over the course of that session, I had begun to again feel the staccato of her speech pattern, reflecting a distance and hesitation in her connection with me, and what I also understood to represent her underlying shame. I told her that I appreciated her wanting to tell me and I also said to her that I had begun to feel her distance, as I had in the early months of the therapy. We talked about the shame in telling me that she had met her and her fear of judgement. She then revealed that she had been briefly married to this woman and that even Sharon did not know about this relationship. As we spoke more about what had happened on this trip, she thought that I would likely ask her if it helped to talk about these circumstances before she left on her next trip or if we should not talk about them. She needed me to know, she said, that although we had talked about the possibility and she acted out anyway, it was important to her that I remain vigilant with her and anticipate with her those circumstances when remaining abstinent would be difficult. She also reported that she and Sharon were not in a good place when she had left to go on this trip, which likely left her more needy and depleted, all of which contributed to her seeing her former partner. Roberta revealed that, in the middle of the dinner with her former wife, seeing her was a fantasy and that having sex with her would have only resulted in her feeling more depleted and worthless. She cut the evening short, without sex. However, when initially confronted with telling me about the encounter, she was still too ashamed and concerned that I would judge her. In telling me at the end of the session, she said that she knew that continuing to meet and not talking about what happened would be pointless. It felt, that there was more to lose by us not talking, which is why she finally needed to talk about what happened. What she was actually saying in the language of ISP, was that she did not want to lose "us", and that we had become a trusted enough partnership to fight through her fears. By talking about her concerns, she wanted to make sure that I understood how powerful her needs were, otherwise both the twinship and idealization would diminish and the selfobject transference would no longer be effective.

In the second therapeutic disjunction, as Roberta was telling me about a disagreement she was having with Sharon and how she felt misunderstood by her, I responded from a perspective that Roberta found difficult to digest. She described a disagreement between herself and Sharon in which Sharon felt the need to meet a friend who had come to town, even though it was an inconvenience for the family and Roberta. Roberta believed that Sharon, meeting her friend, was a capitulation to Sharon's need to please someone else, and not keeping her eye on the needs of her nuclear family and Roberta. This has been a continuing issue in which Roberta believed that Sharon's need to please others all too often superseded the families' needs. I questioned Roberta about this, and as I did so, I remembered becoming very active and essentially telling her that she basically needed to approach Sharon and understand her perspective. She left the session feeling that this was a different tact from the one we had been on, but she wanted to think about it.

Roberta reported in the next session that in the last few days she had become unusually frustrated with her children on a number of occasions, and that she was finding it difficult to connect with Sharon. She then said that she felt that something went wrong between us in the last session. After the last session, I too wondered if I had been more empathic to Sharon's concerns than Roberta's, but I was not sure of its impact on Roberta. Roberta then asked me if I was ok, or had there been something that was bothering me during our last session. I explained to her that I too felt different at the end of the last time we met and would think about my own state of mind. I continued telling her that there was something on my mind that day, having nothing to do with her. I continued and told her that my activity and interest in "solving" Roberta's marital problems, instead of listening and understanding the predicament she was facing, and questioning how she felt, was directly related to her moodiness with herself and with her wife and children. With a smile, she said, "I thought so, it didn't sound like you." I had taken such a different tact in that session, such as telling her what she should do to solve this problem with Sharon, that she thought something must be happening in my life. This led to a discussion of the importance of our relationship. She said that although it was somewhat risky to ask if I was alright, it was more risky, she said, if she did not ask. She also said that she trusted me and the therapy, and that I would not dismiss her feelings out of hand, but engage in a reasonable collegial conversation with her. All of this I believe, suggests that Roberta believed that we would be able to find our way back to the leading edge of the therapy, both the idealization and the twinship that had been guiding our work together.

Roberta is now in the third year of the therapy. I don't want to give the impression that we are in any way done. A new challenge has recently emerged, which Roberta and I acknowledge will be challenging and test the reserve of our relationship and her connection with Sharon. Sharon was recently diagnosed with a debilitating disease, the prognosis of which is not clear at the moment. I do believe that the first two plus years of the therapy have established a foundation for our further work together. Roberta, who initially was ashamed about needing the therapeutic relationship, now at times herself invokes the strength of the connection and how it has helped her weather the crisis in her marriage and her struggle to find fulfilling work. I hope to continue to be able to help her through these issues and to develop the "core" necessary to weather life's expected storms, including managing Sharon's illness and having the "core" necessary to be available to herself, Sharon and their family. From the perspective of this paper, the leading edge involved the evolution of the merger with the idealized father figure, which led into a twinship in which Roberta feels worthy with the vulnerabilities that accompany being human and mortal. As an athlete, Robert's quest had always been to strengthen her "core". She has come to understand a whole new definition of her "core", what she needs and how to remain resilient and strong, even in the face of adversity.

Notes

1 My thanks to Peter Zimmermann for his friendship and collegial support. We are an example of the generative leading edge in action through our rewarding relationship. Specifically his thoughtfulness has been a catalyst for me in further developing these ideas and their application to addiction, and our relationship has always made me a better person and better clinician.

2 One of my colleagues, Peter Zimmermann, and I have had ongoing discussions for years about the nature of the addicts initial selfobject transference. He believes that the therapist has to be almost superhuman to be able to absorb the addiction into a selfobject transference, while I believe that some aspect of the transference must initially be nonhuman, as a recapitulation of the addiction to nonhuman things and activities.
3 The name, identity and the patient's sport with national recognition has been altered or removed to protect her identity.

Chapter 10

Child treatment
Working with the leading and trailing edge

Karen Roser

Intersubjective Self Psychological Treatment is different in working with children than with an individual adult patient. When we talk of trailing edge dreads in adult work, we are referring to those structures of self which develop in response to childhood challenges and become reactivated in the transference with the therapist. Abandonment, trauma, parental shortcomings/misattunements in childhood lead directly to those trailing edge structures getting formed. Similarly, the presence of the tendrils of the leading edge hopes in the transference of adults come from strengths within the original parent/child system: both the child's innate resiliency and the ways in which the parent was able to provide needed selfobject experiences for the child. They become rekindled as hopes within the selfobject transference with the therapist.

But with a child in treatment, the structures of self are still in the process of being formed: the child is, by definition, still entangled in the intersubjective field of the family. As child therapists, we need to understand the leading and trailing edge experiences of both child and parents in the present moment, and how they play out or intersect. These intersections create the complex intersubjective system that is the family. We also need to understand the hopes and dreads of each in relation to our presence in the field, and our own hopes and dreads as they get reactivated in relation to this particular family.

Before we look at the child in treatment, let us first look at the child in development. We already have the well articulated self psychological view of the developing child as having nascent selfobject needs. If they are responded to consistently in a way that provides the needed or longed for selfobject experience in the child, the child's development proceeds from archaic to more mature, and a healthy sense of self and a consolidation of self experience occurs (for instance, see Kohut, 1977, Chap. 4). Implicit in this view is the idea that the child does not develop separately from the bond with the parents. This is made explicit by Stolorow et al. (1987) in their intersubjectivity theory. They make the argument that there is no understanding the child separate from the intersubjective selfobject milieu in which he or she is being raised. The child is part of the intersubjective field and the strengths and weaknesses of the child, deriving from leading edge hopes and trailing edge dreads, develop from within this field and can only be fully understood with an understanding of the relationship between the child and his parents as experienced by the child.

What ISP adds to this conceptualization of development is the awareness of the selfobject needs of both the parents and child. It is not just the needs of the child which must be considered but also those of the parents. The leading edge hopes and trailing edge dreads of the parents interact with the developing child. How the child feels received by his parents, and how his/her hopes and dreads are nourished is half the equation; how the parents feel responded to and nourished by the child is the other half. The parents' experience affects how they engage with their child, which then affects how the child feels responded to, and in turn, how s/he engages with parents, in a cycle of mutual reciprocal influence.

Finally, there is an understanding, implicit here, that the child brings something to the equation. He or she is not just a blank screen of needs, upon which the parents' ability to provide necessary selfobject experiences create a sense of self in the child. The child comes into the world with certain strengths and vulnerabilities, cognitive and physiological as well as temperamental proclivities. These impact the system: both in terms of the child's experience of the parents, and the parent's experience of themselves as being able to provide for their child.

It is thus a two way street. The child with a unique neurological and temperamental make-up develops within the milieu provided by parents with their own specific strengths and vulnerabilities, and selfobject needs, yearnings and dreads. To paraphrase Winnicott, not only is there no such thing as an infant (but only an infant with parents), there is also no such thing as an isolated parent.

Another way to understand this is to look at the different babies conceptualized by different theorists. Mitchell (1988) coins the terms "Freudian baby" and "relational baby", highlighting the discrepancy between the Freudian infant with its focus on instinctual drives, and the baby whose primary influence is early object experiences. Teicholz (2001) updates this by separating the relational baby into the Kohutian baby and the baby of theorists such as Benjamin, Aron and Mitchell. Both give primary importance to the early relationships of a developing child. For Kohut, the parents are expected to be watchful in order to minimize the impact of their subjectivity; there is a clear focus on the parents providing for the child's selfobject needs (Teicholz, 2002, p. 14). When there is a developmental issue, it is conceptualized as a misattunement or failure to correctly address the child's selfobject needs. For the other relationists, the focus is on the parents allowing their subjectivity to be in the room with the child. The emphasis is on authenticity, and the child's experience of the reality of their parents subjectivity, and the impact this has upon their experience. If there is a problem, it is based upon the interaction between the two (or three, or more) subjectivities in the room. Teicholz sees value in both conceptualizations and wonders if there is a way to bridge the gap between these theories. ISP provides the means. We have here a theory that brings in the parents' hopes and dreads as they are triggered by the child, as well as the child's selfobject needs, and how they have been responded to.

To illuminate the ideas just discussed, here is an example from everyday life: I am listening to a mother and her 20-month-old daughter in a shower at the gym. The daughter is complaining loudly, almost screaming, as mother attempts to rinse the daughter's hair. The mother is saying, what's wrong, why are you acting this way, you do this at home ok. Her communication is conveying that she is keenly aware of my silent presence in the space, which is therefore codetermining the interaction between mother and child. The daughter, unperturbed by my presence, continues her screaming and crying, not out of control, just loudly protesting. Finally, the mother gives up and says, ok, just wait a moment while I rinse myself off and we will get out. As soon as the mother focuses on herself, the daughter stops crying and within ten seconds is asking what mother is doing and saying she wants to do it herself. Her mother says just let me finish and we will get out. Child's voice rises as she cries, "I do it!" And mother says ok, you rinse it off, here let me help you. They happily finish rinsing the girl's hair and leave.

What is going on here? There are many different ways to understand this interaction given the limited information we have. Mahler et al. (1975) might have talked about the mother's anxiety (triggered by my presence) influencing her daughter's ability to self regulate, causing her to be more demanding and challenging. In this view, it is the mother's emotional world which is predominantly influencing the field. In the language of ISP, it is the mother's trailing edge anxiety which is emphasized in this conceptualization. Daniel Stern (1985) might look at the ways in which the daughters developing capabilities and neurological and physical plant influence her mother's behavior. We can look at this interaction from a self psychological view. The mother is looking to soothe and care for her daughter, i.e. to be the idealized mother figure. Her daughter's rejection of this causes the mother's disequilibrium and a sense of her own incompetence as mother. She withdraws. On the other hand, from the daughter's vantage point, perhaps she is looking for a mirror to her own developing competency, and her mother's attempts to soothe her miss their mark and puncture her grandiose self. Or she is yearning for an experience of twinship, an experience of working side by side with her mother. Once mother gives up trying to fix the situation, i.e. to be idealizable, daughter's grandiosity and/or twinship needs can emerge AND mother has a sense of competency and perhaps idealizability in getting the job done. In different language, the mother's leading edge hope is activated and the child's is strengthened. My point here is that there are two very active subjectivities in this scenario influencing each other. Who the mother is influences her daughter's developing sense of self which in turn influences mother's sense of herself as mother. Ultimately, this is a successful interaction. Mother and daughter have both been flexible enough to take in the other and come away with a reasonably positive sense of self and other.

In this example, my role is as unseen observer. Despite being unseen, my presence is definitely influencing the field, as mother is clearly aware of me and self conscious. But I am not actively involved. My subjectivity is involved cognitively in formulating theories and emotionally in reacting to their presence in my space. If we were in a room together I would be more a part of the field, influencing mother's ability to access her leading edge, and daughter's self development. And, based on how they responded to me, my sense of myself as competent would be more or less activated. This is what happens in child treatment.

For traditional self psychologists, the focus in child treatment is on empathizing with the selfobject needs of the child, with the goal of helping the child gain a stronger and more resilient sense of self. Many self psychologists have written about the self psychological treatment of children. In carving out the way in which self psychology lends itself to the treatment of children, Morton Shane (1996) says that not only do self psychologists look at internalized conflict as it appears in the transference, they also do not "neglect the power and continuing influence on the child of his mother and father in the here and now" (p. 202). Marian Tolpin (2002) discusses child analysis from within the leading edge of experience. In her description, not only is the therapist experienced like the parents, but there is the potential for a new, more responsive selfobject experience, wherein the child can resume development. She also talks about the analysts trailing and leading edge experiences as well. Jules Miller (1996) adds how to work with fantasy, specifically in the modality of play, in the treatment of children from a self psychological perspective. Anna Ornstein (1984) talks of the use of play in family therapy.

Child treatment from an ISP perspective involves attention not only to the child and his or her developing self, and selfobject needs, but also to the selfobject needs of the parents. Similar to systems theory, we are looking at the dynamics between the various members of the family. However, in the ISP perspective, the focus is on selfobject needs, and how they are met, received and either thwarted or allowed to flourish. The vulnerabilities, as well as the strengths of the child are seen as arising from within this complex intersubjective field and cannot be understood separately; likewise, the strengths and weaknesses of the parents are also only understandable from within this field. For example, a parent's overwhelming anxiety about their child may be understood as arising primarily from within the parent's own unmet needs for idealization OR from their very real understanding of their child's precarious self organization.

In the therapeutic context, the parents, as well as the child, will come to the therapist with their sense of hope and dread vis a vis the therapist. In the initial assessment phase, the therapist will begin working to understand these hopes and dreads, in order to determine how best to meet the needs of the family. In some cases, the therapist's presence helps alleviate the parents' dreads, and with their hopes in the foreground, the parents' other needs can take a back seat. The therapist will then be able to focus on the child's selfobject yearnings. In others, the parents' selfobject needs will be in the picture to a greater extent. Finally, the way in which the therapist defines the needs of the family before her and how she develops relationships with the individuals involved is also dependent on her own hopes and dreads. As the treatment progresses, the therapist will continue to monitor all the members of the family as to how they are organizing the experience.

Alex and his fathers

The gay parents of 8-year-old Alex came into my treatment room, at the end of their ropes. Unlike his older sister, Alex was extraordinarily difficult. His nightly tantrums often lasted an hour, and were triggered by the most innocent of events: a request to pick up his clothes could lead to screaming, kicking his heels on the floor and damage to physical property. Occasionally he was violent, and required physical containment by one of his fathers. He was unreachable at these times: reasoning, requests for him to go to his room to cool off, nothing worked except to let it run its course. Afterwards he was contrite and sorry about the pain he had caused, but felt justified in his view that it was his parents, or sibling at fault.

The parents were looking for me to get through to him so that he would stop these irrational outbursts. Because this behavior was limited to the home, they saw it as something Alex could control, if only he chose to.

During the initial assessment, it was clear that there were very pronounced strengths in this family. His fathers are lovely, highly functional, experienced parents. They work reasonably well together, and have a deep love and commitment to their two adoptive children. Their hopes were clearly present, as they sought an idealized professional, who could help their son. They were looking for answers and information about their son who was bewildering to them. Additionally, they were looking for validation of themselves. They both held their roles as parents at the center of their self organization and Alex was challenging their perception of themselves as good enough fathers. This created vulnerability and intensified the distress in the system. There was a trailing edge dread that they were not good enough parents and that they would be judged by their inability to control their son's outbursts. In order to be able to change so as to meet Alex's needs, they needed to be seen as good enough parents by me.

Alex, right from the start, had gotten many nutrients and was developing well in many ways. Intellectually curious, socially aware and sensitive, he was an excellent student and friend. However, in the home, the relative lack of structure compared to school, particularly the lack of a predictable routine, left him struggling. Whereas his sister responded well to the parents' loose style, Alex felt ambushed when asked to do something such as set the table or take a shower. The request felt out of the blue to him. He would have a big reaction, out of proportion to what the parents thought was "normal". This caused a big reaction in them, and they would accuse him of being irrational and manipulative. The situation escalated to a total breakdown of control in Alex and anger and frustration in his fathers. All three were eager and willing to work with me, and wanted things to change.

Where was I in this intersubjective picture? My empathy for Alex was not hard to find and I felt confident that I would be able to enter his world. With the parents, my twinship needs were triggered. My special needs son, a few years older, presented similar challenges and I was hungry for a feeling of kinship around being a dedicated parent in a situation that felt, on and off, out of control. While I hoped that this would convey my non judgmental stance towards them, I worked hard to keep the twinship needs in the background, aware that the hunger in me to tell them I'd been there, was not where their primary selfobject yearnings lay. I knew that there was a danger that I would lose them in their yearning for an idealization. They needed me to be professional and knowledgeable, as well as non judgmental – not stuck in the same boat! They never asked me anything about myself, not even whether or not I was a parent. However, even in the act of listening and empathizing, my needs were getting met. I felt my humanness as I empathized with their pain. I gave them what I so needed, understanding and empathy. The experience of watching them as they began to strengthen as parents, became healing and strengthening for me. While never stated directly, my similar experience powered my empathic bond with them.

After a brief assessment period, I began my work with the two fathers. The first few months I worked on two tracks with them. One was to respond to the parents need for validation that Alex was extremely difficult. Because Alex was doing so well outside the house, they got nothing but praise from teachers and friends. No one in their world saw what they saw and experienced nightly: huge rage reactions to ordinary requests. They were left alone, with their sense of themselves as adequate parents crumbling in the face of Alex's tantrums. If Alex was so great, then they must be really bad parents.

By describing Alex as having a more fragile neurological structure than their other child, I was able to validate and provide a structure for their reality. This fragility created more vulnerability particularly in the home, which was more unpredictable and unstructured than school.

Understanding this allowed them to organize around me as providing answers, and diminished their vulnerability slightly. They were strengthened enough to look at what was going wrong in what they were doing with Alex, armed with the knowledge that I didn't blame them.

The other track of my early work with parents was to help them understand Alex's emotional needs. This began with an exploration about the meaning to them of Alex's struggles, in light of his having been adopted. Did they see him as foreign, different from them? They did struggle with his being different; however, they had also both been seen as very different in their families of origin. Being gay in families with little understanding, or sympathy, had left them with wounds of their own. Thus, for them, it was a point of connection with their son. They worked harder as parents.

Their struggle centered more on not understanding that he needed something different from them than what came naturally. Since what they had been doing made sense to them and had worked for their older child, they couldn't understand why Alex wasn't responding in the same way. Keeping in mind their latent vulnerability, and with a lot of awareness that I was asking something very difficult of them, I asked them to put aside their ideas of how their family should be structured and what had worked previously, and to reorganize their family around Alex. They struggled with the idea that they needed to change the whole family's structure and routine to help Alex. But gradually they came to understand that it was Alex's wiring, his neurological system that was causing the difficulties he was having. At my suggestion they set up a psychiatric consultation but decided against medication at this time. However this understanding helped them to approach Alex differently. For instance, together we developed a very detailed, nightly schedule around chores. Having this structure helped Alex feel a measure of control, and that he was being treated the same as his older sister. I also worked with the family on how they phrased their requests and what their expectations for Alex were. With the gradual changes and accommodations to Alex's specific needs, the family system became a more empathic selfobject milieu that permitted the leading edge yearning of both Alex and his fathers to begin to unfold. Alex wanted to be a good son, who would feel loved and admired by his fathers, who in turn wanted to feel love and pride in their son.

Gradually the situation at home eased somewhat and the parents felt some measure of relief from their sense of failure. But they were still highly stressed: while the tantrums diminished somewhat in frequency and intensity, they still occurred. It remained difficult for them to stay calm and nonreactive in the face of Alex's rage. I decided to see Alex for individual sessions, which I had not done since the initial assessment period. I felt I needed to address Alex's vulnerabilities, and try and create more resiliency in him, so that it was not such a challenge for him to bear with the relative lack of structure at home. My hope was that this would alleviate enough of the stress on the parents that they would be able to react more calmly to Alex when the inevitable frustrations occurred. I also felt like the emphasis in treatment on the parents was feeding their trailing edge dread that they were being seen as the problem. In preparation, I told the parents that I would be able to work on Alex's self esteem, and on strengthening his sense of self. This would allow him to tolerate better the necessary irregularities and inconsistencies of home life. However, in focusing on this I would not be focusing on trying to change his behavior unless and until Alex brought it up himself and wanted to change. In the language of ISP, I would be working with him on his leading edge hopes not his trailing edge behaviors at least at first. They agreed to this. I would continue to see them, on a monthly basis, and begin to see Alex weekly.

The treatment began with Alex anxious and eager to share his world. It was easy to establish a bond, as Alex readily saw me as an ally. He played and I facilitated, and joined in. I was grounded in my understanding of his need to use me for the selfobject functions I was providing. I was mirroring his, at that point, quite archaic and fragile grandiosity, and enlarging on the themes he unfolded through drawing, storytelling and dramatic enactments. The themes mostly centered around war, and battle, dramatic rescues, and acts of bravery. Alex expanded to fill the space, very lively and engaged in this "room of his own". In addition to the focus on a mirroring selfobject experience, I was very clear about boundaries and expectations, providing the safety of an ideal, highly structured and consistent space. This was particularly in response to Alex's fragile neurological system. I wanted to help him feel strong and capable, minimizing his experience of a demanding and intrusive outside world. Alex stayed within this boundaried space for the most part. For one brief period he tested me, by threatening, playfully, to break some toys, but this was easily dealt with within the play. Within the limits I imposed, he saw the boundless freedom in the space and his imagination, and his relationship with me. All this to say that treatment progressed along classic self psychological lines.

The challenge for me, and where the theory of ISP came in, was in my ability to retain empathy for Alex, while also holding the parents anxiety and concerns in my awareness. I could see in Alex the strengths the parents had nurtured and relished. I could also empathize with him as he played out his frustration and anger with his parents and sister. He saw them being triggered but could not see what he was doing to cause the reactivity. From within his world his anger made sense. But I was well aware of the other side of the story, and what Alex was bringing to the conflict from his side: explosivity and emotional outbursts that overwhelmed the emotional field. I could see how he defended himself from awareness of his emotional liability and saw that he needed the strength of the mirroring bond before he could see his behaviors. And I could see in the intensity and hunger for play the toll the conflict was having on Alex's sense of self. Underneath his veneer of self assurance, Alex was feeling very bad about the disruption he was causing in his home. My dilemma was that I had to empathize truly and genuinely with both sides of the equation: parents and child. This meant listening to the truly scary stories of Alex's rage, and counseling hope and patience to the parents, all the while continuing to maintain the safe and non-demanding space which Alex had come to count on.

My hope here was that Alex's grandiosity would become less brittle, allowing him to be more tolerant of others' different agendas, particularly his parents. And, on the other side, that the parents would feel strengthened by my calm understanding, allowing them to respond to Alex more neutrally and with less emotional reactivity. In the beginning of the treatment this was mostly a theoretical hope. While I could see the strengths in the system, I also could see the profound weaknesses. My dread was that I would not be enough to help this family. That the system needed more: either medication for Alex, or for Alex to be placed in a setting outside the home. These dreads were intense for me, part of a larger trailing edge experience around not being enough. After hearing about a particularly intense fight, I would find myself wavering internally. What I held onto at these times was the theory, which enabled me to speak to the parents from a hopeful place. And increasingly, I could point, both to myself internally and to the parents, to the very real successes: the ability of the parents to hold onto their tempers, and Alex's ability to recover more quickly.

With these hopes and dreads swirling around the treatment room, and with a mirroring selfobject transference strongly in place, Alex began to change. At first the change was only apparent in his relationship with me. He became more flexible, allowing me to have more of an active role in the room. While I was still the mirror of his grandiose fantasies, he was able to tolerate some push back from me, such as when I beat him at a game or made a suggestion. Because of his neurological vulnerability I had needed to create a safe, very boundaried space. As he began to grow stronger, I moved very slowly into changing my stance. I needed to allow Alex a long time to experience the predictability and safety of the room, and not burden him with my subjectivity, and the uncertainty this brought up. Within these constraints, he began to relax his guard. His play became more interactive and I felt more an equal participant. He began to talk: at first mostly to express verbally the frustration with his family, which had previously only been there in his play. And finally, after years of play and saying it was everyone else's fault, he began to approach the idea that he had a problem around controlling his temper. I responded by asking him why he thought this, and joined him on his quest to understand himself better. I brought in my understanding of how difficult this was, both for him and for his parents. I tried to humanize all of them. We worked together to understand what triggered him. I also began to show more of my feelings in the room. I played up my frustration when he beat me, showing anger at myself when I had a bad shot, and played out anger at him for beating me. It was playful and lively and he seemed to enjoy it. There was more of a sense of twinship in the room.

Along with this newfound self-reflection, Alex became more aware of one of his father's struggle for self-control. Initially denigrating, Alex very gradually became aware of their similarities and a sense of twinship became more possible in this relationship as well.

Finally, Alex began to show more resiliency at home. Imperceptibly at first but gradually working up to significant and noticeable progress, he was able to tolerate his parents' requests and demands of him. The tantrums diminished to once a week and then once a month, although they were still there. They also diminished in intensity, with the outbursts becoming more and more verbal rather than physical. His parents also gradually, but significantly, began to change their responses to Alex. His more reactive parent, with my help and support, explored ways he could walk away. He asked his partner to step in, and we talked of ways they could spell each other. I consistently responded to them with, what works? Does it work when you engage Alex when he is out of control? Or does it work better when you walk away? Their need to defend themselves gradually became less evident, as I would empathize with how challenging this must be for them. As a result of our work, Alex began to show more tolerance of the vulnerabilities in his fathers, and they became more able to tolerate his and their own lapses in control. The intersubjective field between parents and Alex was becoming more empathy based, and all concerned were benefitting.

To summarize, child treatment from an ISP perspective involves an understanding that the child and the parents are all participants in an intersubjective field. From within this perspective, understanding the selfobject needs of the parent can be equally important to working with the selfobject needs of the child. While it is not possible or necessary to work with every parent as intensively as I did with Alex's, having this model creates a space to consider both, and respond with empathy to the needs of all members of the family.

Chapter 11

Working with couples in Intersubjective Self Psychology

Nancy Hicks and Louisa Livingston

Although virtually all of the principles of ISP are at play in couples therapy, we think it is important to emphasize three of them. The first is the concept of the selfobject. Stolorow and Stolorow (1987) wrote: "The term selfobject refers to a dimension of experiencing an object in which a specific bond is required for maintaining, restoring, or consolidating the organization of self-experience" (pp. 16–17). The couple relationship is a context in which many people seek a partner who will reliably meet their needs for closeness, support, and understanding. The provision, or lack, of selfobject experience accounts for an immeasurable number of the fluctuations in partners' sense of connection to one another, and to the wellbeing of each. Thus, the capacity to mutually provide selfobject experiences either supports or disrupts a couple's ongoing relational and individual experience. As Leone (2018) has recently written, "The concept of lifelong needs for relationships and experiences that are affirming, vitalizing, strengthening, comforting, regulating, and growth-promoting ... offers couples therapists a clearer vision or depiction of healthy relationships than do other branches of psychoanalysis" (pp. 391–392). Employing the notion of the selfobject, therapists can demonstrate, discuss, and help people learn how to be better partners to one another.

The second concept is the intersubjective perspective. Intersubjectivity refers to "the interaction between the differently organized subjective worlds" of two or more people (Stolorow & Atwood, 1992, p. 2). In our view, the most effective way to address the problems arising between partners is to help them see the ways in which their behavior is mutually created, emerging out of the interplay between their individually patterned, and largely nonconscious, relational selves. In the context of the intersubjective field, each partner's past experiences and her or his present behavior converge. This is often manifest in surface tension, which is underlined by unrecognized conflicts between partners' hopes and fears, their characteristic assumptions regarding others, and their particular modes for seeking connection and protecting against harm. The interplay among these often unrecognized organizing principles can obstruct a couple's capacity to provide mutually effective selfobject experiences for one another. The result is often observed in problematic trailing edge processes such as heightened aggression, distancing, devaluing, and other forms of stalemate. The role of the ISP therapist is to help each partner identify his or her internalized patterns and assumptions, or organizing principles, and to see how these may intersect with those of the partner.

The third concept, which encompasses the first two, is identifying, clarifying, and tracking the alterations between the couple's leading edge, which constitutes their more hopeful selfobject experiences, and the trailing edge counterpart. Simply put, the forward edge transference refers to those relational situations in which an individual has a sense of hopeful trust as a result of experiencing others as reliable selfobjects. The trailing edge transference refers to circumstances in which the dreads and fears emerging from painful past emotional circumstances are elicited by something happening in the present, causing the individual to feel fearful and mistrusting. In couples therapy, trailing edge features tend to predominate early in treatment, often appearing in the form of intense conflict andor withdrawal within the couple dyad. Each partner's trailing edge will usually include apprehensions about the therapist, in addition to his or her misgivings about the other partner.

In individual therapy, the practitioner may spend a great deal of time attempting to grasp a patient's unique subjectivity, as well as how it interacts with that of the therapist. The complexity of tracing the intersubjective interplay among participants increases in couples work. Most notably there are three people rather than two in the room. Thus the intersubjective field may encompass the relationship between partners, the relationship between the therapist and each partner, and the relationship between the therapist and the intricate patterning that characterizes the couple relationship. Trop has written,

> The focus of the couples therapist should be the multiple intersubjective fields that occur in conjoint therapy. The area of investigation of the couples therapist is the interaction between the subjective world of the two partners, as well as the meanings that occur at the interface of the interacting subjectivities of the therapist and each partner.
>
> (1997, p. 101)

Initially, and throughout treatment, the therapist's own trailing edge fears may become aroused, interfering with his or her capacity to provide a selfobject experience for the couple. Three common examples are: "Am I going to fail with these two?", "I want to escape from all this anger!", "I really don't feel like I am able to grasp where she or he is coming from!" The distinctive hopes and dreads of partners, and of the therapist, increasingly emerge as the therapy progresses and the various transferences vacillate between forward and trailing edge. If all goes well, the forward edge will remain more and more in the foreground as therapist and couple, as well as partners, become better able to provide selfobject experiences for one another.

The persistent identification and analysis of the trailing edge interactions, which over time leads to increased awareness and an expanding ability for each partner to sidestep his or her implicit patterns and assumptions in favor of the more positive forms of relating that will be experienced by the other as providing a self object experience. The ultimate role of the ISP couples therapist is to help partners understand such patterning, to identify it as it occurs, and to develop better ways to provide selfobject experiences for one another.

Although ISP couples therapy may appear similar to other forms of couples therapy, there are some important differences. In ISP, the therapist is much less likely to assign homework, carry out role plays, or proceed according to protocols such as those employed in Sue Johnson's Emotionally Focused Therapy for Couples (2004), Harville Hendrix's Imago Relationship Therapy (2005), or John Gottman's Gottman Method (1999). ISP is a psychoanalytic approach, albeit conducted from the perspective of Self Psychology and Intersubjectivity Theory. This generally means that more active interventions, when they happen, will be preceded by practices such as introspection, observation of self and other, and the mutual search for emotional meaning. This type of couples therapy attends more to understanding and reworking the processes arising between two individuals, as opposed to recommending behaviors designed to result in behavioral change. Not that such activities are never recommended in ISP couples therapy, but they depend more upon the therapist's ongoing understanding of what the couple might need in order to move forward. Thus, the emphases are: on the therapist's empathic attunement to the couple and their needs, on providing the couple with opportunities to have self object experiences through their relationship to the therapist, and on the couple's eventually learning to provide selfobject experiences more effectively for one another.

In response to the writings of Kohut, pioneers in the 1980s and 90s expanded the field of Self Psychology to include working with couples. Marion Solomon (1988) explored the role that unmet selfobject needs play in relationship conflict. Her work with couples emphasized developing empathy among therapist and partners, and between partners. She accordingly strove to create a nonjudgmental therapeutic environment in which members of couples could learn to provide selfobject experiences for one another. Around the same time, Philip Ringstrom (1994) introduced a Six-Step Model of Conjoint Therapy in which he applied Intersubjectivity Theory to Self-Psychologically informed couples therapy. Employing empathic attunement, asserting that "neither spouse has a more correct version of reality than the other" (p. 159), and connecting each partner's complaints to an early history of unmet selfobject yearnings, Ringstrom explicitly explored the manner in which each partner's unique way of experiencing the world interacted with and shaped the other's. In a similar fashion, David Shaddock (1998) made use of empathy to decipher symbolic areas of couple conflict. Employing a process of sustained inquiry in order to understand his couples' emotional worlds, he was able to uncover the hidden, unmet selfobject yearnings that frequently underlay their relationship distress. As Intersubjectivity Theory increasingly exerted an influence on Self Psychology, Martin Livingston (2007) developed a method of "sustained empathic focus" to help partners slow down, reach for deeper feelings, and understand their own trailing edge fears. Over time, what he termed their "dyadic capacity" (p. 316) was increased, as each became more self-expressive and better attuned to the other. Carla Leone (2008) found that "a lack of needed selfobject experience underlay most or all couples' presenting problems" (p. 80). She has sought to enhance her couples' relational skills by acting as a model for effective selfobject responsiveness in regards to both members of the couple. In her writings she has explicitly pointed to the importance of affirming any forward edge or "growth promoting" behaviors as they appear in the therapeutic work (p. 87).

In the case examples that follow, each of us details her way of approaching couples from an Intersubjective Self Psychological perspective. Although each psychotherapist was guided by Intersubjective Self Psychology, or ISP, each has her own style of working, in keeping with the idea that each therapist's unique subjectivity shapes the therapeutic exchange in an ongoing fashion. The nature of such exchanges was correspondingly influenced by the subjectivity of each partner and by the particular dynamics of their relationship.

Nancy Hicks' couple

Introduction

The case of Ty and Annie highlights two activities essential to working with couples within the framework of Intersubjective Self Psychology. The first involves addressing the complex interplay among the relational patterns and expectancies each partner brings to the mix. Ty and Annie initially sought help for the difficulties they had collaborating as parents. They subsequently understood that their parenting problems were symptomatic of a more fundamental issue: an ongoing impasse in which the selfobject needs of both partners were repeatedly frustrated. Each partner hoped to be heard by the other, and to have his or her essential worthiness recognized. These longings took on a different cast within partners, reflecting the contours of their respective selves. While Ty sought to be fully seen and accepted without criticism, more in line with the mirroring aspect of selfobject experience,

Annie hungered to have her needs register with Ty, thereby experiencing him as more intimately protective of her and of their son. Her hopes were especially focused along the idealizing aspect of selfobject experience.

Far too often, however, a trailing edge transference characterized their interactions. As Annie felt her needs were unseen by Ty she became increasingly angry and critical, while Ty, feeling misunderstood, focused desperately on regaining Annie's acceptance, and thus his tie to her, rather than on providing what she needed from him. The interaction among these themes led both partners to adopt the behaviors that had served them earlier in development: Annie angrily distanced and gave up trying, resigning herself to never being heard. Ty tried even more fiercely to please, anticipating he would finally be seen for who he was. Thus they reinforced one another's worst fears, as well as the self-protective stances that arose from them. My own subjectivity was a factor in how their impasse came to light and was addressed. For example, my leading edge desire was to experience myself as an effective therapist, one who was uniquely able to help this couple come to a better place with one another. When I felt thwarted in this, I frequently feared I was not up to the task, becoming overly active with the partners in hopes of making them, and thus myself, feel better. This often interfered with their experience of me as an empathic, listening presence. When over time I was able to come to terms with this trailing edge issue in myself, I was more able to attune to them. I could then provide the framework for them to explore issues deeply, ultimately learning to recognize for themselves when they were falling into trailing edge interactions.

The second activity of couple therapy, an indispensable aspect of carrying out the first, is helping each partner uncover, experience, and express unacknowledged affect. As Stolorow and Stolorow (1987) wrote, "the need to disavow, dissociate, or otherwise defensively encapsulate affect arises in consequence of the failure of the early milieu to provide the requisite ... responsiveness to the child's emotional states" (p. 74). When these self-protective emotional adaptations emerge in an adult relationship, they must be understood as arising out of a partner's fear that "emerging feeling states will meet with the same faulty responsiveness" (p. 74) they received from the caregivers. Careful mutual exploration of such trailing edge fears and their resulting adaptatons will render partners more able to share their vulnerabilities with one another in the present. Integral to this process, as always, is the therapist's capacity to maintain an ongoing empathic connection with both members of the couple.

Clinical case

Ty and Annie presented as two very different kinds of people. From the very first moments they spent in my office, Ty was wrought up, edgy, and anxious. His gaze often wandered to his partner, as if trying to gauge how she was responding. Throughout the hour he spoke in a pressured fashion, his eyes beseeching me, and/or Annie, to understand. For all this, when

Annie spoke, Ty usually found a way to cut her short, claiming she was mistaken, or that she had misunderstood him. His nervous monologues took over the relational space. Apparently a woman of few words, Annie sat back in her chair, silent and sulking. When asked for her perspective, she shrugged her shoulders, claiming she wasn't talking much and didn't really want to try, because Ty never listened anyway. This seemed true enough. It was somehow paradoxical that Ty appeared so anxious to connect with Annie, yet made it so very hard for her to insert herself into the dialogue.

On the flip side, Annie's behavior was unsettling. She reminded me of a rebellious adolescent to whom nothing could be said that wouldn't be taken as offensive. The two of them were clearly locked into a trailing edge-dominated pattern that was going to be difficult to address. It was our first session, and already I was feeling unsure of myself, which reflected the activation of my own trailing edge: the sense that I was not going to be competent enough to help this couple. To me, Annie was intimidating. I felt impotent in the face of her scornful style, alternating between wanting to reprimand her and hoping she wouldn't say something mean-spirited to me. Ty's verbal barrage was overwhelming to me. I wanted to run away. I pictured a wall surrounding me, forming a barrier between myself and his needful anxiety. Yet I knew I must not allow my vulnerabilities to shape my response to them, which would involve my reverting to an inclination to try too hard. As the session proceeded, I worked on adjusting my stance to one of calm listening, seeking to understand what might be going on within these two people, and how they made each other feel.

My first step was to try and help them become more comfortable with me and with the concept of therapy as a safe space in which both of them could express themselves. I asked each to give me a perspective on their parenting problems. They looked at one another for a moment. Not so predictably, Annie took the lead. She said that Ty didn't take her concerns seriously. For example, she had suggested to him repeatedly that their 8-year-old son, Elliot, was behaving too aggressively at home and at school. But Ty had pooh-poohed it, claiming she was overreacting. After all, he'd said, Elliot was just a kid. When the school called to report Elliot's having bullied another child, Annie was distraught, and angry at Ty for not having taken her seriously.

That was as far as Annie got. Ty jumped in, vehemently protesting that he was listening to her *now*! Annie slumped into her chair, rolled her eyes, and was silent. I asked her what was going on. At first she said, "I don't want to talk about it!" She glared. I wasn't sure if it were at me or simply away from Ty and out into the blank space of the room. Either way, another trailing edge fear arose in me. Fearing her disdain, I was hesitant to press her further. Then, miraculously, she helped me out. "This is what always happens! This is why I don't even bother! He doesn't let me get a word in edgewise. It always ends up being about him." Then, to him,

"This isn't about you, Ty, it's about our son!" Ty jumps in again: "I was just trying to help. You make it sound like I'm this awful person. I'm sorry I didn't listen earlier ..." Annie: "And you're doing it again now!"

Seeing that their circular exchange was about to take flight, and feeling a need to calm myself as well as them, I stopped them, saying "Let's take a minute and talk about what just happened. Is this how things tend to go between you?" Annie: "Yes. He gives me no space at all. There's no room for me to express myself. He just takes over." Ty once again interrupts; "That's not fair! I'm always concerned about what you think ... !" I gently stop him, believing it necessary to intervene in repetitive sequences of conflict early on in treatment so as to protect each partner, create an atmosphere conducive to reflection, and begin to help each individual see his or her role in the cycle. Me: "Ty, you have to wait your turn and give Annie time to talk. You'll get your turn. Try to hear what she's saying."

If Annie's withdrawn behavior was a reaction to never getting in a word edgewise, Ty was fighting mightily to redeem himself in her eyes. He seemed desperate to stay connected to her, disputing any implication that he was unworthy. I found myself feeling badly for him. Throughout my life I had struggled with my fear of having a woman be angrily critical of me. This was one of my trailing edge apprehensions, and I deeply identified with his dilemma. As the session progressed I reminded myself of the need to stay empathically connected to both partners. I also cautioned myself that Annie was just as vulnerable as Ty, but was displaying it differently. Steering myself back to my leading edge, I focused on creating a safe emotional environment for both. In order to accomplish this I tried to slow down the pace of their interactions while encouraging them to be self-reflective rather than reactive.

I asked each to say more about how they felt in these difficult exchanges. Ty began.

TY: "It used to be that we could talk about anything. Now, she doesn't even seem to like me. And it seems like everything I do is wrong. She's always been a very good listener, but in the past year or two she doesn't listen much at all."
ME: "And how does that leave you feeling?"
TY: "Scared. Scared that I'm going to lose her. I can't seem to get through to her." (Annie listened quietly. Her posture softened a bit. She seemed to be taking in what Ty was saying. In sharing his fears, he had let Annie in, creating a moment when they could have a sense of closeness. For a brief period dread was displaced by hope.)

In retrospect, I see that this slight break in their impasse gave me an opportunity to calm my own anxiety by pointing out the behavioral sequence I'd earlier observed. It's an example of how my trailing edge unease with not feeling competent can move me to try too hard. Thus I become active rather than helping partners reflect on their feelings and experience.

ME: "From where I sit, I think the two of you have gotten into an interaction that just keeps repeating itself. You seem to be trying harder and harder to GET Annie to connect with you, Ty. Annie, you seem to respond by receding further and further."

They both nod in agreement, but say nothing. I ask,

ME: "Does this kind of pattern feel familiar to either of you in any way? For instance, Ty, is there some reason you might keep trying so hard to connect with Annie, even when she's giving you the message she wants you to give her some space? Maybe something from your own history?" (I observe myself focusing on Ty first, doubtless because he's less daunting to me.)

He tilts his head.

TY: "Maybe ..." (I turn to Annie, but before I have a chance to speak, she laughs and shakes her head.)
ANNIE: "I'm not going *there*! I'll talk about what's happening now, but I don't want to talk about the past."
TY ECHOES HER: "She really doesn't want to talk about the past."

I feel a slight queasiness in my stomach, a pang of fear, perhaps. It seems that in this matter, Annie's exploration of her past, they are both aligned. Is the fear I'm feeling my own, Ty's, or something disavowed in Annie? Or all three? Annie surely has misgivings about allowing herself to experience the emotional pain of her past, but even more, she doesn't anticipate she'll get much help with such feelings if she tries to explore them with us now. Thus her trailing edge apprehensions, that her needs will yet again be deemed unimportant and thus remain unheard, keep her from opening up. Her presentation, however, belies her sense of vulnerability. She appears belligerent, even aggressive. Ty's almost hypnotic echoing of her words quite possibly reflects his concern that exploring the past will make Annie upset, which she might subsequently take out on him. Or perhaps he really is implicitly supporting her in protecting herself from something which frightens her. Either way, my trailing edge has been aroused. I briefly fantasize about myself in relation to my own parents, the ultimate triangle. Deeply identifying with my father, I always counted on his support. In that moment with Annie and Ty, it was terrifying to imagine them *both* angry with me. As the session moves on I remind myself that I am the therapist, not a child, and that I have the capacity to manage the situation as I might not once have.

After our first meeting I continued to feel uneasy. I had only a preliminary understanding of what was going on with Ty and Annie. A sense of vulnerability arising from my trailing edge anxieties had been sparked. And the couple's volatility left me feeling somewhat dysregulated emotionally. Often the intense emotion flowing between two highly aroused and antipathetic individuals is difficult for a therapist to absorb. When affects related to the therapist's own trailing edge are stirred as well, it becomes even more difficult for him or her to contain and manage the emotional response. Between sessions, I consciously worked to understand and compose my emotional state. Mainly I was feeling overwhelmed and not good enough, but I also struggled with my own fears of being abandoned by them.

I correspondingly tried to exercise greater empathy in regard to each partner. What had I learned from interacting with and observing them? What were my internal reactions telling me? In light of Ty's frantic attempts to connect with Annie despite her rebuffs, and Annie's stubborn unwillingness to engage, I imagined that both of them must have had some painful emotional experiences earlier in life. I also hypothesized that each was capable of a wider range of emotions when not engaged with the other. Over time their intersubjective pattern had come to restrict their capacity to interact more freely with one another. Of the two I found Ty easier, although I could see how his anxious verbose style could be off-putting, and how it might be experienced by Annie as self-focused. He wore his vulnerability on his sleeve, yet he didn't really listen to her. I felt I could explore this with him, but Annie presented more of a challenge. I struggled with my reaction to her. Her refusal to explore the past left me feeling pushed away, and also devalued. I was sorely tempted to try to "convince" her to dig deep in therapy in much the same way I'd seen Ty try to convince her to hear him. Nonetheless, I knew my response was rooted in painful aspects of my own history. I could not allow this trailing edge issue to shape my interactions with Annie.

Annie opened the subsequent session by asking to discuss their handling of Elliot's problems in school. She said she felt Ty was too easy on their son. Instead of being stern with Elliot, Ty empathized too much with the difficulties he was facing. I asked Annie to give an example, but before she could reply, Ty burst in, "But you're so hard on him!" Annie responded, "He needs some self discipline! And there you go again, not letting me speak!" She turns to me, "You see!" I resisted the temptation to nod a sympathetic "yes." Suddenly I was relating to Annie's side of their experience! This made me feel I was getting somewhere with my own self-exploration. I turned to Ty.

NH: (Sensing there is a trailing edge dread involved.) "Ty, let's explore your feelings about this a little more. I see what Annie is saying. You do tend to interrupt her. Let's talk about what goes on for you that it's hard not to jump in when she's speaking."

TY: "She's so critical. When I hear her talking about Elliot in that tone of voice, I want to protect him."
NH: "What is the tone of voice? Can you describe what you're hearing?"
TY: "She sounds kind of, I don't know, cold. It's a little scary. I think Elliot's a little frightened of her."
ANNIE: "That's not true! He is not afraid of me! You're imagining that!"
NH: (Not wanting to pull attention away from what appears to be a deepening affective moment.) "Just a second Annie. I'm going to come back to you, but let me finish this with Ty first. You okay with that?" (She nods, apparently reassured that she'll be heard. I see her capacity to wait as a sign that she has gained trust in me and is beginning to experience me as a selfobject.) "Ty, so two things here. One, you think Elliot may be bothered by his mother's tone of voice, may find her critical." (Ty nods.) "Second, you might identify with this feeling." (Ty nods again.) "So tell me more about that second feeling, that she's critical of you." (The mood has changed some in the room. Both have become quieter, I believe because each feels more confident of my attunement.)
TY: "Well, it just feels that no matter what I do, she doesn't like it. Actually, that she doesn't *like* me anymore." (Silence. He sighs.)
NH: "That's been hard for you." (Silence.)
TY: "Yes. It makes me feel like I've lost her."
NH: "Maybe that's why you try so hard to get her to see your side of things. It's like you're trying to convince her, to win her back."
TY: (His body sagging, he nods his head.)
NH: (After a moment of silence.) "Annie, is this bringing anything up for you?"
ANNIE: "Well I feel sad that he feels that way. I don't *want* him to feel that way. But this has been going on so long, I don't know how *I* feel anymore."

The mood in the room has moved from antipathy to sadness. As Martin Livingston's work suggests (2007), helping partners reach for vulnerable feelings enables them to be more accessible to self and other. I believe this was made possible once I understood and internally addressed my own trailing edge fears, and thus was better able to sustain empathic connection to Annie and to Ty.

Over the next months, we continue to explore their feelings about the relationship. In part because they've felt heard by me, both partners have become more able to hear and provide selfobject experiences for one another. In most sessions Annie and Ty return to their familiar interactive cycle, but they have become increasingly able to stop themselves before they spiral out of control. Although we have explored very little of her past beyond the basic knowledge that she was the child of a difficult, protracted divorce, Annie has become more accessible during our sessions. Sometimes she laughs or smiles, saying that she really cares about Ty and wishes she could feel differently about being married to him. I find myself feeling warm towards her. Ty seems more able to check himself before speaking, and more content to sit and listen, perhaps because Annie is less prone to be critical of him. Facing his own human frailties is not so difficult for him. Through a process of sustained empathic connection, the three of us are now operating on the forward edge. This moves the treatment ahead.

According to Kohut, empathy is both a capacity for connecting with other human beings, and a "mode of observation" (Kohut, 1981, p. 542). My own empathic awareness tells me that, without overlooking each partner's concerns and vulnerabilities, I should now begin to focus on further delineating the intersubjective field that continue to shape their interactions. This slight shift is based on my observation that Annie and Ty still tend to lapse into their familiar patterns, and that I need to more directly address this. Keeping in mind Self Psychology's emphasis on the adaptive nature of "defenses," I hope to more precisely highlight self-preservative or hurtful behaviors as they occur, stopping the action to help partners explore the trailing edge factors that activated such behaviors. The following clinical example illustrates this shift in emphasis.

In a subsequent session we concentrate on a time earlier in their relationship, when Ty was preoccupied with establishing what turned out to be a very successful career. Annie recalled having begged Ty on numerous occasions to spend more time at home with her and Elliot. She was lonely, and it was getting increasingly difficult for her to manage work and childcare. Ty did not seem to pay much attention to her pleas. Eventually Annie decided to quit her job altogether. She was aware of feeling hurt and angry that her entreaties didn't register with Ty.

NH: "Do you think that is still having an effect on how you feel towards Ty now?"
ANNIE: "Oh definitely. I get mad when I think about it. He just acted like it was up to me to manage on my own. My career, my needs and feelings, they didn't matter much!"
NH: "So you're still pretty angry."
ANNIE: "Yes! And I'm not going to let something like that happen again!"
NH: (to Ty.) "Are you aware of how upset Annie has been about this?"
ANNIE: "Oh he knows. I've told him."
TY: "Yes, she's told me. But what am I supposed to do? It's over and done!"(I decide not to respond to his sense of being hopelessly misunderstood, but this could have been another point of intervention. At the time I was more focused on encouraging Annie to explore her feelings.)
NH: "Annie, can you say more about how this has affected you?"
ANNIE: "At some point I think I just gave up."
NH: "Gave up?"

ANNIE: "I just started handling things myself. I knew what I said wasn't going to register. So I quit my job and focused on Elliot and our home life. I didn't mind that part so much. I mean, I love Elliot." (She looks down. Appears sad. I weigh whether to further attune to her sadness, or, sensing there is more to this, press her gently.)

NH: "But you just stopped protesting. I wonder why you did that?"

ANNIE: "What? I really tried to tell Ty. More than once."

NH: "I believe you. But I wonder why you didn't up the ante when he didn't hear you. Maybe yell really, really loud until he couldn't ignore it?"

ANNIE: "I don't know. I guess I just figured there was no point."

NH: "I think we have to examine your assumption that Ty would never hear you. Maybe he would not have heard you no matter how loud you yelled. But I'm thinking this might connect to something else important in your life. Some other time when you felt you'd never be heard."

ANNIE: "I don't know what you mean."

NH: "What about your parent's divorce? I have the impression you were shuttled around from home to home, even though it made you very unhappy."

ANNIE: "Well *that's for sure!* No one listened to me then, either!"

NH: "So maybe you've been adopting some of the same strategy now. Just keep going, even if your needs aren't being met. Even though you're not being heard."

ANNIE: "That's possible." (Silence.)

NH: "You seem sad." (Silence.) "I'm wondering where your anger and sadness about this gets channeled. I think they might seep out in what Ty hears as your critical voice. Maybe also in keeping yourself more distant from him, more self-sufficient. That way you make sure it never happens again."

ANNIE: "That could be, too." (Silence.)

NH: "Ty, do you have any thoughts?"

TY: (Quietly.) "I feel badly that I didn't listen to her. I don't know why. I don't know what I was thinking …"

ANNIE: (angrily) "You were thinking about *yourself!*"

TY: "I guess that's true. I thought you were okay. And I wanted to do well. To provide for my family, and do well." (Silence.)

This session opened the door for Annie to explore more of her past, and for Ty to think about how he might have overlooked her needs in the interest of pursuing his own goals. In subsequent sessions Annie recalled her parent's very contentious divorce, which included a custody battle over their four children. She described the parents as having been so wrapped up in their animosity towards one another that they paid little heed to the impact of the divorce on Annie and her siblings. As a result of the divorce the children had been forced to give up their home, their schools, and many of their beloved activities and friends. Annie learned to rely even more on herself than she had before.

NH: "Did you ever find yourself wishing you could have more? For instance, wishing you could have your family back? Or wishing your parents would be more attentive to you?"
ANNIE: "Oh yes. But after a while I just felt resentful. I had no respect for them. I think I'd lost all hope they could really be parents to me."
NH: "That sounds familiar. Do you think you've felt something similar with Ty?"
ANNIE: (Silence.) "Probably, yes."

In joint sessions such as these, both partners have moved further from their earlier inflexible and antipathetic positions. Each is more able to be self-reflective, to listen intently, and to extend empathy to the other. This arises out of a sense of hopefulness that the other will continuing to inhabit their forward edge, more reliably creating selfobject experiences within the context of their relationship. The vignette below conveys a core piece of work Ty did around that time. It illustrates how, within an attuned context, he became more fully able to experience his present affect and connect it with his past, which ultimately helped him to stay centered in the here and now, thus making him a better partner.

TY: "I'm trying manage my feelings better. I know I tend to go on and on. And lose it. But I can't seem to rein myself in, especially when it comes to Annie."
NH: "Have you had any thoughts about why that happens, about what happens when you get so emotional?"
TY: "Well, my family was like that. People were always yelling and having lots of feelings."
NH: "What was that like for you?"
TY: "It was awful. You never knew when somebody was going to explode. My parents fought all the time. My dad in particular was really unpredictable, and scary when he yelled at you."
NH: "That must have been really distressing."
TY: "Yes. There was never any physical violence, but it felt like there could be. So I was always scared something would happen. I spent a lot of my time placating."
NH: "Placating ... who?"
TY: "Well, everyone really."
NH: "You were afraid of your mom as well?"
TY: "Not in the same way. She would yell, but I never worried she would hit me."
ANNIE: "But your mom was really cold. You need to tell her about your mom."

TY: "Yes, well I never quite knew where she stood. She never really intervened when my dad lost it. And she never comforted us or anything when he upset us. We'd just sit in our rooms and shake."

ANNIE: "Even now she's very distant. You visit her all the time, but she's never very warm to you, or to Elliot."

TY: (Silence.) "I think I felt like neither of my parents really liked me. I still don't know if they like me. I think they love me, but I'm not sure they like me."

NH: (Leaving some room for this to sink in.) "How do you think this has affected you?"

TY: "I definitely think it's made me more driven. I have more of a need to prove myself."

NH: "What about in relation to Annie?"

TY: "I guess I worry that she doesn't like me either."

ANNIE: "But you didn't seem all that worried about that at first! You didn't seem to care about pleasing me then!"

NH: (Silence. Looks at Ty.)

TY: "No. I just assumed you'd be okay. I thought I'd finally found someone who would be there for me, and I didn't think too much about your needs. That was my mistake." (More silence.)

NH: "But you began to pursue Annie when you felt her withdraw, and when she behaved more as if she didn't approve of you."

TY: "No, as if she didn't *like* me!"

NH: "So it's hard to resist trying to convince her of your worthiness when she doesn't seem to like you anymore. You try to talk her out of it."

TY: "I think that might be what I'm doing. I'm not aware of any thoughts when I'm doing it."

NH: "What if you stop yourself and imagine not trying to convince her. What happens?"

TY: "I can't stand the feeling. I can't describe it."

NH: "Just sit for a minute longer. Try to imagine what it feels like." (Silence.)

TY: "It's kind of ... empty, alone. Not good."

NH: (Waiting a bit longer to see if there's more.) "So then you *really* feel disconnected from her. I'm thinking that trying to *get* her to see your perspective is your way of trying to reconnect. Maybe you worry that if you don't keep trying, nothing will happen. That Annie won't seek you out and meet you halfway."

TY: "That's about right." (Silence.)

Livingston's couple

Introduction

Eric and Jenny appeared to want more from their relationship than simply seeing each other on the weekend. Each of them hoped to resolve enough of their difficulties that they would feel comfortable purchasing a home or apartment together. They wanted help exploring their hopes and fears about living together. Although not verbalized, I suspected that they hoped for greater intimacy. Each one had different backgrounds and differing views of what constituted a good life. Highlights from the first year of a two-year therapy are detailed.

Clinical case

Eric and Jenny, long term girl and boy-friends (their words), both about 60, wished to explore and overcome their fears of intimacy, concretized as their inability to follow through on living together. A large, soft-spoken man with dark skin, Eric owned his home in the Bronx and had begun creating a small dental practice in one room of his home. He chose to work at home three days a week, purposely allowing time to learn hypnosis. He hoped that hypnosis would enhance his practice as well as allow quiet, alone time for himself. Ever since he was a youngster, Eric required time away from both work and his few good friends or he would become, in his words, "too stimulated." Born a decade after his siblings, he was raised and doted upon by his mother, two sisters and a grandmother and grandfather. Consequently, he received lots of love. His raising and the stature of his family in the Bronx provided a strong sense of himself. Jenny's background differed greatly from Eric's. As a child, mostly ignored by her parents, too often she fended for herself. Now she lives in Brooklyn in her home that she purchased, pretty far from Eric's place. Jenny, a social worker, enjoys helping her clients; what's more, when she's home she happily helps friends and neighbors.

First Session: Eric, who made the appointment with me for the couple, began:

ERIC: "I'm afraid that if we lived together, my small world would be disrupted by Jenny's chaotic family. For example, if any of her family or friends call – even in the middle of the night – she immediately goes out and helps them."

Eric forthrightly let us know his trailing edge fear, indirectly telling us what he hoped for – that Jenny would change, choosing to spend time with him more often than with her friends. He usually called Jenny at least once a week and drove from the Bronx to her place in Brooklyn most weekends – no small feat since they each lived in different boroughs outside of Manhattan. Eric definitely seemed to want their relationship to work, spurring his leading edge hope that he and Jenny would live together.

JENNY: "In the past, I've been taken over by strong men, including members of my family and two different husbands. I'm determined not to let that happen again!"

She continued, speaking poignantly about her trailing edge "fear of being swallowed." Jenny also wondered if she, and by implication Eric, would be good-enough partners, giving her pause about moving in together. In general, Jenny seemed pessimistic about the likelihood of their remaining together in the long run, evidencing a strong trailing edge of doubt. Although her doubts and uneasiness appeared problematic for them as a couple, I viewed her ability to speak up for herself as a leading edge.

LL: "Jenny, part of what I hear is that you would feel safer if both of you worked on your own stuff before living together. Is that correct?" (She nodded definitively.)

Within the intersubjective space surrounding the three of us throughout the first session, neither Eric nor Jenny were shy about voicing their thoughts and fears as well as the kind of life they each desired. As a result, I liked and admired both of them, thus creating my leading edge of hope for the couple as well as for our working together. However, because I had little idea about how we three might work out the couple's spending more time together, let alone live together, a trailing edge of doubt was also evident to me internally.

Several weeks later Jenny had cataract surgery and, at her request, Eric stayed with her. Each of them had looked forward to his being there for the week. A few days after Jenny's surgery, she began feeling much better. Eric left to keep a doctor's appointment, unwittingly not thinking about letting her know, either by telling her directly or leaving a note. Worse, because he was tired after the appointment, he returned to his own home to rest, still without contacting Jenny. Understandably, Jenny first worried and then became angry about his thoughtlessness, creating a trailing edge of discouragement and anger. She called and left me a voicemail. Like Jenny, I too was both surprised and perturbed by Eric's thoughtless behavior – my trailing edge that shook me up a bit.

In our next session, Jenny used most of the time to "vent" about her frustration with Eric, declaring that she was angrier and more upset with him than usual, implicitly suggesting that she was often upset with him.

JENNY: "When Eric was with me, he took better care of me than anyone had my whole life! But after the first few days we were home together, he was gone. Not a note, not a word. He didn't even say 'goodbye' or where he was going or when he'd be back. He was gone for several days!"

LL: (Incredulous and aware that in her situation I'd likely react similarly though I tried to remain calm with the couple.) "Jenny, your feelings are very understandable. And of course Eric's being with you stirred up lots of yearning as well as hope that he would continue to be so helpful and loving. That must have made it so much worse when he disappeared."

Noticing their faces light up with my explanation, I continued:

LL: "When he left unexpectedly after being with and helping you a great deal, Jenny, but then stayed away longer than maybe either of you anticipated, I wonder if besides being mad, you also worried about what might have happened; maybe you were also concerned that you might still need some help and reassurance from him."

As the session wound down, I looked directly at both of them and stated: "Jenny does *not* want to be the leader for both of you; she wants you to help with decisions at least part of the time, Eric." Jenny smiled, nodding.

Afterwards, I realized that seeing Eric reminded me of a lover I'd had decades ago, when I lived in a semi-southern state before moving to New York City. That relationship ended in part because each of us tired of the difficulties we encountered as a "mixed" couple – my pale skin contrasting with his dark skin. Too many people stared, looked puzzled or worse, verbally disapproved of us. When my lover became increasingly unreliable, we parted. After moving to New York City, I was both pleased and almost flabbergasted, not only at the wide variety of skin coloring but also that so many people seemed blase about it. My first partner's coloring, and his eventual unreliability, reminded me of Eric's intermittent unreliability as well as his skin color. I hoped and wanted to believe that Eric ultimately differed in important ways from my "ex."

A few months after our first session, Jenny and Eric briefly mentioned what it was like when Eric spent the prior week with Jenny after her second cataract surgery.

JENNY: "It was *great* having Eric here last week; I really missed him after our week together. Especially at night in bed. I wished he was still with me."

Her statements warmed my heart; I was really pleased for both of them. Gently, I asked each of them what they wanted within the relationship.

JENNY: "I prefer spending more time together, seeing how that goes, but it never happens."
ERIC: "The way my brain works, when I'm with Jenny, I'm completely engrossed in her. I *lust* after her. But then I can't focus on other things I want and need to do – like the hypnotism courses I want to take."
LL: "Eric, how can we help you get some of your work done at her place, since you both want that? Maybe try to shut off part of your brain when you're with Jenny? Then you can stay longer *and* also get some work done?"

The couple became lively and open, playing around with spending five days together, and two days apart. All three of us were pleased, enjoying our separate and collective leading edges of hope within our intersubjective field.

Months later, when the couple continued seeing one another only on the weekend, Jenny wondered out loud about getting together in midweek.

ERIC: "That's a great idea; I never thought about meeting on a workday!"
JENNY: "I'm glad you like the idea. At first, I assumed I shouldn't suggest that we meet on your day off."

They were clearly pleased with Jenny's suggestion, as was I, although nothing came of it for months. Nor did they seem interested a couple weeks later when I asked about their taking up Jenny's suggestion. My disappointment at their not following up with meeting mid-week plus their moving at a snail's pace created my trailing edge of doubt that I would be able to help them and/or that their relationship would remain intermittent. Similarly, I didn't think that asking about why they hadn't met mid-week would be helpful at that time because I assumed they weren't quite ready to make the effort to see each other more often.

Weeks later, Eric invited Jenny to see his place; she traveled up to his apartment and spent the weekend. Unfortunately, not only was the location of his place difficult for Jenny to find time and travel to Eric, but his home was *very* messy. Together they decided that Eric would continue going to Jenny's place.

LL: "What a shame it didn't turn out as well as you each hoped."

Inwardly, I was shocked and disappointed that Eric did not make much of an attempt to clean up even his living room or bedroom despite his eagerness for Jenny to see and stay at his home; taken all together, that created a trailing edge of my disappointment in Eric. Moreover, it seemed as though he thought only of himself; that thought created an unwelcome trailing edge for me about whether or not I would be able to help them feel okay either about continuing as a couple or, at some point, one or both of them deciding to break off their relationship. They were both similar to one another yet also differed from each other in important ways.

A social worker by profession, Jenny worked throughout the week. Assigned a variety of people each day within a large area in Brooklyn, she helped each client with whatever was needed and wrote up the findings for herself and the agency. She was good at and enjoyed her job, in part because she cared about the people she saw, thus creating her leading edge of feeling good about herself and her work. Therefore, she didn't she mind having so little time during the week for anything else.

Several weeks later, I asked:

LL: "What's it like for each of you when you're together at Jenny's place?" (They described much of what they did together: going out for a drive, taking a walk together or going uptown, even seeing a movie once in a while.)
ERIC: "I like being at Jenny's place. It's calming. But I wish we spent more time *together* on our weekends."
LL: "What do you mean?"
ERIC: "Whenever anyone asks for her help, she does it immediately. I don't like being alone so *often* when I'm at her place."
JENNY: (speaking almost defiantly.) "If my friends need help, I'm *going* to help. I *need* to help them. Eric, if you don't like it, you can always leave, go home."
LL: "I wonder if we can find a compromise so that each of you would feel better when Eric is at your place."
JENNY: (more calmly.) "There's nothing we can do differently. If my friends need me, I *have* to help then. My only free time is on the weekend. Eric and I do plenty of things together then. I *love* having him here. He calms me."
ERIC: "It's okay with me. I *like* being with you, Jenny."

After the fiasco of Jenny's visit in Eric's home, for a while Eric seemed willing to do almost anything to make their relationship work, thus creating a leading edge of hope and desire. Nevertheless, he was afraid that his small boundaried sphere would be too disrupted by Jenny's chaotic family and friends, constituting his trailing edge of fear and uncertainty.

I understood the important similarities and differences between the couple, yet I was concerned about the outcome. Each member of the couple was smart, cared deeply about some people in their lives and wanted to give to others. Nevertheless, they were also very different from the other regarding free time. Eric's need for quiet as well as time alone at his home were in direct contrast to Jenny's thriving on – perhaps needing to –help others, not only at work but also family and good friends, even in the dead of night. I knew that it gave her not only purpose but also a strong sense of being wanted and included, unlike her experience as a youngster. Regretfully, her way of life at home helping others whenever they asked created an impediment for Eric's living with Jenny, often creating a mild trailing edge of disappointment for Eric. Though I was not a fan of Jenny's spending so much time apart from Eric during their weekends together, I was unable to change that. I tried to persuade myself that it seemed "good enough" to each of them. Nevertheless, within the intersubjective space encircling the three of us in that moment, I was aware of my trailing edge of feeling neither strong enough nor savvy enough to help them weigh their time together that might work out better for them. Because neither member of the couple seemed very concerned, inwardly I breathed deeply and tried to relax, hoping to rid myself of my trailing edge of concern about helping them. Once in a great while, the couple's togetherness worked out wonderfully.

When a horrific snowstorm occurred on a weekend that they spent at Jenny's place, Jenny received a call from her daughter asking for help. Eric tried unsuccessfully to dissuade Jenny from going because of the storm, creating a trailing edge of fearing the storm and fearing for Jenny's wellbeing. Nevertheless, despite his fears and at his own insistence, he drove Jenny to her daughter's house and remained there until she was ready to leave rather than worrying about her driving alone. Because Eric found a solution that assuaged his concern for both Jenny and himself, his leading edge hope overtook his initial trailing edge concern. Moreover, their working it out together helped him feel much better about both himself and Jenny. His thoughtfulness and generosity also created a leading edge of pleasure for Jenny, grateful for Eric's help and support when she needed it. Moreover, they're finding a solution that was successful for each of them gave me more hope for them as a couple, in turn creating my leading edge within our intersubjective arena.

Much later that year, in session, Jenny voiced concern that Eric arrived at her place later and later, as if he didn't want to spend much time with her. Eric adamantly disagreed.

ERIC: "I get caught up doing things and either forget the time or try get to a good stopping point before I go to see you."

He insisted that he enjoyed his time with her, creating a leading edge of pleasure both for him and for her as well. He also said he usually felt sad when it was time to leave: a mixture of his feeling good about being there and sorry to leave, thus simultaneously experiencing both leading and trailing edges. Like Eric, I felt a bit sad yet also heartened by their exchange; I was pleased that each of them spoke up about their fears as well as what they wanted from each other; hence, almost simultaneously, I experienced both a trailing edge fear that they were going to be angry and unresolved with each other, swiftly followed by my leading edge pleasure that they were able to find a solution that worked.

Weeks later, both Jenny and Eric were pessimistic about their relationship, each one experiencing a trailing edge of pessimism. Disappointed, I was quite annoyed with myself about how "pie in the sky" I'd been about their relationship – thus, incurring a strong trailing edge. Silently, I talked to myself in an effort to stop beating myself up, simultaneously trying to listen to and be with the couple. It was almost as if I were on a roller coaster with its ups and downs.

Conclusion

As seen from the preceding examples, each couple presented with somewhat different problems, and each analyst differed in how she approached her work. Over time, Louisa and her couple established a high level of trust, with the therapy proceeding collaboratively. Forward movement occurred very slowly, although it occurred in a reciprocal fashion involving all three persons.

Nancy and her couple also established a level of selfobject responsiveness which served as the foundation for the work they did. The therapy involved intense collaboration among the three, but in contrast to the first case, Nancy spoke up more often even when it was unnerving for her. She actively engaged and challenged the couple when she believed it was necessary. Using questions as well as pointing out the effect of one member's behavior upon the other, she helped ensure that all three of them understood their hopes and fears, and how these affected their ability to form a secure connection.

Chapter 12

Sexuality and Intersubjective Self Psychology
What matters

Gordon Powell[1]

I became a self psychologist to be like the self psychologists I knew—thoughtful, open, smart, and generous. As a gay man, I knew it was difficult at that time to find well-trained and compassionate psychoanalysts who were also gay affirming. I wanted to be one. I wanted to build a private practice open to everyone—a neighborhood practice, as I think of it—but one especially welcoming to gay men.

As I steeped myself in self psychology, I found its basic assumptions about human nature and the curative process sensible and appealing, and my regard has only grown with deepening familiarity. Heinz Kohut, the father of self psychology, broke from his idol Sigmund Freud partly because they viewed human nature very differently. As I will describe in detail, self psychology is built on Kohut's assumptions of the best about people, and I love this about self psychology.

I came to adulthood as a gay man in the 1970s, when sex seemed to be everywhere. In those years of the Sexual Revolution, gay pride was coming into popular awareness, and most Americans seemed to be accepting, discussing, and enjoying the manifold pleasures of sex. Americans in general and gay men in particular were alive to a newfound freedom to explore their sexual desires.

By the 1990s, though, when I began studying and practicing self psychology, AIDS was slaughtering gay men. Sex and sexuality were again very much on our minds, but for much darker reasons. Sex had become terrifying.

To my great dismay, self psychology had little to say about sexuality, though, because Kohut had demoted sexuality and aggression from their exalted status in Freud's theory, where they had reigned as the most important determinants of human motivation. For Freud and his followers, belief in the centrality of the sexual and aggressive drives was the ticket to admission to the psychoanalytic club. Kohut formed another psychoanalytic club, which made attention to the self[2] and the self's needs the most important considerations of treatment. Sexuality was not so important.

But what Kohut wrote about homosexuals shook me: that homosexuals are less capable of forming loving relationships than heterosexuals. He invariably saw analytic progress in extinguishing homosexual fantasies and behavior (e.g., see Kohut, 1977; Miller, 1985).

I struggled to reconcile this damning view of homosexuals with his otherwise non-judgemental view of humankind. I puzzled over how—or whether—self psychology could help me understand and celebrate my patients' sexuality.

For decades, I sought in self psychology an understanding of sexual development that could guide my work. No more. Now I understand that although Kohut threw out the polymorphously perverse baby with the bathwater of sexuality, that same radical act saved sexuality from psychoanalysis and vice-versa. By removing sexuality from its status as one of the two superordinate motivations in human life, he allowed both sex and psychoanalysis to develop in healthy directions. By describing a clinical approach that both hews closely to individual experience and allows clinicians to be open and generous, he gave us the means to promote healthy sexual and gender-identity development. Kohut saved sexuality and psychoanalysis from their failed marriage.

By the time I undertook psychoanalytic training, only a few self psychologists had written about sexuality and homosexuality. Among them, R. Dennis Shelby (1994, 1998) had written articles about homosexuality. In the first, he reviewed the history of psychoanalytic views of homosexuality and wrote, "After World War II, American analysts presented some of their most virulent statements regarding the homosexual psyche" (1994, p. 59), but by the 1990s, "[Psychoanalysts] now have permission to begin viewing homosexuality considerably more benignly than we did during our [psychoanalytic] training period, perhaps even to view it as a given when working with our patients" (p. 63). He asserted that sexual orientation is an innate, not an acquired, characteristic, and the clinician's task is to provide attuned responsiveness to the patient's "gender self" (pp. 76–77).

Betsy Kasoff (1997) questioned Shelby's assertion that homosexuality is innate—it may be for gay men, but is not always for women who identify as lesbian, she wrote. Etiology, however, interested her less than "understanding ... homosexuality as an alternative developmental outcome to heterosexuality and bisexuality. I do not see this outcome per se as indicating developmental derailment or biological difference" (p. 216). I share Kasoff's view.

Marian Tolpin (1997b) wrote about sexuality in self psychological theory, contrasting Freud's belief in the primacy of sexual needs with Kohut's belief that sexual needs are but one of the child's needs for selfobject responsiveness, which allows sexuality to be integrated into a cohesive self.

> The outcome for the development of sexuality and the self is not determined by the genitalia, or by rivalry, anger, envy, or the deflation and disappointment of having to wait: the outcome depends on how the

'naive' wishes, urges, and drives of the 'oedipal-self'—and the inevitable delays, deflation, and disappointments—are responded to, that is, on the nature of the child-parent ties.

(p. 183)

She understood that sexuality develops along with self-development and that, "With sexual maturation come two interrelated forms of intense pleasure—pleasure from sexuality, in and of itself, and pleasure from sexuality as a way of transiently re-accessing the deepest roots of self-experience in primary connections with responsive (selfobject) others" (p. 184).

The relative paucity of papers about sexuality in self psychology reveals Kohut's radical rethinking of psychoanalysis. After he demoted instinctual drives (the drives for sex and aggression) from their standing in Freudian theory, he found a place for aggression in his new theory, with his ideas about narcissistic rage, but he found no place for sexuality.

What happened to sexuality in Kohut's theory? Ironically, while moving sexuality and homosexuality out of the crosshairs of psychoanalysis, he gave us a way of working that allows us to welcome our lesbian, gay, bisexual, transgender, and queer (LGBTQ) patients as full members of the human race, with all the capacities for love and life—and all the hindrances—as everyone else. His thinking allows us to focus on the sexual and gender experiences and fantasies of each individual patient in a way that allows for their full, idiosyncratic development.

Self psychology and sexuality

Psychoanalysis was founded on Freud's attempt to understand sexuality. Sexual desire—the patient Anna O.'s for Freud's colleague Josef Breuer—launched Freud's "talking cure." Eventually, Freud concluded that every important behavior and fantasy could be distilled to sexual and aggressive desires. They are the irreducible givens of psychic life.

Kohut saw a fundamentally different human being. Late in his career, he rejected Freud's veneration of sex and aggression. He believed we are better understood by considering the self and the self's needs. He found that attention to them created lasting change much more effectively than did attention to aggressive and sexual drives. He did not discard Freud's important ideas about oral, anal, and phallic stages of sexual development; the mind as comprising id, ego, and superego; and family dynamics as including an oedipal phase and sibling rivalry, but he subordinated them to considerations of the self and the self's needs. This shift in thinking was monumental and necessary but left sexuality as a bit player in the drama of our emotional lives.

Self psychology posits that we experience relationships in one of two ways. Sometimes we relate to others as if they are separate from us, with their own motivations, desires, and histories. This is the *object-related* aspect of experience, which Freud and most other psychoanalytic traditions address.

Kohut focused on the other aspect of relating: the *selfobject* (or *narcissistic*) aspect. Sometimes we experience someone as providing—or failing to provide—necessary psychological functions for us. At these times, our sense of self (our narcissism) expands to include that person, whom we experience as part of our self, not as an individual in their own right. That person's responses affect us as if they were our own.

At any moment, one of the two aspects of relating—object-related or selfobject-related—will dominate our experience of another person; the other aspect will be in the background. A self is created and held together by incorporation of other's responses to our selfobject needs. Kohut considered this realm of experience more important clinically and developmentally than Freud's object-related realm. Therefore, self psychology mostly concerns itself with the selfobject aspect of relationships.

In the selfobject realm of relating, sexuality is just another selfobject longing. To the extent that sexuality manifests itself as a narcissistic need—the need to be affirmed, admired, accepted, and the like—it is but a sexualized version. Sex and sexual fantasies can also be used defensively, which means they would maintain self-cohesion without allowing further growth.

Sexuality, then, is not much different from other selfobject fantasies and behaviors. It is especially compelling, to be sure, but is not a need in and of itself.

Kohut's focus on the narcissistic aspect of sexuality meant that he paid less attention to its myriad other aspects: its interpersonal expression of love and intimacy; the sensual pleasure; the physicality; the possibility for play and experimentation; its importance in confirming and expressing desire; the ways in which it recreates (or creates for the first time) the earliest bodily sensations; its value for developing mastery over earlier trauma; its use as creative expression; its susceptibility to being pursued addictively; and so on.

By limiting sexuality's meaning to just another expression of narcissism, Kohut effectively removed sex from psychoanalysis.

Kohut and homosexuality

In his first book, *The Analysis of the Self* (1977), Kohut writes about Mr. A., an analysand in his mid-twenties. Although he dated women, Mr. A.'s homosexual fantasies brought him to treatment. In those fantasies, he enslaved a strong, handsome man—rendering him physically helpless—and maintained "quasi-sadistic, absolute control" over him. "Occasionally he achieved orgasm and a feeling of triumph and strength at the thought of masturbating a strong and physically perfect man and of thus draining him of his power" (p. 70).

To Kohut, Mr. A.'s fantasies were not evidence of healthy sexual desire. He viewed Mr. A.'s homosexual fantasies only as sexualized selfobject needs: "The patient's homosexual fantasies can ... be understood as sexualized statements about his narcissistic disturbance" (p. 71). Mr. A.'s homosexual fantasies, to Kohut, were symptoms that could be resolved (i.e., removed) by analysis.

If Mr. A.'s fantasies actually were an expression of a healthy desire for sexual and romantic contact with men, then his leading-edge need (i.e., healthy hope) to have his sexual self acknowledged and accepted by his analyst would have collided with Kohut's trailing-edge (i.e., defensive) belief that his homosexuality was an unhealthy expression of selfobject needs. (See the Introduction to this book for an extensive discussion of leading and trailing edges.)

Like Freud, Kohut (1996) regarded the choice of a same-gendered partner as a choice of someone like oneself and therefore a narcissistic object choice.

> [O]n the whole, homosexuals are weighted more toward a narcissistic concept of interrelationships with other people than heterosexual people are ... [I]n some, *although not very many* homosexual relationships, the other person, the partner, is clearly seen as a separate love object who has his own mode of seeing the world.
>
> (p. 40; italics added)

Kohut took some of the sting out of this view, though, by reasoning that the homosexual's narcissistic relationships are no reason for condemnation, because he did not consider narcissism pathological.

> People are not all cut according to the same plan ... [C]ertain creative people do not develop their object-love capacities to a great degree, but their narcissistic forces lead to the flowering of their creativity. Who is to say that this is less good than the capacity to fall in love with a woman?
>
> (p. 40)

In other words, homosexuals may not be able to love—the pull of their narcissism is inescapable—but greater creativity may compensate for that loss. This strikes me as a lousy deal.

More damningly, Kohut said, "[M]ost homosexual relationships—and this does not mean that heterosexuality cannot take the same form, but homosexual relationships more so (I have no statistics on it)—are quick pick-ups, emergency measures, taken to relieve tension" (Kohut, 1996, p. 84).

Kohut's view of homosexual relationships as transactional—for tension relief or satisfaction of narcissistic needs—reveals his bias that most homosexual desire is an unhealthy sexual expression, a defensive maneuver that precludes mature (i.e., heterosexual) object love and that ought to be outgrown as a healthier self develops.

Kohut himself, though, probably enjoyed a homosexual relationship that he experienced as one of the most importantly beneficial relationships of his life. In "The Two Analyses of Mr. Z.," Kohut (1979) writes about a patient (Mr. Z.) who is now widely accepted as a disguised version of Kohut himself (see Strozier, 2001, pp. 21–26, 308–316). Many facts of Mr. Z.'s life correspond with Kohut's.

Kohut describes Mr. Z. as a heterosexual man "who had some trouble in his relations with women" (p. 397). In his youth, Mr. Z. was deeply lonely, and, according to Kohut, Mr. Z. reported that, "Beginning at the age of eleven, he had been involved in a homosexual relationship, lasting about two years, with a 30-year-old high school teacher, a senior counselor and assistant director of the summer camp to which he had been sent by his parents" (p. 401).

[Mr. Z.] described these years [with the counselor] as extremely happy ones—they might well have been the happiest years of his life ... The relationship to the counselor appeared indeed to have been a very fulfilling one. Although overt sexual contact between them occurred occasionally—at first mainly kissing and hugging, later also naked closeness with a degree of tenderly undertaken manual and labial mutual caressing of the genitalia—he insisted that sexuality had not been prominent: it was an affectionate relationship. The boy idealized his friend (p. 404).

The relationship ended when Mr. Z. approached puberty and their affectionate bond dissolved. Nevertheless, "Mr. Z. felt no resentment against his friend and spoke warmly about him whenever he mentioned him during the analysis. He felt that their affection had been genuine and that their friendship had been mutually enriching" (p. 405).

Today, as then, a sexual relationship between an 11-year-old and a 30-year-old would be statutory rape, and many—maybe most—11-year-olds would be significantly traumatized by the event and would experience it as sexual abuse. But Mr. Z. experienced the relationship as unequivocally good, and his experience is the one considered here. As with Mr. Z., so with all our patients: *their* experiences are the focus of our attention. Psychoanalysts can—we *must*—imagine other possible reactions that currently lie out of the patient's awareness—e.g., did Mr. Z. repress traumatic aspects of the relationship?—but we begin by taking the patient at face value.

Kohut had a relationship in his youth that corresponds with much of Mr. Z.'s with his counselor (Strozier, 2001, pp. 21–26, 308–316). Kohut's mother hired a tutor for Heinz, probably when he was ten or 11. The tutor, Ernst Morawetz, was a college student, between 19 and 23. Their relationship was intellectually stimulating and emotionally essential to Kohut, who later said,

> I had this private tutor, who was a very important person in my life. He would take me to the museums and swimming and concerts and we had endless intellectual conversations and played complicated intellectual games and played chess together. I was an only child. So it was in some ways psychologically life-saving for me. I was very fond of the fellow.
>
> (Strozier, 2001, p. 24)

Strozier writes that, "Kohut himself as an adult talked to many colleagues about Morawetz but was always vague about the details of the relationship … He seems to have been vague even with his family" (Strozier, 2001, ftn., p. 394). Kohut dedicated his last book, written as he knew he was dying, to the memory of two people: Ignaz Purkhardshofer, a history teacher whom he idolized (Strozier, 2001, p. 29), and Ernst Morawetz.

The relationship with Morawetz was "psychologically life-saving" for Kohut, who may have felt with Mr. Z. that those were the "happiest years of his life." Like Mr. Z., Kohut was a lonely boy. Like Mr. Z., he expressed no ambivalence about his relationship with his tutor.

We have no other indication that Kohut had homosexual fantasies or relationships, so conjecture about his sexuality is based on assumptions about the congruence between Mr. Z.'s relationship with his tutor and Kohut's with Morawetz. Mr. Z.'s sexual and romantic relationship with his tutor may have accurately reflected Kohut's experience, or perhaps Kohut felt an unrequited desire for Morawetz that he allowed the imaginary Mr. Z to enjoy. Perhaps Kohut had no homosexual fantasies and no sexual activity occurred with Morawetz. Perhaps the relationship was *more* sexual and romantic than Mr. Z.'s. Many permutations of the historical relationship are possible. We likely will never know the truth.

In Kohut's lifetime, both mainstream culture and psychoanalysis regarded homosexuality with contempt, so if he had homosexual fantasies or experiences, they likely would have received no positive affirmation. With whom would a psychoanalyst hoping to establish himself as a competent professional in the 1950s confide about his homosexuality? Kohut was rejected in his first attempt to attend The Chicago Institute for Psychoanalysis, and Strozier speculates that if he had had a homosexual relationship with Morawetz, that could have been the reason (Strozier, 2001, p. 80). If true, that experience could have taught Kohut to keep his mouth shut about the nature of his relationship with Morawetz.

Whether or not he ever had homosexual fantasies or activity, Kohut did have a more forgiving view of homosexuality than did mainstream psychoanalysts of his time. He presented Mr. Z.'s homosexual relationship as entirely healthy, without second-guessing Mr. Z.'s assessment, and his judgements about homosexuality were less condemning than his colleagues', even though he arrived at his conclusion with some jerryrigged reasoning: homosexuals may be narcissistic, but there's nothing wrong with narcissism, so we need not stigmatize them.

Kohut's view was less harmful than psychoanalytic doctrine of the time, but it was nevertheless harmful enough. He tried to use psychoanalytic theory to remove the stigma from homosexuality, but his theory didn't allow him to go all the way. He died before psychoanalysts could go as far as Shelby, who asserted in 1994 that *some* psychoanalysts, at last, could see homosexuality as innate, not aberrant. Fortunately, we can use the theory Kohut gave us to completely remove the stigma from homosexuality.

The corrective to Kohut's view is one in which homosexuality is seen as "an alternative developmental outcome to heterosexuality and bisexuality," as Kasoff wrote (1997, p. 216). In this view, no one is regarded a priori as more or less capable of object-related relationships than anyone else solely because of sexual orientation. This view asserts that we come to value aspects of our self when they are acknowledged and affirmed by important people around us. Finally, this view prioritizes and values the patients in our consulting room and their actual experiences. We do not judge them by whether or not they fulfill our conceptions of some theoretically ideal sexual development.

This is the view of ISP, the variation of self psychology that I practice and that is presented in this book. ISP is founded on the self psychology derived from Kohut and adds an indispensable idea: what goes for the patient goes for the clinician. Not only does the patient have selfobject needs, but so does the clinician. Not only does the patient bring hopes and dreads to the treatment, but so does the clinician. The clinician's subjectivity must be accounted for in accounting for the patient's, and vice-versa. They affect each other. Every patient and every clinician bring their particular psychological worlds to the consulting room, and each analytic pair creates an alchemical combination that is something new on earth.

Intersubjective self psychology and sexuality: what matters

In the poem "What Matters", May Swenson beautifully describes what we often forget or never learned: that whom we desire and love is not ours to determine, so "the target doesn't matter."

Although early in my career I had balked at Kohut's demotion of sexuality to just another selfobject need, in practice I see selfobject needs as the essential element of psychological change, and I see sexual desire as but one (special) manifestation of selfobject longing. Sex and sexuality are important, but Kohut was right: sexuality is not the alpha and omega of human motivation, but rather another experience that clinically is most usefully seen through the lens of selfobject needs.

In fact, I find that sexual orientation—specific considerations are less important than I had imagined. Many gay men come to me because they want an openly gay therapist. They often assume I can understand them better than my straight or lesbian colleagues would. I do have cultural competence with gay men—that is, I am familiar with the mainstream culture and subcultures of mostly white, urban gay men in America, and I understand the sexual practices, the cultural references, and the argot particular to them. Cultural competence is essential when working with patients of any group. But I connect or fail to connect with gay men just as I do with non-gay patients. Whether or not I understand them, like them, and can help them has, in the end, little to do with sexual orientation, theirs or mine. It has to do with aspects of personality apart from sexuality.

The essential hopes and dreads of LGBTQ patients are no different from those of other patients, except insofar as the former have had to come to terms with their sexual orientation and/or gender identity to themselves and to the world and may still be struggling with that. LGBTQ people suffer and die every day for these struggles, but they are not inherent in being LGBTQ. They are cultural artifacts. They are the result of growing up in families and cultures usually hostile to non-heteronormative sexual and gender identities and expressions.

There is no such thing as the LGBTQ patient, just as there is no left-handed patient or blue-eyed patient. Absent the accidents of outward circumstances, the innate hopes and dreads of all people are the same. We all long for relationships—romantic, sexual, and platonic—in which we are recognized, affirmed, desired, and protected. We strive to create, thrive, and grow. We want to love and be loved. We want to laugh. We hope to contribute something unique in the world. We seek physical, sexual, emotional, esthetic, and intellectual satisfaction and pleasure.

To my surprise, I now see self psychology's lack of a developmental theory of sexuality as extremely useful, for two reasons. First, because psychoanalytic theories of sexual development have historically been hostile to LGBTQ people, and second, because the absence of a developmental theory frees clinicians to engage with each patient in their particularity and without prejudice about their sexual orientation. When we do that, we can understand, promote, and make tolerable each patient's idiosyncratic sexual development. As the late runner-cum-philosopher George Sheehan often said, "We are each of us an experiment of one."

In psychoanalytic theories of sexual development, intercourse-loving, monogamous, cisgendered, heterosexual males are the winners. Everyone else is a loser. This view was codified, hardened, and sharpened by psychoanalysts in the United States into pseudoscientific justification for the derogation of women and the stigmatization of homosexuals and others who did not fit into the procrustean bed of "normal" sexual behavior and gender roles.

Any theory that proposes normative development necessarily divides people into the healthy and the deviant. No matter how well-intentioned the theorizers may be, their ideas will inevitably be used by someone to harm someone else and to keep some group on the outs, and LGBTQ people have been greatly harmed by psychoanalytic theories of healthy sexual development. The theoretical damage done to homosexuals is described above.

Only in 1974 did the American Psychiatric Association deign to declassify homosexuality as a mental disorder, and not until 1990 did the World Health Organization follow suit. Psychoanalytic theory has been hostile to sexual (and gender) variation far longer than it has been accepting.

I do not want psychoanalysis determining how sexual and gender development ought to proceed; my patients and I usually do an excellent job together of understanding their sexual orientation and gender identity.

The causes of sexual orientation have proven stubbornly resistant to our understanding. For some, the object of desire remains stable and consistent over decades or for their lifespan. For others, sexual desire's object, intensity, and aim may shift and bend, depending on selfobject needs, self development, or external circumstances. And changes almost always occur when one feels one's sexuality accepted by others.

We now understand that homosexuality per se is neither healthy nor pathological, just as heterosexuality per se is neither good nor bad. Homosexuality is one of many sexual orientations, all of equal inherent moral valence. Any sexual orientation can have defensive or progressive and development-promoting characteristics.

Patients' acceptance of their sexuality is almost always contingent on acceptance by those important to them. Therefore, a therapist's understanding and acceptance of a patient's sexual orientation greatly affects the patient's understanding and acceptance. We do not develop in a vacuum; we are profoundly influenced by what is accepted and rejected by those important to us: people as well as cultural groups and institutions.

The therapist's failure to accept a patient's sexual orientation or gender expression means that the patient's leading-edge desire to be affirmed as a full human being will collide with the therapist's trailing-edge defense against accepting the patient as the sexual being that the patient is. Some of Kohut's homosexual patients—like Mr. A—may have found themselves in this predicament.

This collision has serious repercussions. The therapist's failure to affirm the patient's sexual orientation (or gender identity) may preclude the patient's recognition or acceptance of it, because thoughts and feelings often remain unconscious if felt to be unwelcome to important others. If patients sense that the therapist cannot accept their sexual or gender identity, then those essential parts of self may remain out of consciousness and therefore unexplored.

As Paul Ornstein explained,

> As the patient feels more deeply understood, unconscious material begins to emerge. But what emerges from the unconscious is fluid and

depends not only [on] the patient's past, but on the relationship between analyst and patient. Something becomes unconscious because of fear of re-traumatization. When development does not proceed because the response to the infant or child was inadequate, there will be a deficit in the development of the psychic structures. So what is unconscious is what's beneath the deficit; it is the consequence of the thwarted need to grow. So the unconscious is the content of all that was never adequately responded to. The dearth of empathic responsiveness creates the deficits in the self, and these deficits are filled in by defensive structures that prevent the emergence of affective states. What was at one time knowledge and part of the patient's experience is kept out of current experience either by repression or dissociation, but this always occurs in the context of a two-person relationship.

(Geist, 2015)

Freud understood the unconscious differently. As described above, he believed that humans are motivated by drives for sex and aggression. A veneer of civility allows us to function in society but prevents us from awareness of these drives, which results in their expression in distorted forms. The therapist must tear away the veneer and show patients their "true" motivations. A fearless confrontation with truth, as defined by Freud, was the goal of interpretation and treatment.

Donna Orange (2011) described this approach as one that falls within the "hermeneutics of suspicion": Freud looked beneath a person's thoughts or actions for the hostile or sexual motives he already knew were there. Frank Lachmann (2008) wrote of his training in this tradition that, "One looks underneath or behind a person's actions to find the 'real' motivation. Behaviors that appear kind, generous, or perhaps even an expression of gratitude and appreciation actually conceal baser, unconscious motivations that are aggressive and narcissistic" (p. 4).

Freud believed that patients deceive themselves and their therapists. They would rather not acknowledge their lust and hostility, and they are trying to get one over on the therapist, who—by virtue of Freudian theory—knows better.

Kohut's view of patients—indeed, of humankind—was fundamentally different. He believed that we strive to form genuine, caring relationships, unless that desire is badly thwarted and thereby distorted by unempathic early relationships. He trusted his patients to know better than he how they felt and how to understand their motivations. He advocated dealing first with the manifest content of what patients tell us—taking them at face value—before considering latent content.

This view belongs to what Orange calls the "hermeneutics of trust," and self psychology has been built upon assumptions of the best about people: that people are doing their best, even when they are doing bad; that the proper starting point for our work is to give patients the benefit of the doubt about what they say, rather than assuming that they are deceiving themselves and us; and that acts or fantasies of violence or disconnected sexuality are not manifestations of the most basic human motivations but are the results of misfires between patients' needs and what was provided by important people.

Clinical example

For the first year of my work with Nancy, my primary task was keeping her alive. Eric, her boyfriend of six years, had abruptly ended their relationship and Nancy was falling apart.

Her early life had been horrific: her mother abandoned the family when Nancy was five; her father physically abused her; and her two older sisters, the only reliable people in her life, fled home at their earliest opportunity, leaving Nancy alone with her father when she was nine. At school, she was teased and bullied by other girls.

She had attempted suicide several times before we met and often felt suicidal when we began working together. After Eric left, Nancy began playing a terrifying "game." She worked on the 22nd floor of a Manhattan skyscraper, and some evenings, after her coworkers left, she would open the window of her office and sit on the ledge. She would lean forward until she felt like she just might fall, catch herself, regain her equilibrium, then do it again. She was not sure whether she wanted to live or die, and this "game" enacted her potentially fatal ambivalence.

It was essential for me to establish a trusting relationship with her, so she could rely on me. But Nancy's early-warning system for abandonment, always extremely sensitive, was working feverishly after Eric left, and any hint that I did not warmly encourage her dependence on me caused her great alarm. Consequently, her trust in me grew awfully slowly, and I was frightened.

This crisis ended when Nancy almost fell from the ledge. One night, as she leaned forward, she lost her balance and, for what seemed an eternity, hung in mid-air, desperately flailing for something stable. She grabbed the window frame and pulled herself back into her office. She had fought to live—that surprised her—and with that, her suicidal fever broke and her suicidal wishes began abating.

With the crisis averted, we settled into the long-term work of *building self structure*. That is, we created psychological capabilities that hadn't existed before; for example, the ability to calm and soothe herself. *Creating new structure* and *modifying existing structure* are the two processes that promote change and growth, according to ISP.

For a long time, Nancy relied on me to reassure her and ease her distress when she was anxious. She was easily dysregulated, and that sometimes led to suicidal wishes. Over time, she was able to manage much of her anxiety herself. In extreme instances, she still needs me to ease her anxiety. This is how new psychological structure is built. I expect this process to continue and for Nancy to be able to manage more and more of her anxiety and fears without me.

This need to be emotionally held—a leading-edge need—meshes well with my leading-edge need to feel effective. This need of mine in regard to patients derives mostly from my relationship with my late father. As my father slipped slowly into the deep darkness of alcohol and depression during my childhood, I tried, in my childlike way, to save him. I would sometimes force myself to sit with him for hours as he drank in the dark and listen with feigned interest to stories I had heard a hundred times before. Maybe if I gave him the attention he needed, he'd decide to rejoin those who wanted to live.

Once, after he'd had a particularly upsetting argument with my mother, we sat on the front steps of the house and I asked him about their honeymoon, thinking that recalling warm feelings about her might restore a loving marriage.

And I believed that one day I would speak the sentence that would fix him, if I could only figure out exactly the right words in exactly the right order, like a magic incantation. I failed.

My hope of saving him continues as a leading-edge wish to feel effective by helping my patients, but my willingness to sometimes take on more than I can manage can result in a trailing-edge fear of being overwhelmed.

Thus I feel great satisfaction when I calm Nancy's anxieties and her symptoms abate. She is happier and less prone to fragmentation, and she expresses her gratitude. These responses confirm my conviction that I *am* helping her, and my conviction helps her to trust and rely on me. Our reactions to each other reinforce one another in an affirming cycle that satisfies both our leading-edge needs.

We encounter rough seas when Nancy feels that I am unwilling or unable to care for her. When I am overwhelmed by trying to do too much, she senses my trailing-edge anxiety, and her trailing-edge fear of abandonment predominates. She withdraws in rage and shame and suicidal thoughts emerge. If I demonstrate my willingness to resume my responsibilities as the idealized selfobject, however, the selfobject transference is eventually restored.

Re-establishing myself as a trusted figure *modifies existing structure* in Nancy's mind. That is, her defensive belief that nobody wants to care for her is slightly altered each time I disabuse her of it. By repeatedly disproving trailing-edge beliefs, they slowly change. This is how existing psychological structure is *modified*. In Nancy's case, the defensive belief that she must not lean on anyone, because no one wants to help, is proven untrue, at least for each particular instance. Many such instances over the years have convinced her that some people *will* help—that I will help.

For over ten years, Nancy has been free of dangerous thoughts of killing herself. She still has suicidal fantasies, but is not at risk of acting on them. I see this as proof of the power of a strong connection that includes the idealizing selfobject transference. Vital psychological structure has been built, existing defensive structure has been modified, and Nancy is freer and happier.

Nancy's sexual orientation required no remediation. Since adolescence, she had identified as heterosexual. She had sex with men, enjoyed it, and never felt sexually attracted to women. Her heterosexuality was a stable characteristic, a given. Until it was not.

About seven years into our work, she found herself romantically and sexually attracted to a woman in her office called Naomi. Her desire and love for Naomi swept her up. Naomi was crazy about Nancy, and they began dating. Sex with Naomi was exciting and left Nancy feeling deeply connected to her.

They dated, were married, and are now a happy, stable couple. Naomi is expecting a child. Nancy is still attracted to men but more attracted to Naomi. She is bisexual. We didn't see that coming.

No theory of sexual development explains Nancy's sudden and unconflicted move from heterosexuality to homosexuality, but ISP helps me make sense of it.

Nancy's sexual orientation is not the object of our attention; her self and the needs of her self are. Nancy needs to idealize me and seeks from me affective qualities she lacks. I soothe her and comfort her fears, provide caring attention, and lend her my confidence. Her self has cohered and developed because I have provided these selfobject functions. From this more stable self, her idiosyncratic development led her to embrace homosexuality.

Some people's sexual orientation and gender identity are more fluid than others. Nancy's sexual orientation had more latitude for expression once her self became firmer. Women had been unavailable to Nancy as potential sexual and romantic partners, I believe, because the most important women in her early life—first her mother, then her sisters—had abandoned her, with devastating results. But many years of a transformative relationship with me allowed Nancy's homosexuality to emerge, because of the new experience of trusting someone (me) and not being let down. Having learned to trust me, she was able to trust women, thus allowing her homosexuality to emerge. Nancy's sexual desire no longer bars females.

Her sexuality cannot be understood apart from an understanding of her self and its needs. Nancy is not much interested in this, though. She is happy, her relationship is healthy, and the reasons for the late-life re-orientation of her sexual compass do not much concern her. Nancy is an experiment of one, and it's going well.

Nancy's gender identity and presentation are another part of this story. She had always hated girls' clothes and eschewed girls' games and toys.

Every birthday, she hoped for a boy's gift—a toy gun or a GI Joe—and was crushed when she unwrapped a dress or a doll. Perhaps because of her unconventional gender presentation, she was shunned and teased by other girls, but she couldn't figure out what she was doing wrong. She thought she would be happier as a boy. In adolescence, she hated her developing breasts, and as an adult, she never felt they belonged to her.

Her discomfort with her body was continuous but not overpowering. She was content talking about it until 11 years into our work together, when she decided to have a bilateral mastectomy.

Breast cancer had killed two friends in adulthood, and she feared she could be next. After learning she was at high risk for breast cancer, she quickly decided to have prophylactic mastectomies. Surgery would remove both the anxiety and risk of cancer and would leave her more comfortable in her body, she believed. I was somewhat less sanguine, because I feared that she was galloping toward significant surgery as a way to relieve her anxiety without enough consideration of the effects. I felt no judgement about Nancy's gender identity nor about her wish to have a flat chest, but I wanted to be sure that she had thought through the consequences of serious surgery.

This time, Nancy soothed my anxiety. She was confident that this surgery was right for her. She wanted freedom from the threat of cancer, and she was certain she would love a flat chest. We talked about it, and I was mostly convinced by the time of surgery.

I needn't have worried; Nancy was right. Her new chest has been a great pleasure to her. She feels fully comfortable in her skin for the first time in her life. She finally feels she has the right body. Naomi encouraged the mastectomies and is also pleased with Nancy's body. For the first time in her life, Nancy wears shirts and blouses that draw the eye to her upper body. She favors sequined tops. She feels more comfortable appearing conventionally feminine without breasts than she did with them.

This has been *Nancy's* developmental trajectory. No developmental theory I know explains her deep pleasure and satisfaction when she looks in the mirror and sees a boy from the waist up and a woman from the waist down. The course of her development has been idiosyncratic and could be neither predicted nor replicated. As Nancy's self has changed and developed—in the context of her relationship with me—so have her sexuality and gender identity, because they are embedded in the broader context of her self. Sexuality and gender identity are aspects of self, not independent qualities that have a developmental course separate from self-development.

Conclusion

For people whose sexuality and gender expression—essential parts of the self—elicit denial, puzzlement, anger, or even revulsion from important people in their lives and the world around them, the gratitude for a therapist who meets them where they are with fellow-feeling is powerful and contributes to a strong, collaborative relationship.

Psychoanalytic attitudes toward gender identity are currently undergoing changes analogous to the changes toward homosexuality in the 1970s, '80s, and '90s. Analysts increasingly support patients in determining their gender identity for themselves, even when they seek our help for that determination. We do our patients a disservice by assuming they must fit into one of two gender boxes. Which box should Nancy check?

This acceptance has two salubrious consequences. First, it obviates the need for the clinician to determine whether a patient's gender identity is pathological or healthy. This allows the clinician to dispense with an inquiry into how the patient's gender identity was created, an enterprise historically undertaken to correct "unacceptable" gender identities.

Second, by assuming that any gender expression can be healthy or defensive, the clinician can concentrate on the most fundamental clinical task: a conscientious focus on the patient's subjective experience (including the patient's experience of the clinician), with the aim of illuminating and strengthening the patient's self, including the patient's sexual self and gender self.

In the realms of gender and sexuality, the clinician's freedom from a priori assumptions of what is healthy or pathological allows us to understand and accept each individual's experience of sexuality and gender, with particular consideration of what is helpful or harmful. We can inquire closely into what it has been like for this particular person—gay or straight or bisexual or asexual or queer, cisgendered, trans, or gender nonconforming—to have had his, her, or their sexual and gender experiences.

This affirming responsiveness to their subjectivity is a balm for LGBTQ people who are likely to have already experienced prejudice and possibly much worse, as it is for anyone whose full self has never been affirmed. This is what matters.

Notes

1 I thank Betty Rothbart for her close reading and great advice on earlier drafts; Kathy Roe for her excellent suggestions; and I am grateful for the support of Kenneth Wampler, who encouraged me through every version of this chapter and long before.
2 Kohut defined the *self* as the I we recognize ourselves to be: a bounded entity with cohesion in space and over time (Elson, 1987, p. 18).

Chapter 13

A suicidal patient
Gasping for air

Laura D'Angelo

"Do you feel like the music has stopped and all the chairs are taken?" So began the ad I had written for my Psychology Today profile. Zoe, sits in my office, quoting the line. Her eyes well with tears. "That's exactly how I feel," she says. At 31, Zoe is a big, beautiful short-story writer. She is dressed in a bright blue dress, cowboy boots and red lipstick. Her arms are sleeved in tattoos. She is a lesbian, she tells me, and fat-positive, active in a movement that fights fat shaming and encourages people to love their bodies at any size.

It pains Zoe to recount her history to yet another therapist. But she is a person, she explains, who needs therapy and medication to be in this world. I am impressed by a directness that seems to override a current of shame. At my prompting, Zoe details a history of depressive episodes, hospitalizations and suicide attempts. At 13, she swallowed a bottle of pills. At 27, following a breakup with a girlfriend, she slit her wrists. My officious note taking is a ruse, masking the anxiety cresting inside me. Images synapse through my brain: I imagine the horrified face of the roommate who discovers Zoe's body on the floor, blood everywhere. My thoughts zoom to a what-if scenario where no one rescues Zoe and her shocked therapist – phone in hand – learns that Zoe is gone. "What am I getting myself into?" I think. Sensing my anxiety, Zoe says: "But I would never do that to you or anyone treating me!"

A year later, Zoe would become profoundly suicidal. Betrayed by a lover and then feeling double-crossed by me, she would rent a car with the intention of killing herself using carbon monoxide emissions. Agonized texts and frantic 911 calls would punctuate ten heart-racing hours culminating with a suicide note and terrifying silence.

Hope and dread

Psychoanalyst Anna Ornstein (1991) wrote that the more we've been traumatized, the more we dread being re-traumatized. Our fear constitutes the trailing edge of the transference in a psychoanalytic treatment, where childhood pathology gets endlessly reproduced. But every treatment contains hope for growth and healing, which constitutes the "forward" or leading edge (Tolpin, 2002). In the intersubjective field, analyst and patient flow back and forth between currents of hope and dread (Mitchell, 1993; Stolorow, 1995). When the wounded parts of the analyst and patient collide the analytic pair is forced to relive the suffering of the past. In this struggle lies the potential for liberation. Little is written about how analysis can activate a bi-directional process that is healing for patient and analyst. What happens between an analytic couple may seem like a private affair, but it has a ripple effect, adding to the healing of our families, our communities and the wider culture.

Circling

I like Zoe right away. She is wildly intelligent and witty. I appreciate the glimpse she shows me of her inner darkness, and the ways she harnesses her fear and fascination of death into a creative force that animates her writing. Death is her muse. "My life is a dungeon," she writes "and I can't stay alive."

But a couple of months into treatment I notice that my fondness toward her hasn't translated into freedom in our work. A force – within and beyond us – molds the intersubjective space. Zoe's dread that our relationship will not hold is rooted in a relationship with an anorexic mother and sister who could not see themselves in her. I am aware of her fear that I, like them, will shame her for her appetites and find her unworthy. Her apprehension hems me in. With shallow breath we circle, touching into one another with caution.

Sitting in the chair across from me, Zoe searches for clues that I cannot be trusted. "I think that clock is a few minutes off," she observes in a helpful tone. Later, she offers: "Two books on your bookshelf are upside down." She apologizes, laughing at her vigilance. I make a mental note to adjust the clock, turn over the books, get my act together. When she talks about how painful it was to discover that a trusted friend once wrote an essay shaming fat people, I stiffen. Zoe no doubt has scoured my writings for signs of anti-fat or anti-gay sentiment. Being a straight, "normatively sized" woman is grounds for suspicion, and Zoe is on guard for any signs that I want her to lose weight. In this space, thick with caution, moments of connection break through. I am touched by Zoe's sense that her girlfriend is about to leave her and this strikes terror into her heart. She takes in my empathy before her eyes glance at the clock that runs too fast and then dart to the more reliable time-keeper on the wall. She panics. "Oh no! We have to end soon," she says. Her eyes widen and I feel guilty that I can't provide what she seems to need. "I'm sorry I'm so needy," she says. Endings scare her, and her alarm sparks my worry that I cannot help her. Maybe it's true that I am flakey and/or judgey. Any spontaneity could uncage my sequestered badness. My unconscious hope is that my goodness and tenacity will be affirmed by her. I, too am fat-positive! Queer-positive!

It is in retrospect that I understand Zoe and I were unconsciously prepping one another for a drama that would cast the most troublesome parts of ourselves: the part of Zoe that wants her to die and another part that pleads for rescue. On my side, there is a part that feels compelled to rescue her and a young self that bears all the badness. Those selves would mix it up on the analytic stage to produce a treacherous act.

Months into our work together, Zoe starts to feel received by me. I am the empathic older sister, someone who sees herself in Zoe and in whom Zoe sees herself (Togashi, 2009). A twinship takes hold in the transference. Relief washes over her when she learns that I am a "Riotgrrl" fan and appreciate the work of her favorite poet. She takes note when I understand something about her experience that she senses I know about myself. The experience of alikeness allows her to yearn for love from a woman she can look up to. I feel valued by her, no longer under suspicion. Glancing at the couch, she asks if I see people three times a week. "Yes," I say. "Wow! You must really like them," she says. I'm tickled by her equation – the patients in analysis – are the favorites. "Would you like to come three times a week?" I ask. She blushes; she had been hoping I would invite her.

Death – tormentor and muse

I learn that Zoe's fascination with death is rooted in existential terror. As a baby, Zoe was rescued by emergency room doctors during asthma attacks. She remembers her mother, perched at her bedside, tethered to her every breath. As she describes this scene, I am brought back to the morning when my mother burst into my bedroom, holding my 1-year-old son. "He can't breathe!" she screamed. My son was white, his eyes bulging, he was gasping for air. His little abdomen was pumping hard and fast. The worst part was the look of terror on his face. We rushed to a doctor's office where he was injected with life-saving prednisone that opened his airways. A few hours later, we were in a pharmacy loading up on the medical supplies that would become daily staples in our lives: a nebulizer, a plastic mask and hosing. Every morning and every evening, he would suck on the plastic mouthpiece at the end of the tube taking in Albuterol and a steroid called Pulmicort. I'll never forget the horror of knowing that at any moment he could suffocate to death. Now, 17 years later, when my son returns from college, I am eerily tuned into the sound of his cough. In a nanosecond, from any part of the house, even from the soundest sleep, I can discern if his cough is productive or squeezing through inflamed bronchial tubes.

I feel for Zoe's mother whom I imagine taking in Zoe's big, air-starved eyes. But more often I am moved by Zoe's desperate bid for her mother's love and acceptance. Zoe's mother – who struggled with an eating disorder – weighed 90 pounds before becoming pregnant with Zoe. The weight she had gained since was an ongoing source of bitter lamentation. By the time Zoe was four, her mother became preoccupied with the fat on Zoe's little frame. She dragged Zoe to Weight Watchers meetings where the little girl dutifully colored in carrots and peppers in her workbook. Zoe and her sister, three years older, came to embody polarized aspects of their mother's disturbed body image. Her sister became life-threateningly thin and Zoe became fat. Cupcakes and chips were in copious supply for Zoe's sister, but the goodies were locked away from Zoe. "If you want to make a kid fat, put her on a diet," Zoe said.

On weekends, Zoe's parents left her at her grandparents' house. She remembers crying inconsolably as they drove away. The horror that came next exists in shards of memory. Zoe recalls her grandfather, scented by alcohol and creepiness, leading her to a clearing in the woods where he sexually abused her, over and over again.

At age five, Zoe refused to go to school; she was sure her mother would die. Zoe's mother reacted to her school phobia – that stretched over years – with fury. She hit Zoe, and locked her in her bedroom letting her out to use the bathroom and to eat. "What else could she do?" Zoe asked. Her father – an absent presence – failed to intervene. The abiding theme in Zoe's story knit itself into mine. We were both children driven to keep our mothers alive so that we could stay alive.

At 13, Zoe began cutting her arms, breasts, abdomen and thighs, "the fattest parts of me," she said. Meanwhile, Zoe's sister – who nearly starved herself to death – was hospitalized for anorexia. Zoe's sister was considered cold-hearted and ambitious. Zoe was defined as the opposite, needy and artistic. After Zoe moved out, her mother adopted two dogs. The "skinny one" was headstrong and independent. The "fat one" was loyal and sensitive. Putting that together in session one day, Zoe gasped, "Oh, my God, my mom made a dog out of me."

Finding salvation in the fat-positive movement, Zoe soaked up the message that people could be healthy at any size, and critiqued a culture that made women starve themselves. In this milieu, she felt lovable and desirable, and most importantly, she felt that she belonged. The cruel inner voice that made fatness grounds for execution softened, allowing Zoe to find a powerful feminist voice.

When the music stopped

That first year of treatment, Zoe was trying to salvage a relationship with her girlfriend, Sam, a playful, duplicitous and traumatized woman. Sam professed to love Zoe's body, but once broke up with her saying she couldn't be with a fat person. Zoe told me that they had googled me and saw me on the Internet playing African drums, I felt embarrassed by my wonton display of vitality when Zoe couldn't lay claim to her life. Zoe and Sam became installed in my psyche. In my dreams, I would find myself on vacation with them and panic. "What have I done?" I'd wake up trying to figure out a way out. "I'll suggest we go to the movies, so we won't have to interact."

As Sam slipped away, Zoe dropped into a desperate state. "I need to be perfectly still to keep her from leaving," she tells me, one day, weeping. I am unsettled by Zoe's self-talk which has grown cruel and punishing. She ruminates about dying, and her veiled threats of suicide become a death grip on Sam who relives her own traumatic history with suicidal women.

Collision

Just days before Christmas, Sam breaks it off. Zoe comes into my office sorrowing. She speaks of her pain in an eerily disconnected way. Deadness lurks in her languid green eyes. The space between us feels foggy and lifeless, and she feels so far away. When we talk about hospitalization, Zoe snaps to. She begs: "Oh please don't make me go! I can't go back there. It was awful!" We agree that she will stay at her parent's house where she won't be alone, and we will be in touch once a day by phone. "I'm sewn to the bed," she tells me over the phone, in a vaporous voice. She describes her fantasy to inhale deadly exhaust from her parent's car in an enclosed garage. The fantasy gives her comfort and knocks me off my center. "I understand your wish to be out of pain," I tell her. "But if you let this suicidal part make that decision, it will be irreversible." Zoe assures me that she will not kill herself, she just needs to talk about it. Her reassurances feel increasingly hollow. "My existence is complicated," she says. "I wasn't made for this world."

Zoe's internal world is the perfect activation for mine. The question about who could live and who could die stalked my childhood. I remember when I was five, my mother caught a heavy glass ashtray that my father had hurled at her with her thumb. I saw blood spurting from her hand, arching in the air like water from a fountain. I didn't have the words to describe what this evoked in me. Like Zoe, at the deepest level, I feared my mother would die, which meant that I would die. I needed to keep her alive so that I could stay alive. I wished that my mother would make my job easier by being cowed by my father's temper. Instead, she was a fearless provocateur, goading him in conflicts, belittling his position as a university professor, calling him "Stanley Kowalski with a Ph.D." I intercepted my father's rage, taking the bullet for her. I was defined as "the brat," relentless and incorrigible. Projecting badness onto me exonerated them, and left me with an unshakable belief that at my core I was bad, the source of their misery. That was the story told to me. That became the story I told about myself. In fact, I had been told by these stories.

For Zoe and I, the cauldrons of our childhoods were churning. She was living in the dungeon of her past, feeling that she was too much for those around her and would be better off dead. I was gripped by the embrace of my past, needing to keep her alive so that I could stay alive. Deadness enveloped her. Despair hunted her. Panic electrified me. Dread, despair and repetition pervaded the intersubjective field. This was anything but generative, for both of us.

Over the phone, she tells me that her scolding internal voice is becoming more cruel, calling her disgusting and worthless. The counterbalance is a sweet-talking suicidal voice offering helpful suggestions like maybe she should starve herself to fit into a standard sized coffin.

Immersed in suicide literature, I weave in new arguments to stay alive. "Suicide is contagious," I say, "when you kill yourself, you indirectly kill hundreds by your influence." Zoe is unmoved. "If you can stick it out through the rough time, your future self will thank you." Across the unembodied distance, I feel Zoe shrug. My interventions are a shield against my own powerlessness. A depressed friend told Zoe "Your suicidality is a fever. It will break." This gives us a metaphor to work with. And, weeks later, the fever does break. Zoe returns home.

The first day back in my office, Zoe is wearing eyeliner that sweeps upward at the outward corners making her eyes appear large and sultry. She hands me a Christmas card. "Thank you for going above and beyond, beneath and below, and for being the best therapist I ever had." I am touched by her gratitude. "I don't think I'd be alive right now without you," she says. When I close the door, I feel flattened by the responsibility of keeping another person alive.

Together, we exhale. Zoe eases back into her life for a while, resuming work, reconnecting with some friends. But the day she finds out that Sam has a lover, she spirals. She rents a car with the intention of killing herself with carbon monoxide emissions. Driving through the city, she and Sam are locked in a painful, high-stakes fight. Sam calls 911, but Zoe refuses to reveal her location. At 11 p.m. Sam alerts me in a panicked text. I call Zoe who doesn't pick up. "Nice try – getting Laura involved," she texts Sam. I am frightened and confused. Is Zoe dangling Sam like a child pinching a spider by its leg? Would she kill herself out of spite? In a final text, Zoe assures me she will see me the next day. I believe her because I don't know how not to believe her.

Sam texts me. "Do I have to keep texting her? When will this stop?" I tell her to do what she needs to do to take care of herself. I go to bed and in the morning discover a suicide note from Zoe in my inbox.

> I love you, but I don't understand why you would tell Sam to stop talking to me tonight. I thought I could trust you ... Please don't worry, and trust that what I'm doing is best. I'm too shattered to be here.

Betrayed by her ex, Zoe now feels betrayed by me. Terrified, I believe this pushed Zoe to a deadly edge. Hours elapsed since she sent me the email. I call her. No answer. I imagine with horror an early morning jogger discovering Zoe's body slumped over the steering wheel. I call hospital emergency rooms, 911, send police to her apartment.

For several hours, I believe Zoe is dead. I finally track her down through her roommate who walks into Zoe's bedroom and hands Zoe her cell phone. "I just want to be left alone," Zoe says. I am so relieved that she is alive! Then furious! I realize that Zoe wanted me to believe that she was dead. Not only had Zoe refused to take in my goodness, she spit it out like so much sour milk.

Taking a seat in the leading edge

I hang up the phone and ricochet back to an old place, where I am the killer, the killable, the one carrying all the badness. And then I see, clearly for the first time, that I am no longer that child. I force into consciousness the awful feelings of being trapped in a dangerous situation and realize that I now can make a different choice. I can sever the enslaving tie that made me my mother's rescuer. In doing so, I liberate myself from the trailing edge, the child who carries all the badness. I decide to stop making accommodations. I have been there for Zoe and now I need her to show up for me. I am demanding something from her. The next session, I tell Zoe I will only work with her if the threat of suicide was off the table.

> I'm tenacious and I care about you. I can go with you to that edge, but I can't stop you from killing yourself. If that happens, I will be sad. But I can't be in a power struggle with you. You will win.

I say this with confidence that is fresh. Zoe needs to hear this as well as my own terrorized parts.

Despondent and defeated, Zoe is barely able to look at me. "I'm not sure I can live up to what you need from me. I'm a little too much right now and always. This isn't going to end well. Let's discontinue. That way I won't be dragging you through the mud," she says.

We muck around in the mud for weeks before reaching an agreement that allows us to process feelings of grief, rage, betrayal and desperation between us. Slowly, Zoe re-surfaces. She begins writing. She is sad, but not suicidal. In contrast to the dark days of motoring toward death, this period feels like a joy ride. Zoe joins me in the twinship and the analytic exploration begins to flow. Together, we talk about her future. She rededicates herself to writing projects, earns awards and prestigious placements. I feel proud of her.

But this is not the end of the story. As we know, old themes find new ways to govern our lives. A year goes by and Zoe sinks into another depression. There is a falling out with her mother. A leader in Zoe's community, a friend whom she admired, kills herself in a hotel room. Shock courses through Zoe's community. Zoe can't resist the pull of the nightly drunken gatherings of mourners who stumble and slur confessions of their own suicidal fantasies. Lulled into an alikeness experience with her dead friend, Zoe obsesses over how the woman killed herself. She has located the online store where the woman purchased an aphyxiation kit. Zoe's immersion frightens me. Her vicious internal voice starts making the case that Zoe should do the same. She is loathsome, it tells her. Killing herself would be doing everyone a favor. I have trouble producing her monthly bill. "Don't tighten the noose," warns my internal rescuer. The fear of hurting Zoe conflicts with my need to get paid. It reawakens the foul fantasy that my needs are bad because I am bad. This time, I track the mechanics of my own thinking so I won't be ground up by the gears.

When someone we know commits suicide, we are at greater risk ourselves, I think. But even this knowledge doesn't hook me in the same way. Zoe misses our next session, I text her and she doesn't respond. I don't feel the usual rush of panic, nor the urge to track her down. My own healthy strivings remobilized, I hold onto myself clear that I can only accompany Zoe into the dark places for as long as she chooses to be alive.

Five days later, she texts me with unabashed fury saying she quit her job, she quit all her medications and is quitting therapy. She adds that there is no need to worry because she is fine. And definitely no need to talk to anyone about this (meaning her psychiatrist, Dr. Bella). She's hurt and angry that I haven't pursued her, I think. She wants to punish me.

I text her, urging her to come in. She ignores me. I follow up, reaching toward her healthy self. "You haven't responded to my text," I say. "I know when someone treats you this way, you feel hurt and abandoned."

Zoe shows up at my office at the appointed time. She tells me that her friend's suicide has shaken her to the core. On top of that, she has been dropped by her mother, then me. Tearfully, she confesses that she has resumed a form of cutting. In a nightly ritual, she injects empty hypodermic needles into her arms. She is rehearsing a heroin overdose so that she can die and people won't blame themselves. We understand that the fraying tie with her mother has caused Zoe to disintegrate into terrible anxiety. Hurting herself is a way of preventing further fragmentation.

The invitation

When the session ends, I feel confused. I recall her earlier text saying (cryptically) that there is no need to talk to Dr. Bella. Wondering about that, I call Dr. Bella and ask how Zoe presented in their session earlier that day. "She seemed fine!" Dr. Bella says. We are stumped. A dedicated psychiatrist who cares deeply about Zoe, Dr. Bella proposes that she join Zoe and I in our next session to sort out what is going on. I love the idea.

Zoe hates it. "Oh fuck! No! I can't let her see this part of me," Zoe says. She is sitting in the chair across from me, head thrown back, eyes skyward. "I do present differently to her. I'm sorry."

"This is not about needing an apology from you," I say. "This is about my wanting you to be curious about what leads you to make decisions about the different presentations. It's our responsibility to dig into that."

Zoe tries to elicit care from me by making me worry and from Dr. Bella by being OK. "I understand deeply from your history that every cell of your being is calibrated toward mistrusting anyone that shows you kindness," I say. "So you try to manipulate care. The problem is you can't trust anything that you've manipulated."

I invite Zoe to trust the evidence that I care: my consistency, my effort to understand her, my generosity around the fee. "There is nothing you can do or not do to make me care about you. I care about you period. What I give from my heart is not manipulated by you," I say. "Besides, when you get caring in response to your own orchestration you feel unworthy and apologetic."

In holding Zoe accountable for her actions, I am showing up for Zoe as the best version of the mother I hold out to my son. I have freed myself from the part of me that wants to rescue Zoe, the trailing edge. Now, I invite Zoe to free herself from her young part that provokes rescue to feel loved. Those internal parts offer us no hope for a changed future, no possibility for genuine love and growth. They offer only repetition, restriction and shame.

A long weekend follows our conversation. Then Zoe comes in bursting with energy. "I had a major breakthrough at my parents' house!" Zoe says. "I feel like years of analysis came together for me in an explosive way."

She tells me that she was angry after the last session, convinced that I didn't understand her. But a small voice inside of her urged her to stay open.

> Then I was sick at my parents' house and I realized that I was milking it to get my mother's attention. Coughing loudly, lying around limply. What you said was true. That's how I try to get her to care and that's what I was doing to you. With my father, I act like everything is OK, like I do with Dr. Bella.

"That is a major insight!" I say, aware of a newfound dignity in Zoe.

> When you told me that I hurt you when I blew you off, something opened up and I saw everything in a different way. At first I felt terrible about it. I thought that I'm such a dick. You are the person who has been the most kind, the most steady and I hurt you. I thought about killing myself but I knew that would confirm that I was a dick.

Then I stopped attacking myself. I was overcome with a sense of calm and sadness. I understood where it came from. Everything made sense. I feel so insignificant, and I assume everyone else sees me that way too. Telling me that I hurt you made me see that I affected you and that you care about me. In some way, and I know that this sounds awful, I didn't see you as a person. I saw you as a care provider.

"It takes real courage to tell me that," I say. She is silent. "Can I ask you … When you were in your own analysis, did your transformations happen like this? Did they happen suddenly after years, or did it happen gradually?" Zoe reveals the depth of her vulnerability, standing naked before me. I see it as a sign that she genuinely trusts that I won't abandon her.

I tell her there were moments in my analysis where everything suddenly became clear. And I am lucky to continue to have those moments in my work with her.

Before leaving the session, she says: "Imagine if you never told me that I hurt you."

The resolution of Zoe's trailing edge activated Zoe's healthy self, curious about how to stay alive. Since then she has been living into the twinship with me, showing signs of a self in progress. She allows herself to freely yearn for what she needs. She doesn't perform for me, nor do I for her. We are freer to be ourselves. We breathe easier.

I remember the moment that signaled this shift, months after our confrontation. A friend, another leader in Zoe's community, killed herself. No doubt the second suicide was inspired by the first. Sorrow descended upon Zoe and her friends. Instead of falling into the abyss, Zoe kept her feet planted on the perimeter. "I'm angry about the systematic injustice. I'm angry at a world that makes it so hard for her to survive," she said. "I'm furious that a poor woman had to work so hard to make money, cutting hair, reading Tarot cards, and still had no access to mental health care. I spoke about this publicly and it really moved people."

"You turned your anger into a call for action," I said.

"It's strange," she said. "I don't know how she killed herself and I haven't asked. I want to know why – not how."

Wanting to know why – not how – was a return to life, a sort of resurrection. Zoe had broken the tie with the woman who killed herself and was ready to join me, a woman fully alive. No longer was Zoe interested in retracing the steps of the suicidal woman's march toward death. Zoe wanted to know why the woman felt she had no recourse, why she had been denied access to resources and how we, as a society, could do better. Zoe was not trying to figure out a way to kill herself. She was trying to figure out a way to stay alive. Zoe broke from the trailing edge of her experience, resisted the pull to the grave and was ready to claim a place among the living. She entered into a twinship with me, creating space between herself the ones who had killed themselves. From across the expanse, she could safely extend curiosity, compassion and care.

Conclusion

Zen Teacher Thich Nhat Hanh says "No mud, no lotus." The blooming flower emerges by pushing through the mud. Likewise, in psychoanalytic treatment, new relational possibilities spring from the muck of old psychic swamps.

Zoe and I cocreated an intersubjective field, a muddy and dynamic system of interweaving parts, that brought together some of the most troubled aspects of our psyches. ISP takes this field – not the isolated mind of the patient – as its subject of inquiry. There is no way an analyst can avoid cocreating and coparticipating in a field with a patient. Zoe and I each brought a particular subjectivity, a way of organizing experience and experiencing ourselves in the world. Our subjectivities were informed by early emotional experiences with caregivers, our temperaments, our traumas and triumphs, gifts and limitations, hopes and dreads. Our complex worlds of subjectivities collided, colluded, complimented and changed one another. Our understanding of this ever-changing field offered a way out of the habituated dance and into a new lived experience.

Standing on the ledge with Zoe shocked me into identifying and then disentangling from a dimension of my own trailing edge, the replay of past trauma. I entered the relationship in a new way, changing the field between. My greater understanding led to inner strength and confidence that Zoe could take in. Once my powerlessness and helplessness diminished, I could offer her an alternative to a dance with suicide. I became more trustable in a generative leading edge experience. I showed up as the mothering one, committed to her well being and setting limits. This changed her experience of me, softening her suspicion and fear, altering the field. Finally, a lifegiving relational possibility, one that Zoe had been searching for all along, transfigured the field in ways that neither of us could have predicted.

Acknowledgements

I want to thank Zoe for granting her permission to publish the story of our work together. I am deeply grateful for her interest in reading this chapter beforehand and for her sharp and sensitive editorial comments. I appreciate Zoe's willingness to collaborate with me to find ways to disguise identifying details and to clarify details that felt way too important to disguise. The narrative of our psychoanalytic work touched Zoe who said she felt "more known, understood and cared about" than ever before. She chose the name "Zoe" because it sounds cool. Zoe means "life" in Greek.

References

Alexander, F. (1950). Analysis of the therapeutic factors in psychoanalytic treatment. *The Psychoanalytic Quarterly*, 19: 482–500.
Atlas, G. & Aron, L. (2018). *Dramatic Dialogue*. London and New York: Routledge.
Atwood, G. & Stolorow, R. (1984). *Structures of Subjectivity*. New York: Routledge.
Bacal, H. A. (1985). Optimal responsiveness and the therapeutic process. *Progress in Self Psychology*, 1: 202–227.
Bacal, H. A. (1990). The elements of a corrective selfobject experience. *Psychoanalytic Inquiry*, 10(3): 347–372.
Bacal, H. A. & Thomson, P. G. (1996). The psychoanalyst's selfobject needs and the effect of their frustration on the treatment: A new view of countertransference. *Progress in Self Psychology*, 12: 17–35.
Carroll, L. (1865). *Alice's Adventures in Wonderland*. New York: Simon & Shuster, 2000.
Elson, M., Ed. (1987). *The Kohut Seminars: On Self Psychology and Psychotherapy with Adolescents and Young Adults*. New York: W. W. Norton.
Freud, S. (1895). The psychotherapy of Hysteria. In J. Strachey (Ed.). *Studies in Hysteria*, pp. 255–288. New York: Basic Books.
Freud, S. (1912). Papers technique. The dynamics of transference. *The Standard Edition*, 12: 97–108.
Freud, S. (1914). On narcissism. *The Standard Edition*, 14: 67–104.
Freud, S. (1917). Mourning and melancholia. *The Standard Edition*, 14: 237–258.
Geist, R. (2015). Conversations with Paul. *International Journal of Psychoanalytic Self Psychology*, 10(2): 91–106.
Gottman, J. (1999). *The Seven Principles for Making Marriage Work*. New York: Crown Publishers.
Greenson, R. (1967). *The Technique and Practice of Psychoanalysis, Vol 1*. New York: International Universities Press.
Hagman, G. (1995). Mourning: A review and reconsideration. *International Journal of Psycho-Analysis*, 76: 909–925.
Hagman, G. (2017). *New Models of Bereavement Theory and Treatment: New Mourning*. London: Routledge.
Hendrix, H., Hunt, H., Hannah, M. & Luquet, W. (2005). *Imago Relationship Therapy: Perspectives on Theory*. San Francisco, CA: Jossey-Bass.

Jeanicke, C. (2015). *The Search for a Relational Home*. London and New York: Routledge.

Johnson, S. (2004). *The Practice of Emotionally Focused Couple Therapy: Creating Connection*. New York: Brunner-Routledge.

Kasoff, B. (1997). The self in orientation: Issues of female homosexuality. *Progress in Self Psychology*, 13: 213–230.

Kernberg, O. (1975). *Borderline Conditions and Pathological Narcissism*. New York: Jason Aronson.

Kohut, H. (1959). Introspection, empathy, and psychoanalysis—An examination of the relationship between mode of observation and theory. *Journal of the American Psychoanalytic Association*, 7: 459–483.

Kohut, H. (1971). *The Analysis of the Self: A Systematic Approach to the Psychoanalytic Treatment of Narcissistic Personality Disorders*. New York: International Universities Press.

Kohut, H. (1977). *The Restoration of the Self*. Madison, CT: International Universities Press.

Kohut, H. (1979). The two analyses of Mr. Z. In P. H. Ornstein (Ed.). *The Search for the Self: Selected Writings of Heinz Kohut: 1978–1981, Vol. 4*, pp. 395–446. Madison, CT: International Universities Press.

Kohut, H. (1981). Introspection, empathy, and the semi-circle of mental health. In P. Ornstein (Ed.). *The Search for the Self: Selected Writings of Heinz Kohut: 1978–1981, Vol. 4*, pp. 537–567. New York: International Universities Press, 1991.

Kohut, H. (1984). *How Does Analysis Cure?* Chicago, IL: University of Chicago Press.

Kohut, H. (1996). *The Chicago Institute Lectures*. P. Tolpin & M. Tolpin (Eds.). Hillsdale, NJ: The Analytic Press.

Kohut, H. (2010). On empathy: Heinz Kohut (1981). *International Journal of Psychoanalytic Self Psychology*, 5(2): 122–131.

Lachmann, F. (2001). *Transforming Narcissism: Reflections on Empathy, Humor, and Expectations*. New York: The Analytic Press.

Leone, C. (2008). Couple therapy from the perspective of self psychology and intersubjectivity theory. *Psychoanalytic Psychology*, 25: 79–98.

Leone, C. (2018). Response to MacIntosh's review and discussion of the psychoanalytic couple therapy journal literature: A self psychological, intersubjective perspective. *Psychoanalytic Inquiry*, 38(5): 387–398.

Lessem, P. & Orange, D. M. (1993). Emotional bonds: The therapeutic action of psychoanalysis revisited, Unpublished Manuscript as cited In: Optimal Responsiveness and Analytic Listening, by H. Bacal (1997) *Progress in Self Psychology, Vol. 13*. Ed. A. Goldberg. Hillsdale, NJ: The Analytic Press.

Livingston, M. S. (2007). Sustained empathic focus, intersubjectivity, and intimacy in the treatment of couples. *International Journal of Psychoanalytic Self Psychology*, 2(3): 315–338.

Mahler, M., Pine, F. & Bergman, A. (1975). *The Psychological Birth of the Human Infant*. New York: Basic Books.

Miller, J. (1985). How Kohut actually worked. *Progress in Self Psychology*, 1: 13–30. Hillsdale, NJ: The Analytic Press.

Miller, J. (1996). *Using Self Psychology in Child Psychotherapy*. Hillsdale, NJ: Jason Aronson.

References

Mitchell, S. (1988). *Relational Concepts in Psychoanalysis.* Cambridge: Harvard University Press.
Mitchell, S. (1993). *Hope and Dread in Psychoanalysis.* New York: Basic Books.
Orange, D. M. (2011). *The Suffering Stranger: Hermeneutics for Everyday Clinical Practice.* New York: Routledge.
Orange, D. M., Atwood, G. & Stolorow, R. (1997). *Working Intersubjectively: Contextualism in Psychoanalytic Practice.* Hillsdale, NJ: The Analytic Press.
Ornstein, A. (1974). The dread to repeat and the new beginning: A contribution to the psychoanalysis of the narcissistic personality disorder. *Annual of Psychoanalysis,* 2: 231–248.
Ornstein, A. (1984). The function of play in the process of child therapy: A contemporary perspective. *Annual of Psychoanalysis,* 12: 349–366.
Ornstein, A. (1991). The dread to repeat: Comments on the working-through process in psychoanalysis. *Journal of the American Psychoanalytic Association,* 39: 377–398.
Rado, S. (1933). The psychoanalysis of pharmacothymia (drug addiction). *The Psychoanalytic Quarterly,* 2: 1–23.
Ringstrom, P. (1994). An intersubjective approach to conjoint therapy. In A. Goldberg (Ed.). *Progress in Self Psychology,* 10: 159–182.
Shaddock, D. (1998). *From Impasse to Intimacy: How Understanding Unconscious Needs Can Transform Relationships.* Northvale, NJ: Jason Aronson.
Shane, E. & Shane, M. (1990). Object loss and selfobject loss: A consideration of self psychology's contribution to understanding mourning and the failure to mourn. *Annual of Psychoanalysis,* 18: 115–131.
Shane, W. (1996). Discussion of 'A self psychological approach to child therapy: A case study'. *Progress in Self Psychology,* Chapter 11, 12: 201–206.
Shelby, R. D. (1994). Homosexuality and the struggle for coherence. *Progress in Self Psychology,* 10: 55–78. Hillsdale, NJ: The Analytic Press.
Shelby, R. D. (1998). The self and orientation: The case of Mr. G. *Progress in Self Psychology,* 13: 181–202. Hillsdale, NJ: The Analytic Press.
Simmel, E. (1948). Alcoholism and addiction. *The Psychoanalytic Quarterly,* 17: 6–31.
Solomon, M. (1988). Treatment of narcissistic vulnerability in marital therapy. In A. Goldberg (Ed.). *Progress in Self Psychology,* 4: 215–330.
Stark, M. (1999). *Modes of Therapeutic Action.* New York: Jason Aronson.
Stern, D. (1985). *The Interpersonal World of the Infant.* New York: Basic Books.
Stolorow, D. & Stolorow, R. (1987). Affects and selfobjects. In R. Stolorow, G. Atwood & G. B. Brandchaft (Eds.). *Psychoanalytic Treatment: An Intersubjective Approach,* pp. 66–87. Hillsdale, NJ: The Analytic Press.
Stolorow, R. (1995). An intersubjective view of self psychology. *Psychoanalytic Dialogues,* 5: 395–396.
Stolorow, R. (1997). Dynamic, dyadic, intersubjective systems: An evolving paradigm for psychoanalysis. *Psychoanalytic Psychology,* 14: 337–346.
Stolorow, R. & Atwood, G. (1992). *Contexts of Being: The Intersubjective Foundation of Psychological Life.* Hillsdale, NJ: The Analytic Press.
Stolorow, R., Atwood, G. & Brandchaft, B. (1987). *Psychoanalytic Treatment: An Intersubjective Approach.* Hillsdale, NJ: The Analytic Press.

Stolorow, R., Atwood, G. & Brandchaft, B. (1994). *The Intersubjective Perspective*. Northvale, NJ: Jason Aronson.

Stolorow, R. D., Atwood, G. E. & Orange, D. M. (1999). Kohut and contextualism: Toward a post-Cartesian psychoanalytic theory. *Psychoanalytic Psychology*, 16(3): 380–388.

Strozier, C. (2001). *Heinz Kohut: The Making of a Psychoanalyst*. New York: Farrar, Straus and Giroux.

Teicholz, J. G. (2001). The many meanings of intersubjectivity and their implications for analyst self-expression and self-disclosure. *Progress in Self Psychology*, 17: 9–42.

Thelen, E. & Smith, L. B. (1994). *A Dynamic Systems Approach to the Development of Cognition and Action*. Cambridge, MA: MIT Press.

Togashi, K. (2009). A new dimension of twinship selfobject experience and transference. *International Journal of Psychoanalytic Self Psychology*, 4: 21–39.

Tolpin, M. (1986). Self-objects and oedipal objects—A crucial developmental distinction. *Psychoanalytic Study of the Child*, 33: 167–184.

Tolpin, M. (1997a). Chapter 1: Compensatory structures: Paths to the restoration of the self. *Progress in Self Psychology*, 13: 3–19.

Tolpin, M. (1997b). The development of sexuality and the self. *Annual of Psychoanalysis*, 25: 173–187.

Tolpin, M. (2002). Doing psychoanalysis of normal development: Forward edge transferences. *Progress in Self Psychology*, Chapter 11, 18: 167–190. Hillsdale, NJ: The Analytic Press.

Tolpin, M. (2009). A new direction for psychoanalysis: In search of a transference of health. *International Journal of Psychoanalytic Self Psychology*, 4S(Supplement): 31–43.

Trop, J. (1997). An intersubjective perspective on countertransference in couples therapy. In M. Solomon & J. Siegel (Eds.). *Countertransference in Couples Therapy*, pp. 99–109. New York: W. W. Norton.

Ulman, R. B. (1987). Horneyan and Kohutian Theories of Psychic Trauma: A Self-Psychological Reexamination of the Work of Harold Kelman. *American Journal of Psychoanalysis*, 47(2): 154–160.

Ulman, R. & Stolorow, R. (1985). The transference-countertransference neurosis in psychoanalysis: An intersubjective viewpoint. *Bulletin of the Menninger Clinic*, 49(1): 37–51.

Ulman, R. B. & Paul, H. (2006). *The Self Psychology of Addiction and Its Treatment, Narcissus in Wonderland*. New York: Routledge.

Walt Disney Productions. (1974). *The Sorcerer's Apprentice*. Burbank, CA: Disney Wonderful World of Reading.

Winnicott, D. (1955). Metapsychological and clinical aspects of regression within the psycho-analytical set-up. In L. Caldwell (Ed.). *Collected Papers*, pp. 278–294. New York: Basic Books, 1958.

Winnicott, D. (1965). *The Maturational Processes and the Facilitating Environment*. New York: International Universities Press.

Index

9/11 terrorist attacks 76

AA 67–68
abstinence goals, addictions 117–118
active listening 63
activities as selfobjects 103–104, 107–108; *see also* art; hobbies; literature; music; physical exercise; sport
Adam's case, depression 99, 106–109
addictions i, xi–xii, 42–43, 58, 113–130; abstinence goals 117–118; *Alice in Wonderland* (Carroll) 114, 118; background i, xi–xii, 42–43, 58, 113–130; case reports 117–130; causes 113–116; definitions 113–114; dissociation 114–115; fake/ersatz selfobject experiences 114–116; fantasies 113–115, 117–130; historical perspectives 113, 117; idealizing line of self development 115–117, 121–129; ISP perspectives 113–130; Joe's case 117; Mark's case 117; masturbation 113, 117, 122; megalomaniacal fantasies 114–115, 119; mirroring line of self development 115–120; model of addictions 114–130; narcissism 113–115, 117, 119–130; psychoactive effects 115–116; relapses 117; Roberta's case 118–129; 'shame bound' language 122, 127; treatments 113–130; twinship experiences line of self development 115–117, 125–129; *see also* alcohol; drugs misuse; eating disorders; gambling; sex addictions
addictive trigger mechanisms (ATMs), definition 114–117
agency 5, 50, 83–84, 94, 100–112, 158; definition 104; *see also* helplessness

aggressive drive 162, 164–165, 172
AIDS 162
alcohol 58, 61–62, 65–68, 75, 90–91, 95, 113–130, 174; *see also* addictions
Alexander, F. 47
Alex's case, child therapy 135–140
Alice in Wonderland (Carroll), addictions 114, 118
American Psychiatric Association (APA) 171
The Analysis of the Self (Kohut) 165
analysts ix, 7–13, 14–24, 25–36, 40–41, 43–56, 57–68, 69–79, 80–96, 105–112, 113–114, 123–129, 142–161, 162–177, 178–188; assessments 40–41; cultural competence skills 169–170; 'good enough' objects 46–47, 79, 84, 156; historical background 46–47, 113, 117, 163–164, 171; homosexual analysts 162–163, 169–177; hopes and dreads 44–45, 51–56, 59–61, 62–68, 69–70, 74–79, 80–81, 86–87, 91–92, 111, 124–125, 139–154, 159–160, 174–175, 181–183, 188; intact selfobject tie exploration 80–96, 113–114; 'new object' notion of the analyst 46; objectives 27–29, 45–47, 51–56, 71–72, 74, 77–79, 80–81, 85–87, 93–96, 100, 110–112, 128–129, 131–132, 134–140, 142–143, 176–177, 179; positive feelings 46–47, 82–83; silence ix, 7, 35, 133–134; skills/qualities 44–47, 50–51, 63–68, 70–78, 79, 81–82, 85–87, 93–96, 100, 105–106, 110–112, 128–129, 134–135, 142–143, 145–147, 169–170; success factors 87–88, 94–96, 113–114, 139–140; 'working alliance' concepts 46–47, 81; *see also*

countertransference; empathy; interpretations; selfobject; transferences; treatments
anger/rage 19–24, 51, 57–68, 70, 74–75, 84, 88, 92, 106–107, 135–143, 148–149, 152–153, 156–157, 164, 174, 176, 187; narcissistic injury 21
Anna O. 164
anorexia 181; *see also* eating disorders
antidepressants 115, 118
Aron, Lewis 53, 55–56
art, selfobject functions 103–104
asexuals 177
assertiveness 63, 90–96
assessments, analysts 40–41
asthma attacks 180–181
Atlas, Galit 53, 55–56
attuned engagement 50–56, 63, 72–73, 79, 82–83, 87–96, 105–112, 114, 117–118, 143–161; definition 50–51, 87, 88, 106; *see also* Leading Edge patient strengths; optimal responsiveness
attunement experiences 7–8, 10–12, 15–16, 18, 30, 50–51, 63, 72–73, 79, 82–96, 105–112, 117–118, 143–161; definition 15–16, 50–51, 82; empathy contrasts 15
Atwood, George x, xiii, 3, 7–8, 17, 30, 38, 45, 48, 50, 56, 70, 106, 110, 141; *see also* Intersubjectivity Theory
autism 76
avoidance defenses 10, 70, 86–87, 91–94

Bacal, Howard 16, 49, 69–70, 78, 82, 87
beliefs 3–7, 8, 72, 84
Benjamin 132
biological psychiatry perspective, depression 100
bisexuals 163, 169, 173–177; *see also* homosexuality; sexuality
borderline personality disorder 46, 51, 53
Brandchaft, Bernard xiii, 17, 38, 45, 50, 110
Breuer, Josef 164

cancer 76, 176
caregivers, selfobject 4–8, 26–34, 37–41, 43, 54–55, 58–68, 72–76, 83–84, 92–93, 101–102, 104–107, 114–130, 131–140, 152–155, 164, 173–174, 179–181, 185–187
Carroll, Lewis 114

case reports xii, 16–17, 19–24, 31–36, 57–68, 74–79, 80, 89–96, 106–112, 117–130, 135–140, 144–161, 165–177
central organizing principles 8, 11–12, 54–55, 71–72, 75–76, 82–83; definition 8, 11–12, 54–55, 71–72
Chicago Institute for Psychoanalysis 168
child sexual abuse 167, 181
child therapy i, xi, 131–140; Alex's case 135–140; background 131–140; conclusions 140; gay parents 135–140; ISP perspectives 132–140; literature 132–133; play 134, 139–140; theories 132–135
children i, xi, 14–15, 23–24, 76–77, 108–109, 118–129, 131–140, 144–154, 180–183, 186; empathy 14–15, 23–24, 76–77, 136–140, 182–183; infant definition 132
circling processes 179–180
clinical applications i, ix–xii, 50, 89, 97–188; overview of the book i, ix–xii; *see also individual applications*
coming out 125, 162, 175
communication styles 121–122, 127–128, 145–146; *see also* listening/exploring
compassion 15–16, 29, 44–45, 58–59; empathy contrasts 15–16
compensatory selfobject experiences 39–44, 81–82; activity types 42; definition 39–42; *see also* Leading Edge patient strengths; selfobject
Compensatory Structures: Pathways to the Restoration of the Self (Tolpin) 81–82
confidence 28, 37, 52–53, 62–65, 84, 109, 136, 150, 175–176, 184, 188
consciousness, the unconscious 8, 37, 46, 54–55, 72–73, 80–81, 171–172
'core strength' 126, 129, 188
corrective selfobject experience, definition 82
countertransference 45, 53, 70–71, 78–79, 80–81, 89, 91–92, 111–112; definition 45, 53; depressed patients 111–112; transference/countertransference neurosis 53; *see also* analysts; transferences
couples treatment i, xi, 118–129, 141–161; background 141–161; case reports 144–161; conclusions 161; Eric and Jenny's case 154–161; focus areas 142–143; ISP perspectives i, xi,

118–129, 141–161; Leading Edge patient strengths 142–161; literature 143–144; Six-Step Model of Conjoint Therapy 143–144; sustained empathic inquiry concept 144, 150; theories 141–144; Trailing Edge repetitive transferences 142–161; Ty and Annie's case 144–154, 161; vulnerable feelings 144, 150; *see also* marriage
cult figures 43
cultural competence skills, analysts 169–170
curative perspectives, therapeutic action in ISP 46–56, 62–68, 80–96, 113–130

D'Angelo, Laura vii, xi, 178–188
David's case, transferences 31–36
DBT (dialectical behavior therapy) 30
decentering notion, subjectivity concepts 85–86
defenses xi, 6–7, 10–11, 18–19, 28–29, 33–34, 37–44, 51–52, 69–79, 81, 86–88, 91–92, 141–142, 151, 166, 171–172, 174–175; causes 6–7, 10–11, 37–39, 40–44, 69–70, 81, 86–88, 91–92, 141–142, 151, 166, 171–172; definition 41–43, 86–87, 151; sequestration defenses 8; temporary aspects 42; types 6–7, 10–11, 18–19, 28–29, 37–38, 42–43, 69–70, 72–73, 86–88, 91–92, 141–142; *see also* Trailing Edge repetitive transferences
deflection defenses 6–7, 42
delusions 42
denial defenses 6–7
depression xi–xii, 10, 28, 40–41, 43, 57–58, 59–60, 63–65, 66–67, 83–84, 89–96, 99–112, 115, 174, 178–179, 183–185; Adam's case 99, 106–109; antidepressants 115, 118; biological psychiatry perspective 100; characteristics 103–104; definitions 99–102, 104, 112; 'empty depression' 101–102; Freud's perspectives 99–102, 112; ISP perspectives 99–100, 105–112; Kohut's perspectives 100–102, 112; Leading Edge patient strengths 105–112; literature 99–101; sadness contrasts 112; Sandy's case 108–109; selfobject 99–112; theories 99–102; treatments 99–112; *see also* helplessness; melancholia; suicidal ideation

despair 19, 57–59, 64–67, 84, 99–112, 117, 183; *see also* depression
devaluation defenses 6–7, 142
disruption-repair cycle 47–48, 49–50, 51–53, 80–81, 84, 118
dissociation 10, 37, 54–55, 76, 84, 114–115, 145–146, 172; addictions 114–115
distancing processes 142
distortions, transferences 25–26
divorces 108, 150–154
Doing Psychoanalysis of Normal Development (Tolpin) 49, 81–82
Dr. Bella, Zoe's case 185–186
dreads/fears 10–12, 14, 28–35, 37–39, 41, 44–45, 51–56, 59–68, 69–81, 83–96, 109, 111, 122–123, 131–140, 142–161, 173–174, 178–179, 188; *see also* Trailing Edge repetitive transferences
drugs misuse 42, 108, 114–130; *see also* addictions
duration of treatments 57, 88–92, 107, 121, 125, 129, 150–151, 155, 184–185
'dyadic capacity', definition 144; *see also* empathy
dynamic unconscious, definition 8; *see also* Intersubjectivity Theory; sequestration defenses; unconscious
dyscontrol 59–68, 83–84, 109, 114–115

eating disorders 40, 42, 90–91, 114–115, 179, 181; *see also* addictions; anorexia
ego 99–102, 112, 164–165; melancholia 99–102, 112
emotional development ix–x, 72, 82–84
Emotionally Focused Therapy for Couples (Johnson) 143
empathy xi–xii, 4–6, 9–24, 26–34, 44–46, 50–51, 75–81, 91–92, 95–96, 100–101, 117, 121, 128–129, 136–140, 143–161, 172, 179–180; case reports 16–17, 19–24, 32–34, 91–92, 95–96, 128–129, 136–140, 144–161, 179–180; children 14–15, 23–24, 76–77, 136–140, 182–183; compassion contrasts 15–16; conclusions 24; definitions 4, 9, 11–12, 14–16, 17, 24, 26, 100–101, 151; examples 14–17, 19–24, 32–34, 75–76, 91–92, 95–96, 128–129, 136–140, 144–161, 179–180; exploration mode of empathy 4, 16, 18–24, 137–140, 145–154; failures 24, 28, 128–129;

feedback loops 18–19, 22–24, 30–31; healing powers 16, 18–19, 24; Intersubjectivity Theory 17–18, 24, 136–140; malevolent uses 24; misunderstandings 15–16; Self Psychology 14–15, 17–19, 26–27, 32–34, 80–81, 96, 100–101, 143–144, 151; sustained empathic inquiry concept 17, 18–19, 144, 150; Tess's case 19–24; *see also* analysts; self concepts
'empty depression', definition 101–102; *see also* depression
Eric and Jenny's case, couples treatment 154–161
'experiments of one' viewpoints 170
exploration mode of empathy 4, 16, 18–24, 137–140, 145–154

fake/ersatz selfobject experiences, addictions 114–116
fantasies 3–8, 11–13, 33–34, 43–44, 54–55, 70–71, 78–79, 84, 91–96, 113–115, 117–130, 163, 165–177; addictions 113–115, 117–130; definition 13; *see also* selfobject
fat people 178–188; *see also* eating disorders
feedback loops, empathy 18–19, 22–24, 30–31
feelings 3–7, 8–10, 14–28, 31–39, 45–47, 60–68, 72–79, 82–96, 115–130, 137–140, 144–161
fever analogy, suicidal ideation 183
flirtations, lesbians 119, 121–122, 126–127
Forward Edge xiii
'forward edge' 39, 142–144, 153, 161; *see also* Leading Edge patient strengths
free association 7, 122, 127
Freud, Sigmund ix, 25, 46, 49, 80–81, 99–102, 112, 162, 163–166, 172; *see also* psychoanalysis

gambling 42; *see also* addictions
gay parents 135–140; *see also* child therapy; sexuality
Geist, R. 172
gender identity, Nancy's case 175–177
generative enactment, definition 55–56, 73
generative transferences xii, 12, 18, 38–41, 44–45, 47–48, 50–56, 57, 71, 82–96, 110–112, 113–130; attuned engagement 50–56, 63, 82–83, 87–96, 110–112, 114, 117–118; definition 38–39, 55–56, 86, 114–116; fake/ersatz selfobject experiences 115–116; *see also individual cases*; Leading Edge patient strengths; transferences
'good enough' objects, analysts 46–47, 79, 84, 156
Good Will Hunting (film) 75–76
Gottman, John 143
grandiose self 6, 11, 27, 43–44, 110, 122, 133–134, 138–140, 165; definition 6, 11, 43–44; *see also* mirroring line of self development; narcissism; selfobject
Greenson, R. 46
grief 76, 99, 102–105, 108–109, 184; *see also* mourning

Hagman, George i, vii, xi, 3–13, 69–79, 80–96, 105
haughtiness 43; *see also* grandiose self; narcissism
helplessness 20–25, 32–33, 54, 59, 102–112, 165, 188; definitions 104; *see also* agency; depression
Hendrix, Harville 143
'hermeneutics of trust' 172–173
heuristics 54
Hicks, Nancy vii, xi, 141–161
Hitler 24
hoarding defenses 42
hobbies, selfobject functions 103–104
homosexual analysts 162–163, 169–177
homosexuality 118–129, 135–137, 162–177, 178; background 118–129, 135–137, 162–177; biases 166, 168–170, 177; case reports 118–129, 165–177; causes 163–169; concepts 162–171; contemptuous viewpoints 168–170, 176–177; gay parents 135–140; Kohut's perspectives 162–169, 171, 172; mental disorders 171; Mr A. 165–166, 171; Mr Z. 167; Nancy's case 173–177; Roberta's case 118–129; tension relief viewpoints 166–167; *see also* lesbians; sexuality
hopes 10–13, 18, 28–29, 31, 37–41, 44–45, 50–56, 63–64, 70–71, 84–85, 86–96, 113, 122–129, 131–140, 142–143, 147–161, 166, 174–188; *see also* Leading Edge patient strengths

How Does Analysis Cure (Kohut) 39, 47, 56
Hulton, Blethyn 56
human suffering sources, selfobject 5, 6, 9–10, 26
humiliation 42, 54, 89, 93–95, 101–112; *see also* melancholia; shame

Id 80–81, 164–165
idealizing line of self development 4–6, 21–36, 39–41, 42–44, 47–48, 50–51, 59, 62–68, 78–79, 83–96, 101–102, 115–117, 121–129, 133–140, 145–161, 174–177; addictions 115–117, 121–129; definition 4, 28, 83, 101; examples 28, 31–36, 39–40, 59, 62–63, 65–66, 67–68, 83, 91–96, 117, 121–129, 133–134, 136–140, 145–161, 174–177; mourning needs 33–34; *see also* self-soothing capacity; selfobject
Imago Relationship Therapy (Hendrix) 143
impotence 90, 95
infant definition 132; *see also* child
intact selfobject tie exploration, Leading Edge patient strengths 80–96, 113–114
interactions 8–13, 30–31, 59–68, 141–161; *see also* Intersubjectivity Theory
interpretations 7, 12–13, 27–28, 29, 30, 43–56, 59–68, 69–79, 80–96, 106–112, 142–143, 172; definitions 86–87, 88–89; guidelines 87–89; indications/contraindications 87–89; prototypes 54–55; repetitive transferences 29, 51–52, 59–68, 69–79, 80–82, 86–88; selfobject 7, 12, 27–28, 30, 59–68, 78–79, 80–96; usage 12, 46–48, 80–81, 86–89, 94–96, 142–143; *see also* analysts; Trailing Edge repetitive transferences
intersubjective context, definition 7–8, 13, 30, 45, 105–106, 123; *see also* Intersubjectivity Theory
intersubjective field 7–8, 13, 34–35, 45, 63–68, 70–73, 80–81, 84–85, 132, 140, 141–143, 157–158, 179, 188; definition 7–8, 13, 34–35, 45, 63–65, 67, 70, 84, 141, 179, 188
Intersubjective Self Psychology (ISP), addictions 113–130; child therapy 131–140; clinical applications i, ix–xii, 50, 89, 97–188; couples treatment i, xi, 118–129, 141–161; curative perspectives 46–56, 62–68, 80–96, 113–130; definitions ix–xi, 3, 8–13, 17–19, 25–26, 31, 37–39, 45, 47, 50, 55–56, 71–74, 77–79, 86, 113–115, 143, 169–170; depression 99–100, 105–112; evolving nature 79; historical background ix–x, 25–26, 38–39, 113, 163–164; introduction 3–13; melancholia 99–100, 105–112; objectives 11, 12–13, 27, 71–74, 77–79, 85–87, 93–96, 110–112, 128–129, 131–132, 134–140, 142–143, 179; overview of the book i, ix–xii; parties 37–56, 69–79, 105–112, 131–140, 142–161, 169–177, 188; pathological narcissism 43–44, 114–115, 164; sexuality perspectives 118–129, 169–177; success factors 87–88, 94–96, 113–115, 139–140; suicidal ideation 106–107, 178–188; supportive process contrasts 12; theory and practice i, ix–xii, 1–96; therapeutic action in ISP xi–xii, 37–56, 57–68, 69–79, 84–87, 88–96, 99–112, 113–130, 142–161, 169–177, 188; *see also individual cases/topics*; Intersubjectivity Theory; Self Psychology
Intersubjective Systems Theory x, 134–135
Intersubjectivity Theory x–xii, 3, 7–13, 17–18, 24, 25–26, 30–36, 45, 48–56, 70, 72, 84–85, 105–106, 131–132, 136–140, 141–161; definition x, 7–8, 9, 13, 30, 31, 45, 49, 84–85, 141–144; empathy 17–18, 24, 136–140, 143–144; overview of the book x–xii; structures 48, 50–56, 72, 81–82, 88–89, 114–130, 136–140, 173–177; transferences 25–26, 30–36, 48–51, 84–85, 123–129, 136–140, 141–144; *see also* dynamic unconscious; Intersubjective Self Psychology; subjectivity concepts
intuition 15–16, 21, 23, 44; empathy contrasts 15–16

Jeanicke, Chris 49
Joe's case, addictions 117
Johnson, Sue 143
joy 84, 112

Kasoff, Betsy 163, 169
Kernberg, O. 42–43

kindness 15–16, 44–45; empathy contrasts 15–16
Kohut, Heinz i, ix, x, xiii, 3–9, 12, 14, 16–17, 24–28, 31, 37–42, 47–50, 56, 80–84, 100–102, 112, 114, 117, 131–132, 143, 151, 162–169, 171, 172, 177; *see also* Self Psychology

Lachmann, Frank 39, 172
Leading Edge patient strengths i, x, xi–xii, 3, 9–15, 19–24, 28–29, 32–35, 38–39, 40–45, 47–56, 57, 60, 62–68, 69–71, 79–96, 105–132, 138–140, 142–161, 166, 171–177, 179–188; case reports 32–35, 57, 59, 60, 62, 63–68, 80, 89–96, 121–129, 138–140, 144–161, 174–177; couples treatment 142–161; definition 9–10, 12–13, 28–29, 38–39, 40, 41, 43, 47, 64, 70–71, 86, 88, 93, 105, 113–115, 131, 179; depression 105–112; guidelines 87–89; historical background 38–39, 47–48; intact selfobject tie exploration 80–96, 113–114; neglected aspects 47–49, 55–56, 80–81; Trailing Edge repetitive transferences 51–56, 63–68, 70–71, 86, 94–96, 122–123, 142–161; 'we'/'us' factors 93–96, 128–129; *see also* attuned engagement; compensatory selfobject experiences; generative transferences; hopes; *individual cases*; optimal responsiveness; Self Psychology; selfobject; transferences; yearnings
Leone, Carla 141, 144
lesbians 118–129, 163–164, 170, 173–177, 178; causes 163, 175; coming out 125, 175; flirtations 119, 121–122, 126–127; marriage 118–129, 175–177; Nancy's case 173–177; open relations 118–119; Roberta's case 118–129; seduction pleasures 119, 121–122; sexual activities 122, 127, 128, 175; 'shame bound' language 122, 127; *see also* homosexuality; sexuality
Lessem, P. 49
LGBTQ 164, 170–171, 177; *see also* sexuality
listening/exploring 4, 16, 18–19, 44–45, 63, 107, 129, 145–148; *see also* communication styles
literature 99–101, 103–104, 132–133, 143–144; child therapy 132–133;

couples treatment 143–144; depression 99–101; selfobject functions 103–104; *see also individual titles*
Livingston, Louisa vii, xi, 3–13, 141–161
Livingston, Martin 144, 150
loneliness 125–126, 151–152
love objects 103–104

Mahler, M. 133
malevolent uses, empathy 24
Mark's case, addictions 117
marriage 32–33, 34–35, 74–79, 89–92, 95, 108, 118–129, 150–154, 175–177; divorces 108, 150–154; lesbians 118–129, 175–177; *see also* couples treatment
mastectomies 176
masturbation 42, 113, 117, 122, 165–166; addictions 113, 117, 122
megalomaniacal fantasies, addictions 114–115, 119
melancholia xi, 99–112; Adam's case 99, 106–109; background 99–112; definitions 99–102, 104, 112; ego 99–102, 112; Freud's perspectives 99–102, 112; ISP perspectives 99–100, 105–112; Kohut's perspectives 100–102, 112; Leading Edge patient strengths 105–112; literature 99–101; narcissism 100–101; sadness contrasts 112; Sandy's case 108–109; selfobject 99–112; theories 99–102; *see also* depression
memories 3–7, 8, 11–12, 20–21, 84
mental disorders, homosexuality 171
mentors 23, 64
Michael's case, Leading Edge patient strengths 89–96
Mickey Mouse, *Sorcerer's Apprentice* (film) 114
Miller, Jules 38, 134, 163
mirroring line of self development 4–6, 11, 26–30, 33, 39–44, 47–48, 50–51, 59–61, 62–64, 78–79, 83–84, 92–96, 101–102, 115–120, 133–140, 144–161; addictions 115–120; definition 4, 27–28, 84, 101; examples 27–28, 30, 33, 39–40, 59–61, 62–64, 84, 92–96, 117–120, 133–134, 138–140, 144–161; *see also* grandiose self; self-esteem; selfobject
Mitchell, Stephen 37, 132, 179

model of addictions 114–130; *see also* addictions
Mooni-like idealization of cult figures 43
Morawetz, Ernst 167–168
mourning i, 33–34, 99–100, 102–106, 109, 112, 185; definitions 99–100, 102–103, 112; idealizing line of self development 33–34; *see also* grief; melancholia; sorrow
Mourning and Melancholia (Freud) 99, 100–101
Mr A., homosexuality 165–166, 171
Mr Z., homosexuality 167
music, selfobject functions 103–104

Nancy's case, sexuality 173–177
narcissism 21, 26–27, 33, 42–44, 46, 84, 100–101, 113–115, 117, 119–130, 164–177; addictions 113–114, 117, 119–130; healthy/pathological forms 42–44, 114–115, 164; melancholia 100–101; sexuality 164–177; *see also* grandiose self; selfobject
narcissistic injury, anger/rage 21
Narcissus in Wonderland (Ulman & Paul) 114, 118
neglected aspects, Leading Edge patient strengths 47–49, 55–56, 80–81
neuroses 46, 53–54, 101–102
'new object' notion of the analyst 46
'no mud, no lotus' saying (Thich Nhat Hanh) 188
normalization 34–35

object-related aspect of experience 165, 169
objectivity, subjectivity concepts 85–86; *see also* reality; truth
obsessive-compulsive ruminations 32, 42
obstacle perspective, transferences 25–26
oedipal phase 46, 164
On Narcissism (Freud) 100–101
optimal frustration, definition 81–82
optimal responsiveness 16, 30, 49–50, 56, 82–84, 87–96, 106, 161, 163–164; definition 16, 30, 49–50, 56, 82–84, 87, 88; *see also* attuned engagement; empathy; Leading Edge patient strengths; selfobject
Orange, D. M. xiii, 49, 72, 172–173
Ornstein, Anna 71, 134, 178–179
Ornstein, Paul 171–172
overview of the book i, ix–xii

parties, intact selfobject tie exploration 80–96, 113–114
parties in ISP 37–56, 57–68, 69–79, 105–112, 131–140, 142–161, 169–177, 188; *see also* analysts; Intersubjective Self Psychology; patients
pathological narcissism, definition 42–44, 114–115, 164; *see also* narcissism
patients, background 37–56, 57–68, 69–79, 80–96, 105–112, 171–177, 188; intact selfobject tie exploration 80–96, 113–114; *see also individual cases*
Paul, Harry ii, vii, xi, 3–13, 55, 80–96, 113–130
perfection 33–34
physical exercise 95–96, 103–104, 118–119, 123–126
play, child therapy 134, 139–140
pornography 122
positive feelings, analysts 46–47, 82–83
postmodern trends, subjectivity concepts 85
Powell, Gordon viii, xi, 3–13, 162–177
prototypes, interpretations 54–55
psychiatrists, Dr. Bella 185–186
psychoactive effects, addictions 115–116
psychoanalysis ix–xii, 46–56, 69–79, 80–82, 100–101, 113, 117, 143–161, 162–177, 178–188; definition 46–50, 80–81, 143; historical background 46–47, 80–81, 113, 117, 163–164, 171; Id 80–81, 164; overview of the book ix–xii; traditional psychoanalysis critique x, 46–50, 80–82, 113, 117, 162–164, 171, 177; *see also* analysts; treatments
psychodynamic therapists ix; *see also* analysts
psychological field, definition 7–8
Psychology Today 178
psychoses 42, 85
psychotherapy 8–13, 37–56, 57–58, 82, 87–96; definition 8, 87–88; success factors 87–88, 94–96, 113–114, 139–140; *see also* analysts; treatments
PTSD 76
Purkhardshofer, Ignaz 168

Rado, S. 113
reactivation retraumatization fears in treatment, selfobject 6–7, 9–10, 21, 41,

69–70, 72–73, 74–79, 81–83, 122–123, 172, 178–179
reality 20–21, 24, 25–26, 73, 75, 85, 115–116, 137–140, 143–144; *see also* objectivity; truth
reason, Id 80–81
references 189–192
regression 25–26
rejection/abandonment dreads 10–11, 70–71, 76–79, 120–121, 125, 131–132, 151–152, 173–174
relapses, addictions 117
relational experiences, definition 5, 8, 13, 30–31
relational mode of empathy 4, 13
Relational Psychoanalysis x
repetitive transferences i, x, xi–xii, 3, 10–13, 18–19, 25–26, 28–29, 32–36, 38–41, 44–46, 48, 51–52, 57, 59–79, 86–88, 92–96, 142–161, 178–179, 186–188; case reports 31–36, 57, 59–63, 74–79, 92–96, 144–161, 186–188; definition 10, 12–13, 25–26, 28–29, 38, 40–41, 45–46, 72–73, 86, 178–179; guidelines 87–89; interpretations 29, 51–52, 59–68, 69–79, 80–82, 86–88; *see also* defenses; *individual cases*; Trailing Edge repetitive transferences; transferences
repression 37, 46–47, 84, 125, 172; *see also* unconscious
resistance defenses 10–11, 18–19, 41, 69–70, 72–73
Restoration of the Self (Kohut) 101
retraumatization fears in treatment, selfobject 6–7, 9–10, 21, 41, 69–70, 72–73, 74–79, 81–83, 122–123, 172, 178–179
Ricky's case, therapeutic action in ISP 57–68
Ringstrom, Philip 143–144
Roberta's case, addictions 118–129
Roe, Kathy 177
Rohde, Aviva viii, xi, 3–13, 14–24, 25–36, 57–68
role-play uses 76, 143
Roser, Karen viii, xi, 3–13, 14–24, 25–36, 131–140
Rothbart, Betty 177
'rubber band effect' 71
running 123–125, 170

ruptures 27–29, 39–41, 49–50, 52–56, 63–68, 72–73, 80–83, 114–115, 117, 122–123

sadness 109, 112; *see also* mourning
Sam, Zoe's case 181–183
Sandy's case, depression 108–109
seduction pleasures, lesbians 119, 121–122
self concepts ix, 3–7, 28–31, 44–45, 57, 72, 79, 83–84, 90–96, 99–112, 125, 134–140, 141–142, 164–165, 173–177; sense of self 3–7, 44–45, 57, 72, 79, 83–84, 99–101, 106, 109–110, 125, 134–140; *see also* beliefs; fantasies; feelings; memories; selfobject; values
self development 4–9, 19–22, 26–31, 37–39, 42, 47–48, 50–51, 56, 80–83, 87–88, 101–102, 105–106, 113–116, 130, 131–140, 163–164, 171; child therapy 131–140; *see also* idealizing; mirroring; selfobject; twinship experiences
self disorders, background 39–41, 46–47, 99–102, 115–117, 171; causes 39, 40–41, 99–102, 115–117
self psychological treatments, basis 5–6
Self Psychology ix–x, 3–7, 8–9, 14–15, 17–19, 21, 25–36, 37–41, 48–50, 80–81, 96, 100–112, 131–132, 134–135, 141–161, 162–177; definition ix–x, 3–7, 8–9, 21, 31, 49–50, 80–82, 96, 143, 151, 162–163, 164–165; empathy 14–15, 17–19, 26–27, 32–34, 80–81, 96, 100–101, 143–144, 151; narcissistic injury 21; overview of the book i, ix–xii; sexuality 162–165; transferences 25–36, 37–41, 80–81, 96, 134–135, 141–144, 151; *see also* Intersubjective Self Psychology; self; transferences
self-actualization 13, 70, 84
self-blame 91–96
self-control 59–68, 83–84, 109, 114–115
self-esteem 4, 5–6, 15, 26–31, 84, 92, 115, 118–119, 126, 138–140; *see also* mirroring line of self development; well-being
self-harm 40, 42, 181–182, 185; *see also* suicidal ideation
self-respect 100
self-soothing capacity 4, 5, 6, 26–31, 59, 63, 115–116, 133–134, 173–174; *see also* idealizing line of self development

self-worth 4, 15
selfobject i, ix, x, xii, 5–13, 14–24, 26–31, 33–36, 37–41, 47–56, 59–68, 69–79, 80–96, 99–112, 113–130, 131–140, 141–161, 163–177, 180–188; activities as selfobjects 103–104, 107–108; addiction perspectives 113–130; caregivers 4–8, 26–34, 37–41, 43, 54–55, 58–68, 72–76, 83–84, 92–93, 101–102, 104–107, 114–130, 131–140, 152–155, 164, 173–174, 179–181, 185–187; child therapy 131–140; compensatory selfobject experiences 39–44, 81–82; couples treatment 141–161; definition 5, 7, 13, 26–28, 29, 37, 59, 72–73, 82–83, 101–102, 141–142, 165; depression 99–112; failures 28, 39–41, 43–44, 49–50, 52–53, 65–66, 72–75, 80–81, 83, 84, 95; fake/ersatz selfobject experiences 114–116; human suffering sources 5, 6, 9–10, 26; intact selfobject tie exploration 80–96, 113–114; interpretations 7, 12, 27–28, 30, 59–68, 78–79, 80–96; major themes 4–6, 27–28; melancholia 99–112; misunderstanding 29; optimal frustration 81–82; optimal responsiveness 16, 30, 49–50, 56, 82–84, 87–96, 161; reactivation retraumatization fears in treatment 6–7, 9–10, 21, 41, 69–70, 72–73, 74–79, 81–83, 122–123, 172, 178–179; ruptures 27–29, 39–41, 49–50, 52–56, 63–68, 72–73, 80–83, 114–115, 117, 122–123; sustained and undisrupted selfobject experiences 82–83, 88–89, 102, 114–130; treatments 26–31, 33–36, 37–38, 49–50, 59–68, 69–79, 80–96; *see also* analysts; fantasies; grandiose self; idealizing; *individual cases/topics*; Leading Edge patient strengths; mirroring; self concepts; self development; transferences; twinship experiences
sense of self 3–7, 44–45, 57, 72, 79, 83–84, 99–101, 106, 109–110, 125, 134–140; *see also* self
sequestration defenses 8; *see also* dynamic unconscious; Intersubjectivity Theory
sex addictions 42, 114–115, 117, 165; *see also* addictions
sex drive 162, 164–165, 171, 172
sexual development stages 164–165, 169

sexual orientation, perspectives 162–164, 169–171, 175–176
sexuality i, 90, 95, 117, 118–129, 135–137, 162–177, 178; background 118–129, 135–137, 162–177; case reports 118–129, 165–177; concepts 162–171; conclusions 176–177; Freud's perspectives 162, 163–166, 172; ISP perspectives 118–129, 169–177; Kohut's perspectives 162–169, 171, 172; Nancy's case 173–177; narcissism 164–177; perspectives 162–177; Roberta's case 118–129; Self Psychology 162–165; *see also* bisexuals; homosexuality; lesbians
Shaddock, David 143–144
shame 15–16, 25, 63–64, 70–71, 84, 89, 90–93, 95, 101–112, 121–123, 127, 178–179, 186; *see also* humiliation; Trailing Edge repetitive transferences
'shame bound' language 122, 127
Shane, E. 112
Shane, M. 112, 134
Sharon, Roberta's case 118–129
Sheehan, George 170
Shelby, R. Dennis 163
shifting sands, treatments 78
sibling rivalries 164
silence, analysts ix, 7, 35, 133–134
Simmel, E. 113
Six-Step Model of Conjoint Therapy 143–144
skills/qualities, analysts 44–47, 50–51, 63–68, 70–78, 79, 81–82, 85–87, 93–96, 100, 105–106, 110–112, 128–129, 134–135, 142–143, 145–147, 169–170
social workers 155–156, 158
Solomon, Andrew 112
Solomon, Marion 143
Sorcerer's Apprentice (film), Mickey Mouse 114
sorrow 84, 102–103, 105–106; *see also* mourning
sport 103–104, 107–108, 118–119, 123–126
Stark, Marth 55
Stern, Daniel 133
Stolorow, Robert x, xiii, 3, 7–9, 17, 18, 25, 30–31, 38, 45, 48–50, 52–53, 56, 70, 72, 78, 84–85, 106, 110, 131, 141, 145–146, 179; *see also* Intersubjectivity Theory
Strozier, C. 167–168

structures, Intersubjectivity Theory 48, 50–56, 72, 81–82, 88–89, 114–130, 136–140, 173–177
subjectivity concepts 7–8, 17, 20–21, 24, 31, 72–73, 77–78, 84–85, 132–133, 145–146, 188; decentering notion 85–86; definition 7–8, 17, 72, 84; objectivity 85–86; postmodern trends 85; truth 20–21, 24, 26, 73, 75, 85; *see also* beliefs; fantasies; feelings; Intersubjectivity Theory; memories; unconscious; values
success factors, Intersubjective Self Psychology (ISP) 87–88, 94–96, 113–114, 139–140
suicidal ideation i, xi, 58, 99, 106–107, 108, 111, 112, 173–175, 178–188; Adam's case 99, 106–107; background 106–107, 111, 112, 178–188; conclusions 188; fever analogy 183; gasping for air 178–188; Nancy's case 173–175; Sandy's case 108; Zoe's case 178–188; *see also* depression; self-harm
suicide notes 183–184
superego 112, 164–165
supportive processes, ISP treatment contrasts 12
sustained empathic inquiry concept 17, 18–19, 144, 150
sustained and undisrupted selfobject experiences 82–83, 88–89, 102, 114–130
Swenson, May 169
systems theory x, 134–135

'talking cure' 164–165
Teicholz, J. G. 132–133
tension relief viewpoints, homosexuality 166–167
Tess's case, empathy 19–24
theory and practice i, ix–xii, 1–96; overview of the book i, ix–xii
therapeutic action in ISP xi–xii, 37–56, 57–68, 69–79, 84–87, 88–96, 99–112, 113–130, 142–161, 169–177, 188; background 37–56, 57–68, 69–79, 84–87, 88–96, 113–130; case reports 57–68, 74–79, 80, 89–96, 106–112; crises 66–68, 76–77, 182–188; curative perspectives 46–56, 62–68, 80–96, 113–130; parties in ISP 37–56, 57–68, 69–79, 105–112, 131–140, 142–161, 169–177, 188; processes 50–54, 79; structures 48–49, 50–56, 72, 81–82, 88–89, 114–130, 136–140, 173–177; therapeutic situation 8–11, 20, 41, 44, 45–46, 59–60, 84–96; types 46–56; *see also individual cases*; Leading Edge patient strengths; Trailing Edge repetitive transferences; treatments
therapeutic situation 8–11, 20, 41, 44, 45–46, 59–60, 84–96
therapists *see* analysts
Thich Nhat Hanh 188
Thomson, P. G. 69–70, 78
timescales, treatments 57, 88–94, 107, 121, 125, 129, 150–151, 155, 184–185
Togashi, K. 28, 180
Tolpin, Marian xiii, 9–10, 27, 38–39, 49, 70, 81–82, 88, 105, 112, 134–135, 163–164
Tom's case 74–79
tough talk 66
traditional psychoanalysis, critique x, 46–50, 80–82, 113, 117, 162–164, 171, 177
Trailing Edge repetitive transferences i, x, xi–xii, 3, 10–19, 28–36, 38–48, 51–68, 69–82, 86–88, 92–96, 113–114, 116, 122–123, 131, 135–140, 142–161, 166, 174, 178–179, 184, 186–188; case reports 32–36, 57, 59–68, 74–79, 92–96, 122–123, 135–140, 144–161, 166, 174, 184, 186–188; couples treatment 142–161; definition 10, 12–13, 28–29, 38, 41, 43, 59, 69–70, 81, 86, 88, 113, 131, 142, 178–179; guidelines 87–89; historical background 38–39, 46–47; Leading Edge patient strengths 51–56, 63–68, 70–71, 86, 94–96, 122–123, 142–161; manifestations 88; necessary work 47–48; *see also* defenses; dreads/fears; *individual cases*; interpretations; shame; transferences; working through
transference/countertransference neurosis, definition 53
transferences, case reports 31–36, 57–68, 74–79, 80, 89–96, 117–130; countertransference 45, 53–54, 70–71, 78–79, 80–81, 89, 91–92, 111–112; definitions 25–26, 30–31, 37–39, 55–56, 72–73; distortions 25–26; examples 31–36, 39–41, 57–68, 117–130; Intersubjectivity Theory 25–26, 30–36, 48–51, 84–85,

123–129, 136–140, 141–144; meaningful relationships 73–74, 84–85; obstacle perspective 25–26; Self Psychology 25–36, 37–41, 80–81, 96, 134–135, 141–144, 151; *see also* generative transferences; idealizing; *individual cases/topics*; Leading Edge patient strengths; mirroring; repetitive transferences; selfobject; Trailing Edge repetitive transferences; twinship experiences
Transforming Aggression (Lachmann) 39
trauma i, 6–7, 9–10, 21, 41, 69–70, 72–73, 76–79, 81–83, 172, 178–179
treatments i, xi–xii, 8–13, 26–31, 33–36, 37–56, 57–68, 69–79, 80–96, 99–112, 113–130, 164–177, 178–188; addictions 113–130; alcohol 113–130; child therapy i, xi, 131–140; depression 99–112; duration 57, 88–92, 107, 121, 125, 129, 150–151, 155, 184–185; melancholia 99–112; 'no mud, no lotus' saying (Thich Nhat Hanh) 188; selfobject 26–31, 33–36, 37–38, 49–50, 59–68, 69–79, 80–96; shifting sands 78; timescales 57, 88–94, 107, 121, 125, 129, 150–151, 155, 184–185; *see also individual cases*; Intersubjective Self Psychology; therapeutic action in ISP
TRISP faculty ix, xii
Trop, J. 142
trust 84, 105–106, 108–109, 128–129, 142–143, 161, 172–173, 179–180; 'hermeneutics of trust' 172–173; *see also* twinship experiences line of self development
truth 20–21, 24, 25–26, 73, 75, 85, 115–116, 172; *see also* objectivity; reality
twinship experiences line of self development 4–6, 27–29, 34–36, 39–41, 42–44, 45, 47–48, 50–51, 59, 61–65, 67–68, 78–79, 84, 91–96, 101–102, 115–117, 125–129, 133–140, 180–188; addictions 115–117, 125–129; definition 4, 28, 84, 101; examples 28, 34–36, 40–41, 45, 59, 61–63, 64–65, 67–68, 84, 91–96, 117, 125–129, 133–134, 136–140, 180–188; *see also* selfobject; trust
Ty and Annie's case, couples treatment 144–154, 161

Ulman, Richard 53, 114–116
the unconscious 8, 37, 46, 54–55, 72–73, 80–81, 171–172; consciousness 8, 37, 46, 54–55, 72–73, 80–81, 171–172; *see also* dynamic unconscious; repression

vacations 123–124
values 3–7
vicarious introspection 4, 14–15; definition 4, 14–15; *see also* empathy

Wampler, Kenneth 177
'we'/'us' factors, Leading Edge patient strengths 93–96, 128–129
Weil, Susanne M. viii, xi, 69–79
well-being 11, 73–74, 94, 101, 104, 114, 118–119, 125; *see also* self-esteem
'What Matters' poem (Swenson) 169
whistle bombs 24
Williams, Robin 75
Winnicott, D. 46, 132
'working alliance' concepts 46–47, 81
working through 10, 12–13, 18–19, 45–46, 48–49, 57–68, 69–79, 80–96; *see also* Trailing Edge repetitive transferences
World Health Organization 171

yearnings 7, 12–13, 20–23, 27–29, 31–39, 41, 43, 44–45, 50–56, 59, 72–79, 86–96, 99–100, 105–112, 115, 122–129, 133–134, 144, 180–188; *see also* hopes; Leading Edge patient strengths; self development
YouTube 95

Zen Buddhism 188
Zimmermann, Peter B. ii, viii, xi, 3–13, 37–56, 68, 80–96, 99–112, 129–130
Zoe's case, suicidal ideation 178–188

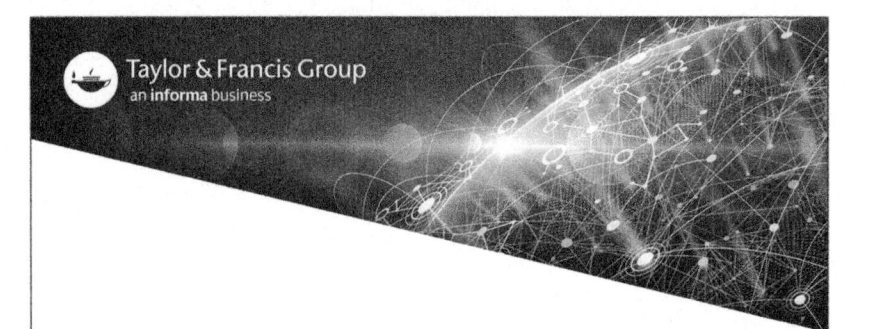

Printed in Great Britain
by Amazon